UNCLE SAM IS WATCHING YOU

Highlights From the Hearings of the Senate Subcommittee on Constitutional Rights

INTRODUCTION BY ALAN BARTH

Public Affairs Press, Washington, D. C.

ACKNOWLEDGEMENTS

This book is based chiefly on extracts from the voluminous transcript of the hearings held by the Senate Subcommittee on Constitutional Rights early in 1971. No copyright is claimed in these statements.

Public Affairs Press is solely responsible for the selections appearing in these pages, but it has benefited by generous advice from Lawrence Baskir, the Subcommittee's chief counsel, Marcia MacNaughton, Christopher Pyle, and Charles Witter.

For permission to include copyrighted material Public Affairs Press is indebted to Ralph Nader, the American Civil Liberties Union, Joseph R. Lundy, Paul Conrad, *The Nation,* and the Des Moines Register and Tribune Syndicate.

M. B. Schnapper
Editor, Public Affairs Press

419 New Jersey Avenue, S.E., Washington, D.C. 20003
Printed in the United States of America
Library of Congress Catalog Card No. 74-173827

INTRODUCTION

BY ALAN BARTH

"There was of course no way of knowing whether you were being watched at any given moment," George Orwell wrote in his nightmare vision of *1984*. "How often, or on what system, the Thought Police plugged in on any individual wire was guesswork. It was even conceivable that they watched everybody all the time. But at any rate they could plug in your wire whenever they wanted to. You had to live—did live, from habit that became instinct—in the assumption that every sound you made was overheard, and, except in darkness, every movement scrutinized."

That grim prophecy has not yet been realized. But there are portents that something like it may lie ahead. Our technology has perfected formidable instruments for intrusions upon privacy and has developed ingenious devices for recording and retrieving the fruits of such intrusions. Increasingly in recent years, and with increasing pervasiveness, governmental agencies acting sometimes in the name of law enforcement, sometimes in the name of national security, have engaged in secret surveillance of American citizens, have eavesdropped on supposedly private communications, and have compiled dossiers on the ideas, utterances, associations and activities of innumerable persons not charged with any violation of law.

This volume reflects, and is prompted by, a grave concern about these impairments of traditional rights of privacy. Its candid purpose is to sound an alarm. It offers the American people a reminder of the values they are in the process of surrendering. Taken as a whole, its contents show extensions of governmental authority which are at once shocking and sobering. Their ominous implications need to be understood. Liberty, it must be remembered, is most commonly lost in the name of national security.

Uncle Sam Is Watching You is based chiefly on testimony given at hearings held by the U. S. Senate Subcommittee on Constitutional Rights early in 1971. Over a period of several months this subcommittee heard a variety of witnesses of diverse points of view, some of them spokesmen for the Department of the Army and the Department of Justice who offered justification of one sort or another for the surveillance practices of their agencies. The extracts published in these pages are exposures of and attacks upon those practices. Their premise is that privacy is one of those inalienable rights which the Constitution of the United States was established to safeguard.

During the 1950s, when it was under the chairmanship of the late Senator Thomas C. Hennings Jr. of Missouri, and in recent years under the direction of Senator Sam Ervin of North Carolina, the Constitutional Rights Subcommittee of the Judiciary Committee has won high repute as a champion of the rights and liberties of individuals. Its recent hearings on governmental invasion of privacy through surveillance, particularly on the part of the Army, was stimulated in part by the publication of two distinguished and arresting articles in the *Washington Monthly* by Christopher Pyle and by an extraordinary television program, *First Tuesday,* by Sander Vanocur of NBC News.

The hearings conducted by the Ervin Subcommittee have been a model of what a congressional inquiry ought to do. There has been no attempt at any time to pillory or prosecute anyone; on the contrary, the committee sessions have been characterized by meticulous courtesy, balance and fairness. They have probed deeply and discerningly into the subject and they have discharged with signal effectiveness the two principal functions of congressional investigation: first, to amass information as a necessary basis for legislation; and, second, to alert the country at large to an emerging national problem. The high quality and character of the subcommittee's conduct are, of course, attributable in no small measure to the urbanity and understanding of its chairman, Senator Ervin; a large measure of credit must go as well to the subcommittee's exceptionally able young chief counsel and staff director, Lawrence Baskir.

Some degree of governmental surveillance is inescapable. Alert police officers, concerned to prevent crime as well as punish it, must sometimes shadow, or otherwise study, suspects in regard to whom they lack sufficient cause to justify an arrest. The essence of counter-intelligence is investigation or surveillance. Anyway, the practice is about as old as government.

The fact about contemporary government surveillance that makes it at once novel and alarming is that its focus today is not upon crime or foreign espionage or sabotage—not upon unlawful conduct of any sort—but upon political ideas, activities and associations, upon the modern bugbear called subversion.

Thus, as the Ervin Subcommittee hearings have dramatically disclosed, the Army, in its zeal to compile all the information it could on every person who could imaginably have some responsibility for possible future civil disturbances, maintained surveillance on such indubitably respectable and law-abiding persons as Senator Adlai Stevenson, Representative Abner Mikva and Georgia State Representative Julian Bond.

"I was elected by the people of the Second Congressional District of Illinois," says Mr. Mikva plaintively, "to be their representative in the Congress of the United States—to voice their concerns and desires regarding the policies of their country, and to try to steer America toward the goals they envisioned. In attempting to do this, I apparently did something which led some employee of our armed forces to decide that I ought to be watched. Was it because I proposed to cut military manpower by 10%? Was it because I co-sponsored H. R. 1000, the proposal to end the war in Vietnam? Is there any political activity, regardless of who is supported or opposed, which justifies the Army in spying on an elected representative of the people?"

These are rhetorical questions and they afford their own answers. But is there any reason why they should be asked regarding an elected representative of the people any more than regarding any ordinary citizen? Is there any political activity, regardless of who is supported or opposed, which justifies the Army in spying on any man or woman in America?

In April 1971, the Ervin Subcommittee's exposure of the Army's vast civilian surveillance machinery brought about a formal transfer of responsibility for such surveillance to the Department of Justice, but it is difficult to determine whether military snooping actually has halted or is merely being carried on with greater circumspection. It is even less certain that the shift to the Department of Justice brought with it any benefit to civil liberties. The FBI which does the actual work of surveillance for the Department of Justice, is just about as primitive and simplistic in its view of what constitutes "subversion" or a threat to domestic order as the Army. And it appears to have even less sensitivity to constitutional restraints. Mr. Pyle tells us that the Justice Department's Interdivisional Intelligence Unit "maintains a political computer larger than the one at Fort Holabird which the Army shut down."

The most significant fact about the FBI's activities in regard to "subversion" is that almost nobody—and least of all any committee of Congress—has presumed to inquire into them for the past 40 years. What the FBI does—and with what effectiveness and efficiency it does it—is shrouded in mystery. Mere citizens of the United States are granted a glimpse of this mystery only when FBI Director J. Edgar Hoover chooses to tell them how many telephones he is tapping and how many concealed microphones he has installed in private premises—or, on the rare occasions when secret reports and memoranda of the FBI come to light through rifling and theft of the bureau's files.

In March 1971 some unknown persons broke into the FBI office in Media, Pennsylvania, stole a considerable number of documents and began sending these documents, anonymously, to a number of newspapers and individuals. These documents may not have afforded a fair sample of the kind of information the FBI normally collects; they may not have been typical of the bureau's work. Nevertheless, they offered the public a peek at some of the surveillance the FBI has been up to. The only previous opportunity accorded the public to look at the quality of FBI investigation and reporting came many years ago, in 1949, when Judith Coplon went on trial for stealing FBI files from the Justice Department, where she was employed, and passing them on to a Russian secret agent. In the intervening 20-odd years, the bureau does not seem to have changed greatly in its view that American internal security is threatened mainly by unorthodoxy and political protest.

The Media papers indicated that the bureau has focused a great deal of its effort and attention on college campuses and particularly on black student groups which, according to a memorandum apparently issued by Mr. Hoover himself, "pose a definite threat to the nation's stability and security." On one college campus in the Philadelphia area, the stolen papers reveal, the FBI enlisted the services of the local police chief, the local postmaster, a campus security officer and a college switchboard operator to maintain surveillance on a professor suspected of "radical" beliefs and associations. Students apparently were used, sometimes on a paid basis, as informers.

One of the memoranda found in the Media office indicates that FBI agents were encouraged to step up interviews with dissenters "for plenty of reasons, chief of which are it will enhance the paranoia endemic in these circles and will further serve to get the point across there is an FBI agent behind every mailbox."

Shortly after the raid on the Media office of the FBI, Rep. Henry Reuss of Wisconsin disclosed that an agent of the bureau came to see him and told him three documents concerning his daughter, Jackie, were among the purloined papers. According to the Congressman, the

FBI agent told him the papers indicated that Swarthmore College, where his daughter is a student, local police and a local credit bureau had been checked concerning certain information about Miss Reuss given to the bureau by an informer. "The FBI representative informed me the investigation had been completed and had developed that no information of a derogatory nature concerning Jackie had been uncovered," Rep. Reuss said. "The FBI has an important responsibility to investigate crime. Its mission is not to compile dossiers on millions of Americans, Congressmen's daughters or not, who are accused of no wrongdoing. They should stick to their mission."

But the FBI takes a very expansive view of its mission. In March, 1971, Mr. Hoover appeared before the House Appropriation's Subcommittee considering his agency's fiscal 1972 budget request of $318.6 million, $44 million more than the sum appropriated for the preceding year. He confided to the subcommittee that on March 1 the FBI was operating 14 telephone taps and two microphone bugging devices in cases involving alleged criminal conduct—installations authorized by courts in conformity with the law. At the same time, according to Mr. Hoover, the FBI was operating 33 telephone taps and four bugs in situations where subversion or some other threat to internal security was suspected. These surveillances were *not* authorized by courts. They were authorized instead by Attorney General John N. Mitchell.

In 1967 the Supreme Court decided that electronic eavesdropping is a form of search circumscribed by the language of the Fourth Amendment to the Constitution. The Fourth Amendment forbids "unreasonable searches and seizures." "Over and again," Mr. Justice Stewart said in his opinion, "this Court has emphasized that the mandate of the [Fourth] Amendment requires adherence to judicial processes and that searches conducted outside the judicial process, without prior approval by judges or magistrate, are *per se* unreasonable under the Fourth Amendment . . ." Thus, the Attorney General has authorized what the Constitution appears expressly to have prohibited.

The rationale by which the Attorney General justifies so arbitrary an exercise of executive authority is that the Presidency carries with it "inherent" power to do whatever the President thinks he needs to do to protect the Government of the United States, or, as the Department of Justice formally stated it, "The President, acting through the Attorney General, may constitutionally authorize the use of electronic surveillance in cases where he has determined that, in order to preserve the national security, the use of such surveillance is reasonable."

This proposition was set forth in a memorandum filed by the Department of Justice with the Sixth U. S. Circuit Court of Appeals asking that court to set aside a ruling by U.S. District Court Judge Damon J. Keith in Michigan that the Attorney General has no authority to conduct electronic surveillance in domestic national security cases without prior court approval. The ruling was made in connection with the prosecution of three "White Panthers" accused of bombing the Ann Arbor offices of the CIA.

The response of the Sixth Circuit Court of Appeals was set forth in an eloquent opinion by Judge George Edwards:

"The government has not pointed to, and we do not find, one written phrase in the Constitution, in the statutory law, or in the case law of the United States, which exempts the President, the Attorney General, or federal law enforcement from the restrictions of the Fourth Amendment in the case at hand . . . An additional difficulty with the inherent power argument in the context of this case is that the Fourth Amendment was adopted in the immediate aftermath of abusive searches and seizures directed against American colonists under the sovereign and inherent powers of King George III. The United States Constitution was adopted to provide a check upon 'sovereign' power. The creation of three coordinate branches of government by that Constitution was designed to require sharing in the administration of that awesome power.

"It is strange, indeed, that in this case the traditional power of sovereigns like King George III should be invoked on behalf of an American President to defeat one of the fundamental freedoms for which the founders of this country overthrew King George's reign."

The doctrine of inherent power is a doctrine of unlimited authority. It is a doctrine incompatible with the idea of a government of laws—and especially incompatible with the idea of a government of limited powers specifically delegated to it by the people through a written Constitution. It constitutes, indeed, the very definition of dictatorship.

In his testimony (included in this volume) before the Ervin Subcommittee, Burt Neuborne, as a spokesman for the American Civil Liberties Union, has summarized the problem: "The wedding of sophisticated information gathering techniques with computerized information storage and dissemination systems has created, for the first time, a very real danger that the sense of privacy which has traditionally insulated Americans against the fear of state encroachment will be destroyed and be replaced, instead, by a pervasive sense of being watched. The emergence of such a police state mentality could mean the destruction of our libertarian heritage."

The fear of surveillance, no less than the fact, produces in the national community a chilling influence on the exercise of those liberties which are the indispensable basis for self-government. And the tragic truth is that honorable and patriotic Americans have come, in some measure, to fear their own government, to fear especially the intrusive reach of the FBI.

The pervasiveness of that anxiety can be gauged in some degree from a news story by Miles Benson of the Newhouse News Service published early in 1971 in the Washington Evening Star. It reported that Senator George S. McGovern, Senator Harold E. Hughes, Senator Birch Bayh, columnist Frank Mankiewicz, NAACP representative Clarence Mitchell, and Attorney Joseph L. Rauh, Jr., all said, when asked, that they suspect their telephones are tapped. A lot of other people have the same anxiety. It is an anxiety far more dangerous than "subversivion." It tends to silence the communication of ideas that makes the American system work.

What is at stake is a weighing of alternative dangers — a danger, on the one hand, that crime may go unpunished, that subversion may go unchecked, against a danger, on the other hand, that lawful comunication among free citizens may be inhibited. The risk inherent in official eavesdropping — the ominous risk for a free people — lies not so much in what it may overhear and record as in what it may silence and leave unsaid.

"When," as Senator Ervin has pointed out, "people fear surveillance, whether it exists or not, when they grow afraid to speak their minds and hearts freely to their government or to anyone else, "then we shall cease to be a free society."

Paul Conrad, Register and Tribune Syndicate

CONTENTS

ABOUT THE AUTHORS

ALAN BARTH, an editorial writer for the *Washington Post,* is the author of *The Heritage of Liberty* (1965) and other books.

SAM J. ERVIN (Democrat, North Carolina), Chairman of the U.S. Senate Subcommittee on Constitutional Rights and a member of the Senate Armed Forces and Government Operations Committees, is a former Justice of the Supreme Court of North Carolina.

BURT NEUBORNE is an attorney of the American Civil Liberties Union.

ARTHUR R. MILLER, professor of law at the University of Michigan, is the author of *Assault on Privacy* (1971).

CHRISTOPHER H. PYLE, an attorney, is a former Army Intelligence officer.

ABNER T. MIKVA (Democrat, Illinois), a member of the U.S. House of Representatives, serves on the House Judiciary Committee.

MORRIS JANOWITZ is chairman of the Sociology Department at the University of Chicago.

RALPH M. STERN formerly served in the Counter-Intelligence Analysis Branch, Office of Assistant Chief of Staff for Army Intelligence.

EDWARD D. SOHIER formerly served in the Counter-Intelligence Analysis Branch, Office of Assistant Chief of Staff for Army Intelligence.

JOHN M. O'BBIEN was formerly an Army Intelligence officer.

JOSEPH J. LEVIN, JR., a former Army Intelligence agent, is a Montgomery Alabama, attorney.

QUENTIN L. BURGESS, a former Army Intelligence agent and Vietnam veteran, is presently associated with a management consultant firm in Washington, D.C.

MALCOLM MOOS is president of the University of Minnesota.

EUGENE EIDENBERG is assistant vice president of the University of Minnesota.

JOSEPH R. LUNDY, Chicago attorney, was formerly a legislative assistant to Congressman Abner J. Mikva.

CHARLES McC. MATHIAS (Republican, Maryland) is a member of the Senate Judiciary and Government Operations Committees.

RALPH NADER is the head of the Center For Study of Responsive Law.

1

FEDERAL POWERS AND CONSTITUTIONAL RIGHTS

By Senator Sam J. Ervin

Our nation is predicated on the fundamental proposition that citizens have a right to express their views on the wisdom and course of governmental policies. This involves more than the currently popular notion of a so-called right to dissent. Our system cannot survive if citizen participation is limited merely to registering disagreement with offical policy; the policies themselves must be the product of the people's views. The protection and encouragement of such participation is a principal purpose of the first amendment.

More than at any other time in our history, people are actively expressing themselves on public questions and seeking to participate more directly in the formulation of policy. Mass media have made it easy for large numbers of people to organize and express their views in written and oral fashion. Rapid means of transportation have aided our mobile population to move easily to sites of central and local authority for the purpose of expressing their views more publicly. The freedom of our form of government and the richness of our economy have made it possible for individuals to move about freely and to seek their best interests as they will in vocations and avocations of their choice, or indeed, to pursue none at all for a time, if that is what they wish. If modern technology has provided citizens with more efficient means for recording their dissent, or for registering their political, economic, or social views, it has also placed in the hands of executive branch officials new methods of taking note of that expression of views and that political activity. For these reasons, those individuals who work actively for public causes are more visible than ever before.

These new sciences have accorded those who control government increased power to discover and record immutably the activities, thoughts and philosophy of an individual at any given moment of his life. That picture of the person is recorded forever, no matter how the person may change as time goes on. Every person's past thus becomes an inescapable part of his present and future. The computer never forgets.

To be sure, recordkeeping is nothing new in the history of government; nor indeed, is the habit all governments and all societies have of surveillance, black-listing and subtle reprisal for unpopular political or social views. Men have always had to contend with the memories of other men. In the United States, however, we are blessed with a Constitution which provides for due process of law. This applies to the arbitrary use of the recordkeeping and information power of government against the individual.

Despite these guarantees, the new technology has been quietly, but steadily, endowing officials with the unprecedented political power which accompanies computers and data banks and scientific techniques of managing information. It has given Government the power to take note of anything, whether it be right or wrong, relevant to any purpose or not, and to retain it forever. Unfortunately, this revolution is coming about under outdated laws and executive orders governing the recordkeeping and the concepts of privacy and confidentiality relevant to an earlier time.

These developments are particularly significant in their effect on the first amendment to our Constitution.

- No longer can a man march with a sign down Pennsylvania Avenue and then return to his hometown, his identity forgotten, if not his cause.
- No longer does the memory of the authorship of a political article fade as the pages of his rhetoric yellow and crumble with time.
- No longer are the flamboyant words exchanged in debate allowed to echo into the past and lose their relevance with the issue of the moment which prompted them.
- No longer can a man be assured of his enjoyment of the harvest of wisdom and maturity which comes with age, when the indiscretions of youth, if noticed at all, are spread about in forgotten file cabinets in basement archives.

Instead, today, his activities are recorded in computers or data banks, or if not, they may well be a part of a great investigative index. Some examples come readily to mind from the subcommittee survey.

The Civil Service Commission maintains a "security file" in electrically powered rotary cabinets containing 2,120,000 index cards. These bear lead information relating to possible questions of suitability involving loyalty and subversive activity. The lead information contained in these files has been developed from published hearings of congressional committees, state legislative committees, public investigative bodies, reports of investigation, publications of subversive organizations, and various other newspapers and periodicals.

This file is not new, but has been growing since World War II. The Commission has found it a reasonable, economical and invaluable tool in meeting its investigative responsibilities. It is useful to all federal agencies as an important source of information. The Commission chairman reports: "Investigative and intelligence officials of the various departments and agencies of the Federal Government make extensive official use of the file through their requests for searches relating to investigations they are conducting."

In its "security investigations index," the Civil Service Commission maintains 10,250,000 index cards filed alphabetically covering personnel investigations made by the Commission and other agencies since 1939. Records in this index relate to incumbents of federal positions, former employees, and applicants on whom investigations were made or are in process of being made.

The Commission's "investigative file" consists of approximately 625,000 file folders containing reports of investigation on cases investigated by the Commission. In addition, about 2,100,000 earlier investigative files are maintained at the Washington National Records Center in security storage. These are kept to avoid duplication of investigations or for updating previous investigations.

For authorization for these data banks, the Commission cites Executive Order 10450 promugated in 1953.

Another department, the Housing and Urban Development Department, is considering automation of a departmental procedure. According to a report made to the subcommittee:

"The data base would integrate records now included in FHA's Sponsor Identification File, Department of Justice's Organized Crime and Rackets File, and HUD's Adverse Information File. A data bank consisting of approximately 325,000 3x5 index cards has been prepared covering any individual or firm which was the subject of, or mentioned prominently in any investigations dating from 1954 to the present. This includes all FBI investigations of housing matters as well. In addition, HUD maintains an index file on all Department employees which reflects dates and types of personnel security investigations conducted under the provisions of Executive Order 10450."

In the interest of preparing for possible civil disturbances and for protecting the armed services from subversion, the Department of the Army and other military departments have been collecting information about civilians who have no dealing with the military services. While the full extent of this surveillance is not yet known, it is estimated that records of the political activities of some 13,000 persons were kept in computerized form by the Army, and countless thousands of other manual files were maintained at regional and local military offices. The program of keeping information on the lawful political activities of Americans has been substantially reduced and many of the files destroyed. However, much of the information gathered still remains in government hands. In addition, the Army is the custodian of 25,000,000 records of all persons who have undergone security investigations as present or former members of the armed forces, civilian employees of the Department of Defense, and employees of defense contractors.

The Secret Service has created a computerized data bank in the pursuit of its programs to protect high government officials from harm and federal buildings from damage. Their guidelines for inclusion of citizens in this data bank refer to "information on professional gate crashers; information regarding civil disturbances; information regarding anti-American or anti-U.S. Government demonstrations in the United States or overseas; information on persons who insist upon personally contacting high Government officials for the purpose of redress of imaginary grievances, and so forth."

In the area of law enforcement, the Bureau of Customs has installed a central automated data processing intelligence network which is a comprehensive data bank of suspect information available on a 24-hour-a-day basis to Customs. The initial data base, according to the Secretary of the Treasury, is a "modest" one comprising some 3,000 suspect records. He states: "These records include current information from our informer, fugitive and suspect lists that have been maintained throughout the Bureau's history as an enforcement tool and which have been available at all major ports of entry, though in much less accessible and usable form. With the coordinated efforts of the Agency Service's intelligence activities, steady growth of the suspect files is expected."

This data bank, used by the Bureau to identify suspect persons and vehicles entering the United States, is considered an "essential tool" in performance of Customs officers' search and seizure authority.

The Department of Justice is establishing comprehensive law enforcement data systems in cooperation with state governments, and is funding state data programs for law enforcement, civil disturbance and other surveillance purposes.

Under the Federal Bureau of Investigation, a national computer center is being established. This will contain information on the records of persons with criminal histories at the state and local level. In addition, the Bureau operates a criminal identification and fingerprint file, soon to be automated, containing the fingerprints of 87 million persons; the National Crime Information Center on wanted persons and stolen property; a Civil Disturbance Center containing information on over 13,000 persons and 14,000 incidents; an Organized Crime Intelligence System containing information on some 200,000 persons; and a number of other data banks in various stages of automation and computerization.

The National Science Foundation has created a data bank of scientists.

The Department of Health, Education, and Welfare has established a data bank on migrant children to facilitate the transfer of school records.

The Passport Office of the Department of State has a computerized data bank of 243,135 individuals in its "Lookout File." Individuals are placed in the file because they are defectors or expatriates wanted for criminal investigation, involved in child custody or desertion cases, indebted to the United States, subversives, AWOL, noncitizens, or for a variety of other reasons.

The Department of Transportation's National Highway Safety Program operates the National Driver Register Service which contains the names of more than 2½ million persons whose driving licenses have been denied, revoked, or suspended for over six months. The Bureau plans to install direct access terminals in police headquarters, courts and driver licensing offices in all states so that the full record of every driver can be obtained automatically.

During our subcommittee hearings in 1969, case after case was documented of the vast programs to coerce citizens into supplying personal information for statistical data banks in the Census Bureau and throughout other federal agencies.

These are only a few of the data programs which have raised due process of law questions from Congress and the public.

How do these things come about? It would be unfair, perhaps, to attribute suspicious political motives, or lack of ethics to those responsible for any one program or for any group of programs for collecting and storing personal information about citizens. Frequently, they just grow over the years. Sometimes, executive department data banks are either merely good faith efforts at fulfillment of specific mandates from Congress or they are based on what some officials think to be implied mandates to acquire information necessary for Congress to legislate. If so, then Congress has no one to blame but itself when such programs unnecessarily threaten privacy or other rights. But it then has an even greater responsibility for acting, once its own negligence is discovered.

Perhaps the most such officials can be charged with is overzealousness in doing their job within narrow confines, to the exclusion of all other considerations.

Sometimes the issue of threats to individual rights is presented only after a data system has developed, and only after practical problems are raised which were not envisioned on paper.

At times, due process may be threatened by the failure of the computer specialists to consider only the information on a person absolutely essential for their programing.

There are political reasons also. One is the failure of heads of executive departments and agencies to mind their own stores and stay out of the business of other agencies. Each department does not need to seize the total man when it administers a program; only those portions of him necessary for the job. Another reason is the tendency of executive branch officials in the interest of political expediency and shortcuts to law and order goals, to seize upon the techniques of data banks, intelligence gathering, and surveillance activities as a substitute for hard-hitting, practical law enforcement work by the proper agencies, and for creative administration of the laws.

All of these excuses will not help the law-abiding citizen who, at the whim of some official, is put into an intelligence-type data bank which is part of a network of inquiry for all manner of governmental purposes.

No one would deny that the government of such a populous and farflung country should not avail itself of the efficiency offered by computers and scientific data management techniques. Clearly, government agencies must, as Congress has charged them, acquire, store, and process economically the information it obtains from citizens for administrative purposes. There is an ever-increasing need for information of all kinds to enable the Congress to legislate effectively and the executive branch to administer the laws properly.

Furthermore, there is an obvious need in such a complex mobile society for recording and documenting amply the official relationship between the individual and his government.

More and more frequently, misguided individuals are resorting to violence and violation of the law. Communities are faced with rising crime rates. Local, state, and federal government have a right and a duty to know when a person has a legal record of violation of the law which, under the law, would deny him certain rights or benefits. They should be able to ascertain these matters quickly.

There are always some problems of accuracy and confidentiality with such records, especially when automated. It is not the carefully designed individual law enforcement data banks which concern the public. Rather, subcommittee study is revealing that data programs which have aroused the most apprehension recently are those—

- Which bear on the quality of first amendment freedoms by prying into those protected areas of an individual's personality, life, habits, beliefs, and legal activities which should be none of the business of government even in good causes;
- Which are unauthorized or unwarranted for the legitimate purpose of the agency;
- Which keep the information they acquire too long and which by the very retention of unknown data may intimidate the individual subject;
- Which are part of a network of data systems;
- Which make little, if any provision for assuring due process for the individual in terms of accuracy, fairness, review, and proper use of data, and thereby may operate to deny the individual rights benefits, privileges, reputation, which are within the power of government to influence, grant or deny.

There is growing concern that the zeal of computer technicians, of the systems planners, and of the political administrators in charge of the data systems threatens to curtail the forces of society which have operated throughout our history to cool political passions and to make our form of government viable by allowing free exchange in the marketplace of ideas.

The new technology has made it literally impossible for a man to start again in our society. It has removed the quality of mercy from our institutions by making it impossible to forget, to forgive, to understand, to tolerate. When it is used to intimidate and to inhibit the individual in his freedom of movement, associations, or expression of ideas within the law, the new technology provides the means for the worst sort of tyranny. Those who so misuse it to augment their own power break faith with those founders of our Constitution who, like Thomas Jefferson, swore upon the altar of God eternal hostility against every form of tyranny over the mind of man.

It has become dangerously clear in recent times that unless new controls are enacted, new legal remedies are provided, and unless federal officials can be persuaded to exercise more political self-control, this country will not reap the blessings of man's creative spirit which is reflected in computed technology. Rather, if the surveillance it encourages is allowed to continue without strict controls and safeguards, we stand to lose the spiritual and intellectual liberty of the individual which have been so carefully nourished and so valiantly defended, and which our Founding Fathers so meticulously enshrined in the Constitution.

I say this out of my conviction that the undisputed and unlimited possession of the resources to build and operate data banks on individuals, and to make decisions about people with the aid of computers and electronic data systems, is fast securing to executive branch officials a political power which the authors of the Constitution never meant any one group of men to have over all others. It threatens to unsettle foreover, the balance of power established by our federal Constitution.

Our form of government is the fruition of an ideal of political, economic, and spiritual freedom which is firmly rooted in our historical experience. Basic to its fulfillment has always been the monumental truth that such freedom is truly secure only when power is divided, limited, and called to account by the people. For this reason the central Government was divided into three separate and equal branches.

For this reason, the bill of rights was added to secure certain areas of liberty against incursion by government and the exercise of federal power was limited to certain purposes.

For this reason, we cherish and protect the legal freedom of each citizen to develop his mind and personality and to express them free of unwarranted governmental control.

I differ with those who say that there are no existing checks on this developing power of computer technology, for I believe they already exist in our form of government. The guarantees are established in our Constitution.

The forthcoming hearings will help Congress determine how these guarantees may best be implemented to meet the demands of the computer age.

In the interest of responding to the many inquiries from scholars, reporters and members of the public who are working on this subject, I should like to refer to other sources of materials which provide useful background information.

The subject of how government manages its information systems, and its paperwork, how and when it uses computers and automation to assist in this effort, has been a continuing subject of concern by a number of congressional committees and their efforts should interest those working on this subject.

The Senate Administrative Practice and Procedures Subcommittee has contributed valuable hearings, reports and studies on the subject of computers, privacy, and government dossiers. Particularly informative is their 1967 report "Government Dossier: Survey of Information on Individuals Contained in Government Files."

The Senate Government Operations Committee has, in other years, conducted comprehensive hearings and issued reports on government information systems and management uses of computers.

In the House of Representatives, the Committee on Science and Astronautics has held a provocative and stimulating series of hearings and panel discussions on the impact of technology, especially on the management of government information.

The House Government Activities Subcommittee of the Government Operations Committee, has produced valuable hearings, reports and legislation on "Data Processing Management in the Federal Government."

More than anyone else, Representative Cornelius Gallagher has continually pointed out the dangers to individuals rights and privacy of the establishment of a national data center, and his Special Subcommittee on Invasion of Privacy, after stimulating hearings produced a classic and concise report entitled, "The Data Bank Concept." The record of his hearings contains testimony from many expert witnesses on the philosophy of privacy and computer technology.

The Census and Statistics Subcommittee of the House Post Office and Civil Service Committee produced a thought-provoking and influential report in the 89th Congress entitled "The Federal Paperwork Jungle." Scholars will find most informative that subcommittee's hearings and reports dealing with the paperwork requirements placed upon business, industry, and the public by the federal departments.

I commend the publications of all these committees and the thoughtful speeches of the chairmen and the members of these committees to persons interested in this subject.

It is my hope that the hearings and study by the Constitutional Rights Subcommittee will add a unique and valuable dimension to the public and congressional dialog on the role of data banks, information systems, and computers in our constitutional form of government.

2

PRIVACY AND INDIVIDUAL FREEDOM

By Burt Neuborne

Government surveillance of individuals is not a new phenomenon. The governmental process of gathering, storing, retrieving and disseminating data on individuals has always existed—and has always been recognized as a significant threat to the functioning of a free society. What is new, however, is the incredible advances in technology which have enabled governmental agencies to achieve surveillance capabilities undreamed of only a few years ago.

Innovations in electronic and photographic techniques have made possible the collection of vast amounts of data on the day to day activities of all citizens, without so much as an inkling that the data collection is occurring.

Innovations in computer technology have made possible the storage, retrieval and dissemination of personal dossiers on millions of Americans. Thus, the practical deterrents of cost and storage space can no longer be relied upon to check the growth of a national dossier system.

The wedding of sophisticated information gathering techniques with computerized information storage and dissemination systems has created, for the first time, a very real danger that the sense of privacy which has traditionally insulated Americans against the fear of state encroachment will be destroyed and be replaced, instead, by a pervasive sense of being watched. The emergence of such a police state mentality could mean the destruction of our libertarian heritage.

The Importance of Privacy in a Free Society

Civil libertarians are often asked why they regard unrestricted governmental surveillance of the individual as an evil. After all, it is said, if a person has done nothing wrong, what has he to fear from governmental surveillance?

The simple answer to such a question is that a libertarian democratic society simply cannot exist, unless its citizens are encouraged to act free from an all encompassing sense of being observed and recorded. The tone of life and spontaneity of spirit which characterizes a free society cannot survive in an atmosphere where all deviations from the norm are immediately noted by the State and stored for future reference. The "chilling effect" of pervasive surveillance will inevitably destroy any society's capacity for dissent, non-conformity and heterodoxy. Subtract those elements from a libertarian democracy and you have totalitarianism.

From the very beginning of the Republic we have recognized that a sense of anonymity *vis a vis* the government was a practical precondition to the proper functioning of a political democracy.[1]

Even the debates over the ratification of the Constitution were carried on anonymously in the Federalist Papers and Anti-Federalist Papers.

It has been estimated that between 1789-1809, six Presidents, fifteen cabinet members, twenty Senators and thirty-four Congressmen published anonymous political materials.[2]

In *Talley v. California,* (362 U.S. 60, 1960), the Supreme Court protected the critical role which a sense of anonymity plays in the free exercise of our political freedom by invalidating a California ordinance prohibiting the dissemination of anonymous political leaflets. The Supreme Court stated:

"Anonymous pamphlets, leaflets, brochures and even books have played an important role in the progress of mankind. Persecuted groups and sects from time to time throughout history have been able to criticize oppressive practices and laws either anonymously or not at all. The obnoxious press licensing law of England, which was also enforced on the Colonies was due in part to the knowledge that exposure of the names of printers, writers and distributors would lessen the circulation of literature critical of the government. The old seditious libel cases in England show the lengths to which government had to go to find out who was responsible for books that were obnoxious to the rulers. John Liliburne was whipped, pilloried and fined for refusing to answer questions designed to get evidence to convict him or someone else for the secret distribution of books in England. Two Puritan ministers, John Penry and John Udal, were sentenced to death on charges that they were responsible for writing, printing or publishing books. Before the Revolutionary War, colonial patriots frequently had to conceal their authorship or distribution of literature that easily could have brought down on them prosecutions by English-controlled courts. Along about that time the Letters of Junius were written and the identity of their author is unknown to this day. Even the Federalist Papers, written in favor of the adoption of our Constitution, were published under fictitious names. It is plain that anonymity has sometimes been assumed for the most constructive purposes."

– In NAACP *v. Alabama,* (357 U.S. 449, 1958), the Supreme Court refused to permit Alabama to compel disclosure of the membership list of the Alabama NAACP. Mr. Justice Brennan, writing for the Court, stated: "This Court has recognized the vital relationship between freedom to associate and privacy in one's associations . . . Inviolability of privacy in group associations may in many circumstances be indispensable to preservation of freedom of association particularly where a group espouses dissident beliefs."

– In *Briswold v. Connecticut,* (381 U.S. 479, 1965), the Supreme Court explicitly recognized a constitutional right of privacy emanating from the penumbral application of the fundamental rights guaranteed by the First, Third, Fourth, Fifth and Ninth Amendments to the Constitution. The Court noted that the First Amendment erected a zone of privacy protecting freedom of speech and association; the Third Amendment erected a zone of privacy against governmental quartering of troops; the Fourth Amendment erected a zone of privacy against unreasonable searches and seizures; and the Fifth Amendment erected a zone of privacy in the area of interrogation.

The Supreme Court in *Griswold,* therefore, accelerated the trend of NAACP *v. Alabama, supra* and *Talley v. California, supra* in recognizing that a libertarian society, as we know it, cannot exist unless its citizens enjoy a sense of privacy.

The evolution of privacy as a constitutional imperative continued in the Supreme Court with the decision in *Stanley v. Georgia,* 394 U.S. 557 (1969). In *Stanley,* the Court invalidated a Georgia statute rendering it criminal to possess pornography. The decision of the *Stanley* Court was explicitly founded upon the inherent limitations on the States' power to inquire into the "private" lives of its citizenry.

Mr. Justice Marshall, quoting from Justice Brandeis' brilliant dissent in *Olmsteid v. United States,* (277 U.S. 438, 478, 1928), wrote: "fundamental is the right to be free, except in very limited circumstances, from unwanted governmental intrusions into one's privacy. 'The makers of our Constitution undertook to secure conditions favorable to the pursuit of happiness. They recognized the significance of man's spiritual nature, of his feelings and of his intellect. They knew that only a part of the pain, pleasure and satisfaction of life are to be found in material things. They sought to protect Americans in their beliefs, their thoughts, their emotions and their sensations. They conferred as against the Government, the right to be let alone—the most comprehensive of rights and the right most valued by civilized man.'"

The evolution of privacy as a right of constitutional dimensions received its most recent Supreme Court recognition in *Wisconsin v. Constantineau* (1971). In its decision the Court invalidated a Wisconson statute which permitted the "posting" by the police chief of names of persons to whom the sale of liquor was forbidden. The Court explicitly recognized limitations on the ability of the state to collect and to disseminate potentially derogatory information about individuals by stating: "Where a person's good name, reputation, honor or integrity are at stake because of what government is doing to him, notice and an opportunity to be heard are essential. 'Posting' under the Wisconsin Act may to some be merely the mark of illness, to others it is a stigma, an official branding of the person. The label is a degrading one . . . Only when all proceedings leading to the pinning of an unsavory label on a person are aired can oppresive results be prevented."

The acceptance by the Supreme Court in *Talley*, NAACP *v. Alabama, Griswold, Stanley* and *Constantineau,* of the existence of privacy as a constitutional right renders the widespread surveillance practices currently engaged in at all levels of government of highly questionable legality. Simply put, if it was unconstitutional for Alabama to compel the disclosure of the NAACP membership lists, it would be equally unconstitutional for it to assemble the identical information by photographing NAACP meetings. If it was unconstitutional for California to outlaw anonymous political activity by statute, it is equally unconstitutional for it to achieve the identical result via sophisticated surveillance. If it was unconstitutional for Wisconsin to assemble and disseminate derogatory information about individuals without any procedural safeguards, it is equally unconstitutional for it to engage in the identical practice via surveillance.

Before the technological revolution in information gathering and storage, physical searches and interrogation constituted the primary forms of governmental surveillance. Our society evolved the Fourth Amendment protection against unreasonable searches and seizures and the Fifth Amendment protection against compulsory self-incrimination as the primary devices to safeguard the sense of privacy from those "primitive" surveillance techniques. (*Boyd v. United States,* 116 U.S. 616, 1886). Given, however, the revolution in surveillance techniques — e.g. *Olmstead v. United States, supra* — the Fourth and Fifth Amendments as they have been traditionally viewed, fail to afford sufficient protection against burgeoning state surveillance techniques which threaten to destroy the veil of privacy needed to insulate the dissenter; the non-conformist and the unorthodox from the fear of sanction.

We must, therefore, evolve new safeguards if libertarian values are to be secure in the latter half of the 20th century.

First, we must evolve a modern concept of the roles of the Fourth and Fifth Amendments in regulating surveillance.

Second, we must evolve substantive limitations upon the government's use of the "new" surveillance, especially in the areas of politically sensitive activity.

Finally, we must evolve procedural guarantees which minimize the potential for abuse inherent in any system of governmental surveillance.

The Role of the Fourth Amendment

When surveillance consisted primarily of physical searches, the Fourth Amendment provided a staunch bulwark for our right of privacy. Unfortunately, however, the Supreme Court has failed to extend the Fourth Amendment's prohibition against unreasonable and warrantless searches to be coextensive with modern notions of government surveillance. Despite a brilliant dissent by Mr. Justice Brandeis in 1928 in the *Olmstead* case, the Supreme Court failed to extend the scope of the Fourth Amendment to encompass wiretapping. In 1967 the Supreme Court abandoned this restrictive interpretation and held that wiretapping did constitute a "search" under the Fourth Amendment. (*Katz v. United States,* 389 U.S. 347, 1967). Nevertheless, despite the fact that the sophisticated surveillance techniques currently in vogue involve equally intrusive searches, substantial confusion continues as to the role of the Fourth Amendment in controlling modern electronic and photographic searches.

It is increasingly apparent that the Fourth Amendment must be read to protect individuals from all unreasonable and warrantless surveillance. In short, no surveillance should be permitted if it fails to satisfy the strictures of the Fourth Amendment.

Thus, prior to utilizing any modern surveillance, an appropriate official should be required to appear before a magistrate and given sworn testimony that probable cause exists that the proposed surveillance will uncover specific evidence of a designated serious crime; that the surveillance is directed at a specific individual and that no less drastic means exist to obtain the evidence in question. The warrant would authorize surveillance for a limited period, and would not be renewable except upon a showing of strong probability that evidence of a serious crime would be uncovered.

In each instance in which court approved surveillance of any kind failed to uncover evidence, a report to that effect would be required to the authorizing magistrate, and unless he ruled to the contrary, to the individual against whom the surveillance was directed.

Finally, all material obtained pursuant to Court authorized surveillance would be required to be destroyed unless actually introduced as evidence in a criminal matter.

In connection with any criminal prosecution, a defendant would be entitled to a copy of all surveillance directed against him, to determine whether the fruits of unlawful surveillance are involved in his case. (*Alderman v. United States,* 1969).

The recent assertion by Attorney General Mitchell of power to engage in warrantless electronic surveillance and wiretapping in situations involving "national security" is, of course, an immense danger to the free exercise of our political freedoms. The traditional existence of a narrow exception for warrantless surveillance of foreign intelligence operations has been dramatically extended by the Attorney General into a *carte blanche* to engage in electronic surveillance of Americans whenever he deems it important from a national security standpoint. It is to the resounding credit of two District Court judges that they have flatly rejected the Attorney General's attempt to drive a repressive tank through the narrow hole in the constitutional dike. Judge Warren J. Ferguson in *United States v. Smith* and Judge Damon J. Keith in *United States v. Plamondon* have vigorously affirmed the rights of Americans to be free from warrantless electronic searches and have declared the Attorney General's activities unlawful.

We must recognize, however, that even if we imposed a fully developed set of Fourth Amendment controls across the spectrum of modern surveillance, we would have only begun to deal with the problem. In addition to Fourth Amendment controls, a set of substantive limitations must be imposed upon the nature and scope of the information gathering and storage process.

What Forms of Information Gathering Can Be Tolerated?

Modern surveillance consists primarily of watching devices, such as cameras and lenses; listening devices such as wiretaps or electronic bugs; and the widespread use of under-cover agents who infiltrate and report upon certain groups. Each technique carries with it particular dangers, expecially to the robust exercise of First Amendment freedoms. Before any technique is resorted to, a form of social accounting must be considered to determine whether the danger to the basic tenets of our society inherent in the particular technique outweighs its value as a law enforcement device.

Thus, for example, in assessing the desirability of wiretapping, one must question whether the results justify the massive destruction of privacy caused by even court supervised wiretapping. For example, in New Jersey during 1970, court approved taps on over 24,000 separate conversations involving over 19,000 persons produced only two convictions—each for a gambling offense. Often the tap is place upon a public telephone, thus ensnaring large numbers of totally unconnected persons in the surveillance net. The statistics for Arizona, Colorado, Florida, Georgia, Maryland, New Jersey and New York for 1969 are not much better. Of 304 requests for court authorizations to tap, 302 were granted. 192 were extended beyond the original 30 day period and some taps continued for as long as 220 consecutive days. Over 13,000 persons were overheard. No reports of convictions have been released, but 95 percent of the participants overheard were clearly beyond the proper scope of the investigation.

As Mr. Justice Holmes eloquently said in his dissent in *Olmstead*: "it is better sometimes that crime should go unpunished than that the citizen should be liable to have his premises invaded, his desks broken into, his private books, letters and papers exposed to prying curiosity, and to the misconstructions of ignorant and suspicious persons."

If we are to continue to tolerate wiretapping and eavesdropping we must take a long hard look at the reality of their impact and decide whether the concomitant massive loss of privacy is worth it.

In assessing the social accounting aspects of watching devices a second set of considerations come into play. Watching devices have been utilized with increasing frequency to monitor and to record the identities of persons engaging in lawful political activities. Thus, the

New York City Police Department attempted to videotape last year's May Day celebration in Union Square, ostensibly to provide classroom footage for a course in crowd control. Only a court order prevented the videotaping. Police in Toledo, Ohio, photographed peace demonstrators and are alleged to have shown the pictures to the demonstrators' employers. FBI agents openly take moving picture footage of demonstrations as a matter of course. Police in Richmond, Virginia, photographed the license plates of demonstration participants.

If we are to continue to tolerate the use of watching devices, we must balance their unique propensity for political surveillance against any alleged law enforcement benefit.

Finally, in assessing the use of undercover agents, especially in the area of political associations, the devastating effect of infiltration upon free association must be weighed. The "chilling effect" of the fear of infiltration is an ever present danger. Moreover, infiltration seems to have a strange propensity for ripening into actual entrapment. In a recent trial in New York, my colleague Paul Chevigny represented a member of the Black Panther party who was alleged to have conspired to rob a bank. The jury acquitted on the ground that the police undercover agent who obtained the evidence had, in fact, entrapped the defendants into an illegal conspiracy by suggesting the robbery, drawing the map and supplying the car.

Who May Be Permitted to Conduct Surveillance?

We have witnessed a distressing tendency for each organ of government to attempt to develop an independent surveillance network.

The most glaring example of the proliferation of surveillance organs is the repeated disclosure of military intelligence operations designed to gather dossiers on civilian political figures. Thus, in addition to the widely publicized antics of the 113MI Group in Illinois and the existence of the military data bank at Fort Holabird, the 108thMI Group engages in widespread surveillance of civilian political activity in New York City.

The 108thMI Group maintained a domestic intelligence arm, CONUS, headed by a female civilian employee of the Department of Defense with the equivalent rank of Captain. She dispatched agents to monitor and report on virtually every political demonstration in New York and compiled, with the active cooperation of the Bureau of Special Services of the New York City Police Department, a massive dossier system on politically active New Yorkers. At her direction a military intelligence agent was directed to register as a student at New York University to monitor political activity on that campus in the Fall of 1968.

In addition to the Military Intelligence dossier system, virtually every other arm of government, including the Passport Section of the Department of State, is busy gathering dossiers on individual Americans. If we are to avoid a national dossier system, legislation narrowly circumscribing the persons authorized to gather, store, retrieve and disseminate information must be enacted. Surveillance activities, including data storage, should be confined strictly to designated law enforcement officials.

Who May Be Placed Under Surveillance?

The surveillance process should be confined to individuals who are suspected of actually engaging in, or being about to engage in, serious crime.

Blanket data collection of persons engaged in controversial political activity should be absolutely prohibited. Such data collection is currently so widespread as to be epidemic.

The police force of virtually every city in America contains a department the major function of which is the compilation of dossiers on political activists. In New York City the dossier preparation function is performed by the Bureau of Special Services, fondly known as the Red Squad.

The states of Oklahoma and New Jersey have recently publicly embarked upon the preparation of computerized dossiers on political activists. Under pressure from the American Civil Liberties Union, Oklahoma has abandoned its project after collecting 6,000 names. The New Jersey intelligence network is currently under attack by the ACLU in the courts.

The massive extent to which the Army collected dossiers of politically active Americans was revealed by the ACLU in *Tatum v. Laird.* The Army has promised to destroy its dossiers.

Unless specific prohibitions against the blanket surveillance of Americans engaged in protest activities are enacted, the sense of anonymity which the Supreme Court sought to preserve in NAACP *v. Alabama* and *Talley v. California* will be irretrievably lost.

What Information May Be Gathered and Stored?

There currently exists no check on the nature of the information being fed into our existing dossier system.

First, legislation absolutely prohibiting the gathering or storage of information relating to lawful political activities is desperately needed.

The common practice of monitoring demonstrations in order to permanently record the participants is so widespread that the FBI brazenly photographs demonstrators without fear of criticism. A recent meeting of the Suffolk County Chapter of the New York Civil Liberties Union was tape recorded by the Suffolk County Police Department without permission. During the 1967 March on Washington, military intelligence agents, disguised as demonstrators were instructed to photograph demonstration leaders. When the photographs were developed, the New York agents had photographed the New Jersey agents and vice versa.

Another common surveillance practice involves the compilation of membership lists in controversial political groups. Although NAACP *v. Alabama* precludes the government from requiring the disclosure of membership lists in controversial organizations, modern surveillance techniques attempt to attain the identical end covertly.

Second, legislation outlawing the storage or dissemination of hearsay or anonymous derogatory information is desperately needed. Current surveillance practices invite the inclusion of anonymous, subjective characterizations of an individual. Such information must be excluded.

Third, legislation regulating the storage and dissemination of arrest records is desperately needed. Current surveillance techniques provide for the wide dissemination of all arrest records, even those occurring many years ago.

The practice of permitting the dissemination of arrest records is a self-defeating process which has the effect of fencing out arrested persons from society. The existence of an arrest record renders it virtually impossible for a member of an ethnic or racial minority to find a decent job. Despite the presumption of innocence, an arrest record acts as a punishment which stigmatizes an individual for life. Studies by the New York Civil Liberties Union and by the Capitol Area affiliate of the American Civil Liberties Union document the fact that arrest records act as a form of punishment by depriving an individual of social and economic mobility. No more heartbreaking cases come into the NYCLU office than the stream of persons who have been denied employment because of an arrest record. I currently represent two applicants for city employment—one as an ambulance driver, the other as a taxi driver. Each has been denied the opportunity to earn a living because of arrests occurring many years ago.

Pioneer decisions by Chief Judge David Bazelon, by Judge Nanette Dembitz of the New York Family Court and by Judge Sol Wachtler of the New York State Supreme Court have questioned the validity and propriety of the unquestioned maintenance of arrest records. Judge Bazelon's suggestion that the judge who dismisses the criminal charges be vested with power to expunge the arrest record is a highly promising method of minimizing the injustice of arrest records.[4]

Especially as to those arrests which occurred as the result of First Amendment activity, no sufficient justification exists for the imposition of a "badge of infamy" upon a citizen by saddling him with the stigma of an arrest record. (*Wisconsin v. Constantineau, supra.*)

How Long May Information Be Retained?

Much of the folklore of this nation turns on the concept of putting a person's past behind him and beginning a new life. This nation was settled by waves of immigrants who chose to begin a "new life" in the new world. The vastness of the nation and the existence of the frontier posed numerous opportunities for a fresh start.

Given modern technology, however, it has become virtually impossible for any citizen to escape from his past. As surely as the scarlet letter was once branded on the flesh, our computers now impose an electronic brand upon us. There is no escape from our past; no opportunity for a fresh start. Truly, we live imprisoned in a web of imperishable data.

We must evolve a social procedure, analogous to the economic bankruptcy process, whereby an individual can gain a "discharge" from his past. Just as the commercial process could not function without a procedure enabling participants to attempt a fresh start, the social system cannot function without a procedure enabling individuals to obliterate the residue of their past errors. That procedure was once the simple expedient of moving to a new town. A shrinking world has destroyed that procedure; and we must evolve a new one. Thus, an informational statute of limitations should be an integral part of any surveillance system, automatically expunging "stale" information after a given period.

Even the imposition of careful substantive limitations upon the surveillance process cannot remove its capacity for abuse. In order to minimize that capacity, the surveillance process must be hedged with rigorous procedural safeguards.

Procedural Safeguards Governing the Storage, Retrieval and Dissemination of Information

Every person about whom personal data is being stored by the government must be notified of that fact and must be permitted access to his dossier to check its accuracy and propriety. An individual, upon receipt of a notice of dossier compilation, must be permitted an opportunity to challenge the propriety of the mantenance of a dossier.

Notice of a request for personal information must be given to an individual prior to its dissemination. The notice must describe the putative information recipient and summarize the requested information. An individual, upon receipt of such a notice, must be afforded an opportunity to challenge the proposed dissemination.

An individual must be afforded an expeditious opportunity to challenge the accuracy or propriety of information contained in his dossier. Such opportunity should take the form of an "accuracy hearing" or "propriety hearing" at which an individual could rebut the contents of his dossier and move for its expunction. Such a procedure would be highly useful to remove "stale" information from a dossier.

To the extent information is gathered in violation of the expanded Fourth Amendment or the substantive statutory limitations imposed upon surveillance, it should be subject to an "exclusionary rule" and stricken from the records.

To the extent information is disseminated in violation of procedural and substantive safeguards, an individual should have the option of either recovering his actual damages or settling for a statutory liquidated amount. Justice Felix Frankfurter aptly observed that the history of liberty is inextricably intertwined with the history of procedure. Only by establishing secure procedural controls over the surveillance process can its dangers be minimized.

Conclusion

As with almost every field of technological advance, we are faced in the area of surveillance with the dilemma of controlling the technological Frankensteins we have created. In the industrial area, production technology threatens the physical ecology of our continent; in the political area, surveillance technology threatens the psychological ecology of the democratic spirit. If we are to survive as a libertarian society, we must insure that the delicate sense of freedom which is dependent upon a commitment to individual privacy is not destroyed in the often spurious name of "efficiency."

1. See, generally, note, *The Constitutional Right to Anonymity,* 70 *Yale Law Journal* 1084 (1960); Notes, "Anonymity: An Emerging Fundamental Right," 36 *Indiana Journal* 306 (1961).

2. A. J. Beveridge, 4 *The Life of Marshall* (1919), 313-319.

3. For a discussion of the *Griswold* case see "Symposium on the Griswold Case and the Right of Privacy," 64 *Michigan Law Review* 197 (1965).

4. Similar considerations militate against the maintenance of records of confinement to a mental hospital. In New York State all involuntary state mental patients are immediately fingerprinted and duly recorded. The records remain even though the confinement may be immediately terminated by a psychiatrist. The maintenance of general medical records, and the possible introduction of "genetic printing" in the coming decade pose similar threats to the sanctity of individualism.

3

THE SURVEILLANCE SOCIETY

By Arthur R. Miller

Someone with limited vision might be tempted to say, as did a federal judge recently, that army spying on the lawful activities of civilians is "much ado about nothing." Viewed in isolation, perhaps the judge was right in characterizing the army's activities as an "assemblage of keystone cops" or as a mild irritant, especially since the public mea culpas by former intelligence agents *may* have helped to abort their expansion. But military spying cannot be viewed in a vacuum—unfortunately, it is symptomatic of growing governmental intrusion and heightened threats to our constitutional freedoms.

Consider the implications of these three propositions: First, Americans are scrutinized, measured, watched, counted, and interrogated by more governmental agencies, law enforcement officials, social scientists, and poll takers than at any time in our history. Second, probably in no nation on earth is as much individualized information collected, recorded, and disseminated as in the United States. Third, the information gathering and surveillance activities of the federal government have expanded to such an extent that they are becoming a threat to several basic rights of every American—privacy, speech, assembly, association, and petition of the government.

As recently as a decade ago we could smugly treat Huxley's *Brave New World* and Orwell's *1984* as exaggerated science fiction having no relevance to us or to life in this country. But in the last few years this comforting, but self-delusive, mantle has been stripped away. Revelations before congressional subcommittees and in the news media have presented a disheartening panorama of the ways in which the intruders of our society, aided by modern science, have destroyed many of our traditional bastions of privacy. The widespread use of spike and parabolic microphones, the emergence of various gadgets for electronic eavesdropping, and the ready availability of cameras equipped with esoteric optical devices have made it clear that we no longer enjoy *physical* privacy in our homes, offices, or remote country retreats. And now, ever increasing resort to the computer, laser technology, and microminiaturization techniques has begun to erode our *informational* privacy and to threaten several of our most fundamental rights guaranteed by the Constitution.

The hearings on governmental questionnaires and related matters held by the Senate Subcommittee on Constitutional Rights during April, 1970, and the wealth of material presented in my new book, *The Assault on Privacy: Computers, Data Banks, and Dossiers* (University of Michigan Press, 1971) demonstrate the spiraling pattern of data collection in this country, and no purpose is served by redocumenting here what now is self-evident. Whether he knows it or not, each time a citizen files a tax return, applies for life insurance or a credit card, seeks government benefits, or interviews for a job, a dossier is opened under his name and an informational profile on him is sketched. It has now reached the point at which whenever we travel on a commercial airline, reserve a room at one of the national hotel chains, or rent a car we are likely to leave distinctive electronic tracks in the memory of a computer—tracks that can tell a great deal about our activities, habits, and associations when collated and analyzed. Few people seem to appreciate the fact that modern technology is capable of monitoring, centralizing, and evaluating these electronic entries—no matter how numerous they may be—thereby making credible the fear that many Americans have of a womb-to-tomb dossier on each of us.

Even though the threat to our informational privacy is growing constantly, most Americans remain unaware of the extent to which federal agencies and private companies are using computers and microfilm technology to collect, store, and exchange information about the activities of private citizens. Rarely does a day go by without the existence of some new data bank being disclosed. In recent months we have read of the Department of Housing and Urban Development's Adverse Information File, the National Science Foundation's data bank on scientists, the Customs Bureau's computerized data bank on "suspects," the Civil Service Commission's "investigative" and "security" files, the Secret Service's dossiers on "undesirables," and the surveillance activities of the United States Army—to name only a few of the federal government's data banks that have been brought to light. Even now only the tip of the iceberg may be visible.

The lack of concern over these data gathering activities probably reflects the fact that by and large they are well intended efforts to achieve socially desirable objectives. For example, the law enforcement agencies can claim that filebuilding is necessary to combat organized crime and restore "Law and Order." In a similar vein, the FBI and the Army can justify their intelligence activities in terms of combating subversion or quelling campus disruptions and riots in our urban centers by knowing who to watch or seize in times of strife.

But there is a negative side to these mushrooming data banks—particularly those that bear the imprimature of a governmental organization. Consider the information practices of the United States Army. Early this year it was revealed that for some time Army intelligence systematically was keeping watch on the *lawful* political activity of a number of groups and preparing "incident" reports and dossiers on individuals engaging in a wide range of *legal protests.* It must be emphasized that this monitoring not only covered society's "crazies" but extended to such non-violent organizations as the NAACP, the ACLU, the Southern Christian Leadership Conference, and the Women Strike for Peace.

The Army's intelligence system apparently came into existence as a by-product of the military's role in ending the civil disorders of the mid-1960's. Although there is considerable justification for certain types of information collection that are directly relevant to the Army's duties, the development of dossiers on people pursuing lawful social and political activities bears little relationship to the function of the military during periods of social unrest—especially when many of those being scrutinized are extremely unlikely to be involved in riotous conduct. Not only is the Army's filebuilding difficult to justify, but it appears to have been undertaken without sufficient appreciation of the fact that the creation and exposure of dossiers on people who are politically active could deter them from exercising their First Amendment freedoms of free speech and assembly, as well as their right to petition the government. If a citizen's conduct and associations are put "on file," and perhaps used to harass or injure him, he may become more concerned about the possible content of that file and less willing to "stick his neck out" in pursuit of his constitutional rights. The effect may be (to paraphrase a thought expressed by Justice Brennan in an analogous context) to encourage Americans to keep their mouths shut on all occasions (*Lopez v. United States,* 373 U.S. 427, 450 dissenting opinion). If we really take or constitutional guarantees seriously, we cannot afford to stand idly by and allow them to be debilitated any further by this type of coercion.

After a flurry of publicity about the Army's activities, the institution of a lawsuit by the American Civil Liberties Union, and a number of sharply worded letters from members of the Congress, the Army announced that it was abandoning the data bank. But as has been pointed out repeatedly by Senator Ervin, many of the Army's statements have been vague and leave the status and future of its intelligence activities in doubt. Add to this uncertain state of affairs the existence of the Secret Service's unregulated computerized system containing dossiers on "activists," "malcontents," and "potential presidential assassins," as well as the recent disclosure that the Justice Department's civil disturbance group is maintaining an intelligence data bank, and no one should be surprised if some suggest that these surveillance efforts contain the seeds of the much dreaded police state or a return to McCarthyism.

The rapid development of a number of other information systems in the law enforcement arena also threatens personal privacy. The Federal Bureau of Investigation has established a National Crime Information Center (NCIC), which provides state and city police forces with immediate access to computerized files on stolen property and wanted persons. In the few years since its establishment, NCIC has become the keystone of an elaborate crime information network that eventually will integrate intelligence information centers throughout the nation into a single system. By the end of 1969 the FBI's Center was exchanging data with state and city police computers in every state except Alaska. In a recent speech to the Association of Computing Machinery (ACM) an FBI representative announced that there are already aproximately 3,000 remote access terminals linked to the FBI's computer. Apparently 1,000 of these are in police stations that are tied directly to NICI and 2,000 terminals are connected to state computer systems, which in turn have access to NCIC.

There is no doubt that in its present form NCIC, as is true of many other law enforcement data banks, is highly utilitarian and justifiable. No one can quarrel with the notion that a policeman in a squad car should be able to call his dispatcher for an NCIC check on a vehicle he stops on the highway and its registered owner before he personally approaches it. How else is he likely to be warned that the driver may be armed and dangerous?

But if these data banks expand to include sensitive information about people who have not been branded as fugitives from justice and precautions are not taken to insure the security and integrity of NCIC and other law enforcement systems, the dangers may begin to outweigh the benefits. In the speech before the ACM mentioned earlier, the FBI spokesman also revealed that police arrest records probably will be computerized and added to the NCIC data base next year, assuming that Congress provides the necessary funds. Despite the notoriously misleading character of many arrest records (many people who are arrested are never prosecuted, even fewer are convicted, and many arrests are of the dragnet variety that occur during *perfectly lawful* demonstrations), it was admitted that there currently are *no* plans to insure the security of the NCIC network or to upgrade the quality and accuracy of the data that is recorded. That, it was said, is the responsibility of the user.

State and local law enforcement computer systems also are becoming increasingly sophisticated. New York already has in operation the essential features of a network built around a single computer center—the New York State Identification and Intelligence System (NYSIIS). This unit is designed to store information for state and local law enforcement agencies and permit them to retrieve data through their own terminals. In Ohio the Cincinnati-Hamilton County Crime Information Center allows 38 city and state agencies to share its computerized information. This system is tied both to NCIC and the Ohio State Highway Patrol Computer Center in Columbus, Ohio and plans are under way to connect the Cincinnati-Hamilton County Center to systems in Kentucky and Indiana. Going farther afield, Scotland Yard is developing an information system that will be available to law enforcement agencies throughout the British Isles and similar computer systems are being developed in other nations and by multi-national organizations such as INTERPOL. Satellite or cable transmission will enable these centers to exchange data with NCIC, which can then forward them to state and local systems.

The same pressures of efficiency and expediency that are encouraging the exchange of information among agencies on the same and different levels of government will lead to even more comprehensive networks in the future. Direct federal funding already is contributing to this trend—the Office of Education is supporting a Migrant Worker Children Data Bank, the Department of Housing and Urban Development is sponsoring prototype computerized municipal information systems and building files on housing loan applicants (with particular attention to those who prove to be ineligible), and President Nixon's welfare reform proposal (the Family Assistance Act) would give the Department of Health, Education and Welfare authority to collect and exchange data on individuals with state welfare agencies. It would be foolish to ignore the ease with which each of these data centers could be integrated with the law enforcement and surveillance information flow.

Other combinations are on the horizon. In light of the polarity of today's student activism and public and governmental reactivism, it is even conceivable that federal surveillance systems and educational data centers will be linked, either formally or informally. If anyone thinks that this notion is farfetched, let him consider the implications of President Nixon's request of September 22, 1970 for funding and increased statutory authority to use 1,000 new FBI agents on university campuses. Conceeding the need for reinforced investigative manpower to restore peace to our institutions of higher learning, what controls will there be on the massive amount of potentially damaging personal information this type of operation is bound to generate and what assurance do we have that the integrity of university records will not be compromised?

The Need for Regulation

At present there are no effective restraints on the national government's information activities and no one has undertaken to insure that individuals are protected against the misuse of the burgeoning data banks. Indeed, a survey by the Senate Subcommittee on Administrative Practice and Procedure revealed many instances of agency demands for information that had not been authorized by Congress and concluded that most "government forms require either nonessential or too detailed information from the individual citizen." Similarly, the authority for the Army's surveillance of civilians is obscure. Neither the executive orders relating to security checks for government employment nor the so-called "Delimitations Agreement" between the military and the FBI, which allocates jurisdiction over personnel security investigations, seems to encompass the Army's file building.

What is more, muscle flexing has become a common government technique for furthering some of its data-gathering activities. Information collectors often deceive people by intimating that the law requires a response to questionnaires that in fact are voluntary, or use coercive practices (such as subtle threats of a loss of government benefits) to extract information. Even among citizens who are offended by certain inquiries or practices, there is a natural reluctance to "buck the system."

No one seems to be immune from these activities. For example, in an effort to trace the movement of American funds abroad—particularly to Swiss banks, draft evaders, and the Viet Cong—the FBI keeps watch on large numbers of domestic banking and credit transactions. Financial institutions rarely object to these intrusions on their files, perhaps in part because many bank and corporate security officers are former FBI and law enforcement agents. Furthermore, since the FBI has jurisdiction over bank fraud cases, the banks may find it to their advantage to "cooperate"—especially if they might want an information favor from their government friends tomorrow. Thus, it is not surprising that the FBI is able to examine over 25,000 credit bureau files annually without first securing subpoenas.

Nor is the government's hyperactivity in collecting information offset by its exercise of restraint in using it. On one occasion the FBI publicly released 1,200 pages of transcripts of electronically recorded conversations among reputed Mafia figures in which numerous prominent people were talked about, often disparagingly. Even conceding the desirability of informing the public of the threat organized crime poses to our society, need it be done by encouraging the daily press to publish unsworn conversations procured by governmental bugging? In a similar vein, why shouldn't citizens have doubts about the government's handling of personal information when presidential advisors have access to their federal tax returns and they are exchanged with state and local taxing agencies without taking any serious precautions to insure their confidentiality.

The data bank problem is being magnified by the computer. The trend toward computerization of personal information is resulting in a marked increase in the quantity, sensitivity, and variety of data that will be found in the electronic dossiers of the future, as well as expediting their exchange. Moreover, gaining access to these systems will be a desirable objective for a snooper, muckraking newsman, or political operative since a printout of someone's file may well contain public record information intermingled with subjective intelligence reports, data given by the subject or an informer with the assurance that its use would be limited, and information transferred from other computer systems. And it simply is unrealistic to assume that the managers or proprietors of computer systems—governmental or private—will take it upon themselves to protect the public against misuse of the data in their custody.

Approximately twenty federal agencies, bureaus, and departments already operate time-sharing computer systems or are in the process of establishing them. Additional systems are certain to spring up both within other governmental organizations and as a result of a number of proposed legislative programs calling for the collection of new bodies of personal data. Thus, the roots of a federal information exchange network have taken hold and the Bureau of Management and Budget has extensive authority to promote its further development. In view of the recent disclosures relating to the insensitivity of some government information handling practices, the prospect of an omnibus, de facto, federal data network evolving without prior comprehensive congressional review or the formulation of any policy guidelines that impose an obligation to protect privacy and the various rights guaranteed by the Constitution is not a pleasant one. Yet in spite of the obvious implications of this growing governmental computer power, in critical areas involving fundamental personal rights, federal agencies are still operating in an environment of policy by default and inaction. Information is being gathered, recorded, and disseminated with a Let-George-Worry-About-It philosophy that is putting us on the pathway toward a dossier dictatorship.

The irony of all this is that several years ago a proposal to establish a National Data Center was blocked by a combination of congressional opposition and public outrage. In retrospect, that suggestion has proven innocuous compared to the reality of some of the systems already functioning in the executive branch of the government. The phoenix that has arisen from the ashes of the Data Center proposal is the unregulated and haphazard proliferation of governmental data banks and machine interconnections that already is posing a threat to some of the pillars of our democratic society.

The Inadequacy of Common-Law Remedies

If some of the constitutional protections we have enjoyed in this country are to survive in a data based, electronic world, the law must begin to adjust to today's realities. As I have attempted to demonstrate in my book, the existing patchwork of common-law remedies, constitutional doctrines, statutes, and administrative regulations is not capable of dealing with the problems raised by the accelerating pace of federal information gathering and the emergence of computerized information systems. Today's legal structure is characterized by uncertain application, lack of predictability, frequent inconsistency, unawareness of the ramifications of the new communications media, and an almost total disregard for the individual's right to participate in information transactions that may have a profound impact on his life. To take but one of many examples of this, the existing common-law tort theories deal almost exclusively with the public dissemination of previously acquired data, and ignore the implications of the unrestrained governmental collection of information. To be effective, a regulatory scheme must reach the latter problem and this simply may be impossible or may evolve too slowly from the right-to-privacy tort as we know it today.

But the law books are not entirely barren. The Supreme Court has recognized the individual's right to object to certain governmental attempts to extract information from him. Perhaps the most clearly developed of these notions is the citizen's right of associational privacy, which seeks to recognize the "vital relationship between the First Amendment freedom to associate and privacy in one's association." (NAACP *v. Alabama,* 357 U.S. 449, 462, 1958). Thus, when the government attempts to gather data concerning an individual's association with a group dedicated to the advancement of certain beliefs in "political, economic, religious, or cultural matters" (Id. at 460), it must "convincingly show a substantial relation between the information sought and compelling state interest." (*Gibson v. Florida Legislative Investigation Committee,* 372 U.S. 539, 546, 1963). These cases certainly contain the doctrinal seeds needed to curb the excesses of those federal surveillance activities that are likely to inhibit the exercises of First Amendment freedoms. It must be noted, however, that the successful assertion of a violation of one's associational privacy appears to depend upon a showing that disclosure will result in a restraint on an individual's ability to exercise his freedom of association.

Closely related to the right of associational privacy is another judicially recognized individual interest—the right to possess ideas and beliefs free from governmental intrusion. As the Supreme Court stated in *Schneider v. Smith,* 390 U.S. 17 (1968), First Amendment guarantees and the concept of associational privacy "create a preserve where the views of the individual are made inviolate. This is the philosophy of Jefferson that 'the opinions of men are not the object of civil governments, nor under its jurisdiction. . . .' "

This judicial recognition of privacy in one's associations and beliefs should not be narrowly construed; if it is, the people will receive only limited protection against highly inhibiting governmental intrusiveness. It seems to me that these Supreme Court cases announce an expansive principle, one that is part of a tradition basic to the nation's philosophical fabric—the conception of government as an institution of limited powers that is obliged to meet a heavy burden of justification when it undertakes a program or course of action that will inhibit the freedom of its citizens. It is axiomatic that in terms of effect of widescale governmental surveillance or information control can chill the exercise of an individual's constitutional rights. Thus, agency supplications based on claims of economy or gains in governmental efficiency or justified in terms of the current quest for the holy grail of "Law and Order" simply do not justify every demand for greater power to extract, manipulate, store, and disseminate data relating to the lives and activities of people and groups.

Unfortunately, the trends in the information surveillance field are altering the citizen-government balance so drastically that even if the common-law privacy remedies were refurbished and the First Amendment freedoms of association of belief were expanded, it still would be unwise to rely exclusively on private lawsuits for damages or an injunction against further intrusion on constitutional rights. In addition to the difficulty and imprecision of attempting to convert a loss of freedom into monetary terms, the right of an injured person to seek redress is hollow indeed because he is so completely excluded from the information gathering-recordation-dissemination cycle that in many instances he may never learn how his life is being affected by the circulation of personal data relating to him.

Possible Legislative Approaches

Direct legislative action based on the congressional power to safeguard constitutional rights clearly is indicated. Statutory protection might take a number of different forms. One relatively simple statutory approach is to prohibit governmental organizations from collecting designated classes of sensitive personal data—an approach that is bound to incur the ire of the agencies, all of whom believe that their data gathering activities are imperative for the success of some national policy.

One variation would be a statute prohibiting data collectors from using, or threatening to use, coercion to compel individuals to disclose data they are not legally obliged to furnish. This would also require reappraising the existing statutes that make disclosure of certain information by citizens mandatory, presumably with an eye toward reducing their coverage. Some aspects of the bill introduced last year by Senator Ervin (S. 1791) illustrate this approach. The same is true of the proposals seeking to eliminate the criminal penalties for failure to answer many of the questions on the decennial census. Although eliminating some of the harsh sanctions for noncompliance with governmental demands for information appears to be desirable, doing so is not a panacea. Prohibitions against coercive data collection will only remedy some of the more blatant abuses; they will be of no assistance in assuring better data handling and dissemination practices or limiting the government's right to collect information from sources other that the data subject.

A different, and in some ways more drastic, legislative approach involves requiring computer manufacturers, users, and data networks to employ prescribed technical and administrative safeguards for maintaining the integrity of personal information. This also could take the form of imposing a general statutory duty of care on every federal official connected with the processing of data, which would have the effect of encouraging sensitivity to the dangers of information abuse, or of enacting detailed requirements that would have to be followed by all computer manufacturers, handlers, and users of personal information.

It would be very difficult at this time to employ any of these legislative formats in a statute that was to have general application. Personal information is used for so many different purposes that it may be impossible to draft a single body of statutory rules to govern all data systems carrying individualized data. The problem is compounded by the chameleon-like character of many types of information—data collected in one context may carry an entirely different meaning when transplanted to another.

Extremely complex legislation therefore would be necessary if specific privacy safeguards are to be prescribed for different information environments. This would be a particularly useful way, for example, of insuring that the sophisticated protective schemes that do exist for safeguarding computerized data are employed. A variety of access regulations, personnel controls, and mechanical devices are available that can discriminate among users and differentiate data on the basis of its sensitivity. To protect a system adequately, a combination of these techniques will have to be used so that a weakness in one aspect of a system's security will not compromise the other protective schemes. Along the same lines, any legislation that purported to prescribe how sensitive personal data—whether computerized or not — should be protected would have to deal with every phase of information integrity and draw distinctions in terms of the various levels of information sensitivity.

Thus, a potpourri of statutory controls might well prove necessary; some would establish degrees of confidentiality for different kinds of data and others might prescribe the technical and procedural safeguards to be employed by the system. This type of refined legislative structuring presumably would be based on an evaluation of how much "privacy" the data in a given system deserves and a balancing of the damage that could be caused by misuse of the information against the importance of the information to some legitimate government objective, as well as the cost and loss of efficiency that might result from implementing various safeguards. Alternatively, separate statutes could be framed in terms of the different types of information that is collected—e.g. health, military, internal security, financial—or to deal with the activities of the various groups that gather data—e.g., law enforcement agencies, military organizations, administrative agencies, statistical organizations.

But a detailed congressional assessment along these lines becomes an overwhelmingly complex undertaking, especially if it must be made against the background of massive surveillance data banks or highly sophisticated computer networks that carry information from numerous sources and are used by different governmental organizations for highly disparate purposes. Our very limited experience with data centers and computer networks, however, makes the job of drafting sound comprehensive national legislation that will stand up under the pressure of rapid technological change virtually insurmountable at present.

Administrative Regulation

Although various factors make detailed federal legislation in the near future both difficult to compose and a potentially unsatisfactory technique, they do not preclude the possibility that the current threat to our privacy and constitutional freedoms may be amenable to administrative regulation. In addition to obviating the need to make highly sophisticated policy judgments in statutory form, which may become obsolete shortly after going into force, giving the problem over to administrative control might have the effect of putting it in the hands of a watchdog group, composed of experts in the field who can exercise continuing supervision over governmental data activities. Moreover, if well drawn, administrative regulations should provide sufficient flexibility to permit experimentation and require less time for revision when new problems present themselves than do statutes.

Unfortunately, there is a negative side. Administrative regulation has fallen into considerable disfavor in the United States because it frequently takes on a highly bureaucractic character. All too often resort to agency action has become synonymous with delay, red tape, and arbitrariness, with the hoped for supervision of a field by an informed cadre giving way to the reality of politicized administrators who have little understanding of the complex problems under their governance. The situation typically is made worse by inadequate staffing and funding, which prevents many federal agencies from acquiring the expertise necessary for rational decision making. Despite these deficiencies, however, I believe that administrative regulation holds the most promise as a means of coming to grips with the important problems confronting us in the information arena.

It is not immediately apparent where regulatory power should be placed or what form it should take. Certain basic principles provide some guidance, however. Because of the national character of the citizen-surveillance problem and the computer-communications industries, there is no doubt that control at the federal level is essential. Yet a regulatory approach based on a general legislative directive to all of the agencies, but that leaves each of them responsible for establishing rules governing their own information activities, is likely to produce such significant variations in philosophy and practice that little may be gained. Thus, regulation must come from a single source having jurisdiction over all of the federal government's information activities.

It also seems axiomatic that regulatory power ought not be given to an agency having operating responsibilities that are dependent upon or involve the handling of a flow of personal information. The debate over the proposed National Data Center and revelations before congressional subcommittees concerning the intrusive activities of the Internal Revenue Service, the Post Office, and the Immigration and Naturalization Service make it abundantly clear that the rights of the individual often get short shrift from agencies that have a vested interest in gathering and using personal data. The result, of course, is that most of the existing information agencies should be disqualified from a leadership role in formulating regulatory policy for governmental data banks.

Is there any organization to which the problem can be entrusted? I have given careful thought to the possibility that an existing federal bureau, agency, or department, such as the Census Bureau, the Bureau of Management and Budget, the Federal Communications Commission, or the Federal Trade Commission, might be given responsibility for developing an administrative scheme for regulating the federal government's information activities and computer systems. But I have sadly come to the conclusion that none of them would be an effective guardian of the rights of our citizens, either because they are obligated to various institutional "clients" or because they are philosophically committed to the paramount importance of administrative efficiency.

If this is true, then the conclusion is inescapable: regulatory control must be lodged outside the existing administrative channels. As repugnant as it may sound in an era of expanding governmental involvements, it may be necessary to establish a completely new institution—perhaps modelled after the semi-autonomous Government Accounting Office—that can operate under a set of legislative guidelines and establish policy for the protection of individual privacy and the preservation of Constitutional rights. A new agency might well succeed in regulating the nature of the data about citizens that can be collected, recorded, and stored by various governmental organizations, enforce a congressional standard of care for insuring the accuracy of the government's information store, and make certain that all federal data centers employ the latest and most appropriate technological safeguards to protect files against breaches of security.

In addition, there are several necessary characteristics that any administrative body must possess in order to be effective as a guardian against undue informational surveillance, and it might be useful at this point to suggest what some of them are. The agency should be staffed by people who are versed in a wide range of disciplines—technology, science, law, and the humanities (particularly psychology and sociology). The agency commissioners or directors themselves should be drawn from various fields. The agency also must have access to all federal data banks and maintain a close liason with other governmental organizations as well as the data gathering and using communities in the private sector. This is essential in order both to stay abreast of the nation's information needs and to be in a position to recommend a revision of the regulatory scheme when changing conditions make that necessary.

One of the basic tasks of an agency of the type I am suggesting is to attempt to educate the data worshippers, the privacy paranoids, and the general public in the hope of achieving some common understanding of society's data needs and the growing public concern over the preservation of individual privacy and the First Amendment freedoms. At present there is considerable anxiety throughout the nation about the specter of a fishbowl environment and a lack of sensitivity to the problem on the part of information managers and system designers.

To further this educative function, it might be desirable to hold public hearings on a broad range of subjects, undertake technical and social science research projects, and act as a clearinghouse for information concerning activity in each of the many fields that bear on the question of governmental information policy. By use of these and other methods, the proposed agency could implement a principle analogous to that embodied in recent proposals before the Congress to create a Technology Assessment Board.

Another basic ingredient for evolving a rational regulatory policy is that the agency must have authority to engage in rulemaking relating to the technical features, personnel qualifications, and administrative procedures employed by all data centers that handle significant quantities of personal information. If airplanes and pilots must be certified, if automobiles are required to meet safety standards and their drivers obliged to pass tests and obtain licenses, why shouldn't governmental data collectors, computer systems, and information managers be obliged to meet and be pledged to honor requirements relating to the preservation of personal privacy and constitutionally based freedoms?

Ideally, the agency's power should be broad enough to embrace the activities of nonfederal information gatherers that might adversely affect the rights we are trying to protect. The regulators should be particularly attentive to the interlocking relationships that have begun to spring up between federal and local data handlers in the law enforcement field and the fact that many of the nation's major corporations maintain dossiers on millions of Americans. Close scrutiny of the latter category of data banks is becoming imperative because there is growing reason to believe that these files are exchanged both within the private sector and with law enforcement and surveillance groups at all levels of government. In short, once standards are established for federal systems, I believe that it eventually will become necessary to apply them to certain non-federal systems.

To implement the controls and regulations ultimately adopted, the federal agency I am describing will have to provide a method for handling grievances brought to its attention by members of the public. One obvious method would be to give statutory authority to the information agency to investigate, direct correction, and award appropriate relief for any abuses brought to its attention by individual citizens. Through the use of these procedures, its ability to negotiate with the information managers, and its status as a governmental organization, the agency could play the role of an information ombudsman, a device that is well known in the law of several European countries and is beginning to be recognized in the United States.

The agency also must develop and place heavy reliance on measures that provide the citizen some degree of control over personal information relating to him. The objective should be to develop procedures that give the individual a voice in the important transactions concerning his life history—transactions that often may drastically affect his economic and social well-being. Our society's traditional dedication to ideals of fair play and due process indicates that any set of rules regulating the handling of personal information should accord the individual, or someone who can represent his interests adequately, the right to receive notice and an opportunity to be heard before important decisions are made concerning his informational profile. The federal government should be held to no lesser standard.

The right to be heard must include the ability to rebut damaging evaluations, or to show that a particular information practice deters his exercise of rights protected by the Constitution, or to demonstrate that the data does not sufficiently further any legitimate government objective so as to warrant its retention, or to demand that recorded personal information conform to minimal standards of accuracy. In order to be meaningful, an administrative means of resolving conflicts between the citizen and the government must be expeditious and inexpensive.

The effectiveness of an agency that is intended to protect individual citizens against information abuses obviously depends upon its ability to avoid becoming a captive of the governmental units and private interests that have a stake in the data networks and systems that are to be regulated. The tendency of the so-called independent regulatory agencies to be captured by the industries they supposedly stand vigil over is a disheartening, but not totally bleak, prior history from which to proceed. With proper staffing and well-chosen lines of authority, an information agency may be able to achieve the degree of independence needed to perform its vital watchdog role. I have tried to explore this possibility in some detail in my book, *The Assault on Privacy*.

The other extreme must be avoided as well. A governmental agency cannot be permitted to become an island unto itself—neither responsive nor responsible to anyone, populated by technocrats whose conduct is shielded by their alleged expertise and the supposed importance of the governmental functions they perform. It must be accessible and be responsive to everyone. Above all, the agency's activities and its regulations must not be permitted to ossify. For the foreseeable future the key to effective regulation will be the ability to maintain sufficient flexibility and resiliency to adjust to changes in our technological and social environment.

4

THE DOMESTIC INTELLIGENCE COMMUNITY

By Christopher H. Pyle

The United States today possesses the intelligence apparatus of a police state. This apparatus is not something of the future; it exists now in the hands of a loose coalition of federal, state, municipal, and military agencies. Together, these law enforcement, counter-intelligence, and internal security agencies have developed to the point where authoritarian government is an operational possibility.

I do not mean to suggest that the emergence of this domestic intelligence community has turned the United States into a police state. On the contrary, I find it somewhat paradoxical that as this apparatus has proliferated, the civil liberties of most Americans have also grown. The reason for this apparent contradiction may be that the men who have developed these agencies are, by and large, decent and well-intentioned men. However, the fact that we may trust them is no guarantee that the apparatus which they have created will not someday come under the control of others for whom the investigatory power is a weapon to be wielded against political and personal foes. As Mr. Justice Brandeis once wrote: "Experience should teach us to be most on our guard to protect liberty when the government's purposes are beneficient. . . . The greatest dangers to liberty lurk in the insidious encroachment by men of zeal, well-meaning, but without understanding."

Accordingly, without questioning the motives of the officials who make up the domestic intelligence community, it makes sense to see what they have been up to, and to contemplate what might come of their endeavors.

Domestic Intelligence Operations

What they have done in their eagerness to protect us from subversion, espionage, and civil disorder is to impose a blanket surveillance upon nearly all political dissent throughout the United States. Today it is almost impossible for a private citizen to sign a newspaper ad protesting the war or to speak at a peaceful demonstration of any kind without being subjected to the government's surveillance. The fact that he signed the ad will be noted by the state subversive activities control board, some legislative committees, and the United States Civil Service Commission. If the demonstration is large, or relates to a controversial topic, the citizen can expect to be photographed by the local police intelligence unit, the Federal Bureau of Investigation, and, until recently, the United States Army. In many instances, the photography will involve both still pictures and videotapes, and the photographers will be posing as members of the press. Later they will get together with their counterparts in other agencies to identify the dissenters and to swap pictures. Eventually some of these will find their way into personality and organizational files, civil disturbance estimates, and mug books on dissenters.

But this is not all. If the local paper writes an article describing the demonstration and the citizen's role in it, the article is likely to become a permanent part of one or more data banks. Political archives are now kept by municipal police, state police, the National Guard, subversive activities control boards, internal security committees, each of the armed services, the Civil Service Commission, the Secret Service, the FBI, the Passport Office, and the Justice Department. In addition, information from the article may be recorded in card indexes, computer indexes, personality files, organizational files, and mug books.

Like their counterparts in foreign intelligence, the domestic intelligence agencies depend upon the press and each other for most of their information. On occasion, however, they find it necessary to conduct their own covert operations. Sometimes these are justified, as when an agent of New York City's Bureau of Special Services successfully infiltrated the Revolutionary Action Movement and foiled a plot to blow up the Statue of Liberty. But sometimes covert operations are not justified.

An especially outrageous covert operation came to light recently in upstate New York when an inquiry into the destruction of an ROTC building on the Hobart College campus disclosed that an agent from the Ontario County Sheriff's office had posed as an organizer for the Students for a Democratic Society and had incited campus violence by offering students bombs, guns, and lessons in guerrilla tactics. In New York City last May, defense counsel for 13 Black Panthers charged with conspiracy to bomb public places alleged that an agent or informer for the FBI had given one of the defendants an unsolicited gift of 60 sticks of dynamite. The FBI's use of wiretaps to collect information pertaining to what it alleged to be the sexual liasions of the late Rev. Martin Luther King is well known.

Less sinister, but no less violative of the rights of law-abiding dissenters is the conduct of surveillances that intimidate and harrass. Examples include:

- The detention, by Army agents, of a busload of demonstrators preparing to leave DuPont Circle in Washington, D. C. for Wilmington, Delaware, following the Counter-Inaugural of January 1969.
- FBI and Army inquiries at banks and bus companies concerning the identity and finances of persons and groups chartering buses to carry demonstrators to Washington, D. C. to participate in the November 1969 Moratorium. Lawsuits filed in New York allege that these investigations led to the cancellation of some charters, thus depriving some citizens of their right to petition their government for redress of grievances.
- Close-in surveillance and photography of law-abiding demonstrators that serves no peace-keeping function, but lets the demonstrators know that the price of dissent is the recording of their activities in political data banks. For example, when approximately 100 demonstrators marked the 25th anniversary of the destruction of Hiroshima last August by planting a locust tree near the laboratory in which the bomb was built, they were watched by undercover agents and filmed by thirteen government cameramen. Harrassing photography is now the subject of suits for injunctions against the police in New York City, Buffalo, Richmond, Virginia, and New Orleans, while data banks are being challenged in Los Angeles, New Jersey, and Oklahoma. The New Jersey police intelligence system seeks not only the identity of law-abiding demonstrators, but the identity of their employers as well.

The domestic intelligence community within the United States is composed principally of police intelligence units, military counterintelligence units, subversive activities control boards, internal security committees of legislatures, National Guard intelligence units, the FBI, the Secret Service, the Civil Service Commission, the Passport Office, and the Justice Department's interdivisional intelligence unit. Associate members of the community include a host of organizations in the fields of industrial security, campus security, preemployment reporting, and retail credit.

Police Intelligence Units

Most metropolitan police departments and almost every major state has a bureau engaged in the collection of political intelligence. Some of these date back to the First World War, when they hunted anarchists, Communists, and aliens. Others have been established more recently in response to the growth of mass demonstrations and the occurrence of urban riots. The National Advisory Commission on Civil Disorders urged their establishment: "An intelligence unit staffed with full-time personnel should be established to gather, evaluate, analyze, and disseminate information on potential as well as actual civil disorders. . . It should use undercover police personnel and informants, but it should also draw on community leaders, agencies, and organizations in the ghetto."

Some of these units are surprisingly large. New York City's Bureau of Social Services, for example, employs over 120 agents and has an annual budget in excess of $1 million. Chicago's is not quite as large.

Because their operations are rarely limited by city hall, these units sometimes carry their investigations beyond the territorial bounds of their jurisdiction. New York police undercover agents, for example, went to Chicago during the 1968 Democratic National Convention.

Similarly, their curiosity can be quite broad. Frank Rizzo, Philadelphia police chief, boasted to NBC-TV last April: "We know everything about the people who are going to cause problems in our city. . . no police department could be successful without the information we glean from . . . our Intelligence Squad. We know, generally, who's going to do what before they do it. . . We know who comes into the town, we know who's going to leave it, when they're going to leave it. . ."

State subversive activities units, unlike police intelligence units, function primarily as clearing houses for data collected by municipal and state police. The Subversive Activities Division of the Massachusetts State Police is typical of many of the older units. It employs five men, operates on an annual budget of $43,000, and spends much of its time conducting "security name checks." In 1967, 2,194 were run, and in 1968, 4,034. The division's annual report for 1969 describes the extent of its information swapping: "the files in this division have grown to such an extent that the FBI, the Immgration and Naturalization Service, Department of Defense, U. S. Army Intelligence, Federal Civil Service Commission, Treasury Department, several departments of the Commonwealth, industrial plants, and educational institutions now clear with this division on security checks."

The Oklahoma Office of Inter-Agency Coordination represents a newer breed of agency which is principally concurred with civil disorders. Established in 1968 as part of the State's Military Department, it coordinates the intelligence activities of municipal and state police and issues regular intelligence reports on protests, marches, demonstrations. It employs a staff of two professionals and has set aside a portion of its $45,808 budget to hire part-time investigators and informants. It exists to inform the governor, police, and National Guard about political activities in Oklahoma but has been forced by a lack of activism in that state to devote much of its regular intelligence reports to events occurring elsewhere in the country. The report for June 30, 1970, for example, alerted Oklahoma authorities to a pop festival in Atlanta, a Black Panther Convention in Philadelphia, and anti-war demonstrations planned for numerous cities in the fall. In addition, it called attention to the activities of a candidate for Congress, a group called Oklahomans for Indian Opportunity (founded by the wife of Sen. Fred Harris), and the Coalition for Civic Leadership of Oklahoma City. The agency was established without legislative authorization by the governor through the disbursement of funds appropriated for the State's Military Department. Since then it has received a grant of $18,347 from the U. S. Department of Justice's Law Enforcement Assistance Administration. Like its Massachusetts counterpart, it also swaps information with a variety of agencies including the FBI, the National Guard, and the Army.

The National Guard

The part-time nature of most National Guard units makes the sustained collection of domestic intelligence difficult. Those units with the most extensive files depend heavily on state agencies like the Oklahoma Office of Inter-Agency Coordination. A zealous intelligence officer, however, can make a difference. In 1968 a Major C. Allen March, the G-2 (intelligence officer) of the California National Guard, made headlines by regularly publishing an intelligence summary of protest politics inside and outside of California. March's summaries appeared to be drawn from newspapers and police reports, but were written from an ultra-right wing point of view. They eventually became the subject of controversy in the state legislature and were discontinued.

Stateside Military Units

The commander of each military unit, installation, base, or activity in the United States has an understandable curiosity about protest politics in the surrounding civilian community. This curiosity is heightened if the protests threaten to undermine the morale, discipline, or security of the post. The anti-war, anti-draft, and soldiers' rights movements, not surprisingly, have been perceived to pose such a threat. Accordingly, installation and unit intelligence offices have for many years collected information on persons and organizations supporting these causes. This activity is separate from, and addition to the very extensive collection efforts of the U. S. Army Intelligence Command, which I will describe in detail later in this statement.

One of the main foci of stateside military intelligence, then, has been the "RITA" program. "RITA" is short for "Resistance in the Army," and takes its name from a group of deserters in Europe who first organized under the name to encourage other soldiers to follow their example. The activities of the American Servicemans Union and the antiwar coffee houses have been primary objects of RITA surveillances, which frequently make use of informants and undercover agents drawn from military intelligence, military police, the Criminal Investigation Division, and the barracks.

A secondary focus of the domestic intelligence activities of stateside military units is race relations. In Europe, Vietnam, and the United States, military posts have been the scene of serious racial violence, and reporting systems have been set up to keep field commanders and the Pentagon informed of racial tensions. Like the civil disturbance and RITA intelligence efforts, this system also has an inherent tendency to probe into the private beliefs and associations of individuals both inside and outside the armed forces.

In addition, a number of stateside units—particularly those with riot control duties—have taken an active interest in civil disturbances which they suspect might grow into riots. Chief among these is the Continental Army Command (CONARC), which is the holding company for most stateside Army units, installations, and activities. It would seem that CONARC, which is responsible for defending the United States against invasion, should also defend it against insurrections and riots. But that is not the case. CONARC was deprived of this responsibility back in 1968 by the creation of the unit which runs the Pentagon's domestic war room. Three years earlier, CONARC also had lost much of its capacity to set up a civil disturbance early warning system when six counterintelligence groups (occupying some 300 offices coast to coast) were taken away from the major Army commands under its jurisdiction and reassembled to make the U. S. Army Intelligence Command. The main purpose for this shift of personnel to an independent support command was to facilitate the conduct of personnel security investigations. But during the Newark riots of 1967, the Intelligence Command also got the assignment to accelerate its occasional monitoring of potential civil disturbances into a full-fledged early warning system, complete with a nationwide teletype hookup and a computerized storage system. Miffed by this turn of events, CONARC resolved to create its own civil disturbance reporting system. It did so by giving domestic intelligence assignments to combat intelligence units in training and to post intelligence staffs. Eventually, it even installed its own computerized civil disturbance data bank at its headquarters at Fort Monroe, Virginia. All of this preparation was to be a hedge against the day when command of its own troops in time of riot might be returned.

In the summer and fall of 1969 it was one of CONARC's units (the 5th Military Intelligence Detachment of the 5th Mechanized Infantry Division. Fort Carson, Colorado) that infiltrated the Colorado Springs peace movement, sent agents to peace vigils in the chapel of Colorado State College, and placed both an agent and an informant in the Colorado Springs Young Adults Project, a coalition of church youth groups which ran a recreational center for emotionally disturbed young people.

At Fort Hood, Texas, another CONARC unit computerized its files on civil disturbances and civilian politics.

To a lesser extent, the Marines, Air Force, and Navy also have been involved in similar domestic intelligence activities. The Marine Corps, like the Army, has been plagued by serious internal racial strife. Accordingly, to keep commanders, the Commandant, and the Pentagon informed of these matters, the Corps has set up an internal system not unlike CONARC'S. The Air Force has followed suit. In a memorandum dated May 25, 1970, entitled "Subversive Activities," the Commander of Sheppard Air Force Base in Texas called upon his subordinates to report:

"—personnel making conversation about the overthrow of the United States government!"

"—personnel making statements which indicate disloyalty;"

"—personnel making threats against the President of the United

States, or other high government officials, or high-ranking military personnel;"

"—congregations of unauthorized persons;"

"—persons attempting to spread anti-war sentiment in public places on Sheppard Air Force Base;"

"—persons making statements with racial overtones."

This memorandum led to a protest by Senator Sam J. Ervin, Chairman of the Senate Subcommittee on Constitutional Rights. The Air Force replied that such reporting systems were not Department policy, and ordered the memorandum rewritten. But the revised text, published on August 7, 1970, was also conspicuously overbroad. It extended the monitoring of supposedly "disloyal" statements to the civilian dependents of Air Force personnel, and continued to require reports on all persons who "unlawfully make provoking statements with racial overtones," or who make threats against the President or other high government or military officials. What constituted "disloyal," "unlawful provoking," or "threatening" statements was not spelled out. Further protests from Congress persuaded the Air Force to rescind the revised text, but similar directives remain in force.

The Navy, like the Air Force, is mostly concerned with anti-war, anti-military sentiment. Its curiosity with these matters has sometimes been excessive. For example, when the Naval Investigative Service sought to find a way of dealing with Roger Priest, a young seaman who published an anti-war newspaper with a Pentagon address, it assigned twenty-five agents to monitor his every move. When Priest spoke at an anti-war workshop in Cleveland while on leave and out of uniform, six of the fifteen persons in his civilian audience were NIS agents. In Chicago at the time of the Democratic National Convention, a civilian employee of NIS tape-recorded speeches by demonstrators in Grant Park. He later testified against some of them at the Chicago Eight (minus One) trial. But neither he nor the Navy has ever satisfactorily explained what a naval intelligence agent was doing monitoring the political activities of civilians wholly unassociated with the Navy.

Internal Security Agencies

Wherever state secrets need protection, domestic intelligence units have undertaken security checks of personnel assigned to sensitive positions. These checks are required by Executive Order 10450 and delve into matters of "loyalty" and "suitability." All of the military departments, the FBI, CIA, Civil Service Commission, Atomic Energy Commission, as well as other agencies, are involved in this kind of inquiry which, like the civil disturbance, RITA, and racial inquiries, has a great potential for invading privacy and inhibiting people in their beliefs, expressions, and associations.

Typical of these personnel security agencies is the U. S. Army Intelligence Command, which investigates most of the Army's military and civilian personnel, as well as persons holding sensitive jobs with firms doing work on classified Army contracts. (It was the Intelligence Command's future agents whom I taught at Fort Holabird).

The Intelligence Command has never been sensitive to the constitutional implications of its conduct. This was demonstrated by the excessive zeal with which it established its civil disturbance early warning system and political computer, and it is no less true for its conduct of personnel security investigations.

Part of the problem undoubtedly lies in the imprecise wording of Executive Order 10450 and the corresponding Army regulation (604-10) which permit the denial of a security clearance—and the job that goes with it—on less evidence than would support a magistrate's finding of "probable cause." In other words, it is not a question of whether reliable evidence indicates that the individual cannot be trusted with state secrets, but of whether the granting of the clearance would be "clearly consistent with the interests of national security." No one knows what this ambiguous phrase means.

In an attempt to clarify it for the entire Department of Defense, Walter T. Skallerup, Jr., Deputy Assistant Secretary of Defense (Security Policy), wrote a memorandum on November 26, 1962, addressed to the under secretaries of each of the services. He said:

"Persons conducting security investigations and inquiries normally have broad latitude in performing these essential and vital functions. This places a high premium upon the exercise of good judgment and common sense. . . .

". . . For example, religious beliefs and affiliations or beliefs and opinions regarding racial matters, political beliefs and affiliations of a nonsubversive nature, opinions regarding the constitutionality of legislative policies, and affiliation with labor unions are not proper subjects for such inquiries.

"Inquiries which have no relevance to a security determination should not be made. Questions regarding personal and domestic affairs, financial matters, and the status of physical health, fall into this category unless evidence clearly indicates a reasonable basis for believing there may be illegal or subversive activities, personal or moral irresponsibility, or mental or emotional instability involved. The probing of a person's thoughts or beliefs and questions about his conduct, which have no security implications, are unwarranted. Department of Defense representatives always should be prepared to explain the relevance of their inquiries upon request. Adverse inferences cannot properly be drawn from refusal of a person to answer questions the relevance of which has not been established."

As a direct result of Ekallerup's memorandum and accompanying inquiry into the training of the Army's personnel security investigators, the 30-hour course in "Investigative Legal Principles" which I taught at the Intelligence School was instituted. The Skallerup memorandum was part of the curriculum.

Unfortunately, much of what Skallerup said and what the legal instructors at the Intelligence School have taught has been countermanded by the colonels and lieutenant colonels who command the military intelligence groups which do the actual investigations. Sometimes the orders come from the Army Personnel Security Group and related offices inside the Intelligence Command headquarters at Fort Holabird. Typical of the questions which they have required agents in the field to ask are the following, which were written last March by officials in the Intelligence Command's headquarters and given to an agent of the 109th MI Group to ask a young officer:

"Have you ever read the *Berkeley Barb?*"

"Have you ever read the *Los Angeles Free Press?*"

"What is your attitude toward publications of this sort?"

"What are the names of all publications to which you are a subscriber?"

"What is your attitude toward the war in Vienam?"

"Why did you display on the rear of your car the two inverted United States flags?"

". . . the Department of the Army desires an explanation concerning the display of the two inverted United States flags because your association with a vehicle displaying these symbols might lead to the conclusion that you are disloyal to the United States . . ."

"Why did you display the 'peace' symbol on your car?" [2]

Interrogations of this sort are among the papers used by security clearance adjudicators to reach a decision regarding the individual loyalty and suitability. The adjudicators themselves have no legal training, and receive a minimal education at the Intelligence School before undertaking their sensitive tasks. The most highly trained-civilian adjudicators employed by the stateside army command—receive only nine days of job instruction on loyalty determinations. They receive no training on the subject of suitability whatever. The least trained adjudicators — intelligence officers assigned to field commands — receive exactly two classroom hours on loyalty and two on suitability. Because of this extremely brief training, it is not unusual for an adjudicator to conclude that a person arrested in connection with a political protest is not suited for a security clearance, regardless of the circumstances of his arrest, the legality of his detention, or his innocence of the charges.

Thus the right to due process when applying for a security clearance is tenuous at best. It has been made even more precarious by the use to which newspaper clippings and other often unreliable sources of information are put. For example, until recently, the Army has made a practice of taking "spot reports" on demonstrations, protests, and various kinds of civil disorders, which happen to mention someone whose security clearance dossier is on file, and filing them in that dossier. (The Army has between 7 and 9 million of these dossiers). Then, whenever that person's loyalty and suitability is reconsidered by the Army or any other federal agency the adjudicator gets to see the unsubstantiated report and to take it into account.

The Civil Service Commission has a different practice. According to its chairman, the Commission maintains a "Security File" of some 2,120,000 index cards containing "lead information relating to possible questions. . . involving loyalty or subversive activity. The lead information contained in these files has been developed from published hearings of Congressional committees, State legislative committees, public investigative bodies, reports of investigation, publications of subversive organizations and various other newspapers and periodicals."

On the face of it, this file might seem like a sensible way to focus investigations. It probably is. But at the same time it poses a substantial threat to individual liberties because there are no criteria for determining what is evidence of "disloyalty" or "subversive activity." The decision is a wholly personal one which the Commission's security staff makes on the basis of its own judgment as to what is proper politics and what is subversive. Asked by a newspaper reporter for an example of someone with questionable politics, Ed Knazik, one of the Commission's evaluators responded: "An extreme example would be Linus Pauling." Pauling is the Nobel Prize-winning chemist who revealed the structure of complex protein molecules in the early 1950s and who has more recently been an outspoken critic of American strategic policy, the atomic bomb, and recent wars.

The Federal Bureau of Investigation

The FBI has been the chief domestic intelligence agency of the United States almost since its inception. Its authority for intelligence gathering is drawn from:

• Formal and informal Presidential directives dating back to 1936 ordering it to gather information "concerning subversive activities being conducted in the United States by . . . organizations or groups advocating the overthrow or replacement of the government of the United States by illegal means."

• Criminal statutes, such as the espionage, sedition, selective service, and anti-riot acts, which authorize the Bureau to investigate political activities which may involve violations of federal law.

• The Emergency Detention Act of 1950 under which the FBI has authority to assemble lists of persons to be rounded up and confined in detention camps should the President declare an "Internal Security Emergency."

• The Internal Security Act of 1950 which authorizes the FBI to gather information to be used by the Attorney General or the Subversive Activities Control Board in designating "subversive" groups.

• Executive Order 10450 authorizing federal agencies to investigate the loyalty and suitability of persons being considered for sensitive government positions.

• Presidential requests for investigations into the backgrounds of persons being considered for political appointment to high government positions.

Unlike the Army, which established its civil disturbance early warning with little thought to its legal basis, the FBI usually has been careful to tie its domestic intelligence activities to some statutory or executive authorization. Thus the main focus of its intelligence efforts has been on possible threats to national security or threats of violence. The activities of foreign intelligence agencies, the American Communist party, its fronts, and affiliates, the Weatherman, Minutemen, and Black Panthers currently receive its closest attention.

Surveillance of New Left groups is predicated on the hypothesis of Communist infiltration, exploitation, or support, or the expectation of large-scale civil disorder.

The Bureau's principal sources of domestic intelligence include newspapers and periodicals and the files of state and local police. Its reliance on the police has at times been heavy. Until recently, one official confided to the *New York Times,* 80 percent of the FBI's information about the Black Panthers came from the subversive units of the local police departments.

Nonetheless, resort is made to covert operations—so much so that agents are rated on their skill in developing informants. Wiretapping is also used on domestic political groups when the Attorney General is persuaded that the group, or individuals in it, pose a threat to national security. Groups tapped during recent years include the Black Muslims, the Southern Christian Leadership Conference, and the Black Panthers; individuals include the late Rev. Martin Luther King, Cassius Clay, and David Dellinger.

While other domestic intelligence agencies have moved toward computerization of their files, the FBI's Domestic Intelligence Division keeps its data in "raw" form. However, its reports do go to the Justice Department's Interdivisional Intelligence Unit where they are fed to a computer.

To the extent that political dissidents are also criminal suspects, records concerning them will be found in the Bureau's new computerized National Crime Information Center (NCIC). The Center's computer provides 40,000 instant, automatic teletype print-outs each day on wanted persons and stolen property to 49 states and Canada; it also "talks" to 24 other computers maintained by local and state police departments for themselves and about 2,500 police jurisdictions. Other NCIC clents include the Immigration and Naturalization Service, the Internal Revenue Service, and the Federal Narcotics Bureau. The FBI says that its information is based wholly on federal and local warrants, complaints, arrests and convictions, but the potential of this system for non-criminal intelligence is virtually unlimited.

Plans for the new FBI headquarters on Pennsylvania Avenue suggest the priority now assigned to domestic intelligence. Of the space set aside, 35,000 square feet is for the domestic intelligence staff—as opposed to 23,000 square feet for criminal and other investigations.

The Justice Department

The principal consumer of FBI reports on political activists in the Justice Department's Interdivisional Intelligence Unit. Other recipients include the Criminal, Internal Security, and Civil Rights Divisions, the Community Relations Service, and the so-called Black Panther Task Force set up in 1969 to monitor the activities of all radicals.

The Interdivisional Intelligence Unit operates on a budget of $274,-000, employs 12 intelligence analysts, and works in a domestic war room in the Justice Department on the sixth floor. Its director is James T. Devine who works directly under Deputy Attorney General Richard G. Kleindienst. Since the November 1969 Moratorium in Washington, D.C., it has supplanted the Army's Counterintelligence Analysis Detachment as the government's headquarters for civil disturbance and political protest information.

To fulfill this duty the Unit maintains a political computer larger than the one at Fort Holabird which the Army shut down. Most of the information in this computer comes from the FBI. The rest is supplied by 93 U. S. attorneys around the country and by other government agencies, such as the Treasury Department's Alcohol and Tobacco Division (which enforces federal firearms laws), the Secret Service, and the Army.

Each week the Justice Department's computer disgorges a huge print-out which describes coming events on the protest circuit. It is divided into four volumes, each about two inches thick, and is bound in brown cardboard covers. Each book covers a region of the country and presents a city-by-city assessment of the potential for civil disorder. It details what marches, rallies, or meetings are scheduled, the organizations and individuals sponsoring them, and the city's history of civil disturbances.

The books are then culled by analysts in the Interdivisional Intelligence Unit who abstract and forward data of interest to the Attorney General and various divisions of the Department. For example, the Community Relations Service receives information on potential racial problems which it might be called upon to conciliate. The Civil Rights Division is alerted to possible violations of the laws it enforces, while the Criminal Division gets data on such offenses as draft card burning and the crossing of state lines with intent to incite a riot.

In addition to the weekly civil disturbance estimate, the computer can produce a rundown on almost any past or coming demonstration of size which will include all stored information on the membership, ideology, and plans of its sponsors. This was done, for example, prior, to the November 15, 1969 anti-war demonstration in Washington organized by the Vietnam Moratorium Committee and the New Mobilization Committee to End the War. Special print-outs have also been done on the Black Panthers.

The Secret Service

In its zeal to protect the President and other high government officials from assassins, the Secret Service has developed one of the most versatile—and constitutionally offensive—political data systems in the government. Built around a Honeywell 2200 computer, this system is capable of sorting and retrieving by name, alias, method of operation, affiliation, and physical appearance. As a result the Secret Service is able to detect, investigate, and, if necessary, detain in advance persons whom it suspects might try to harrass, harm, or embarrass officials under its protection.

Starting with computer-printed lists of persons of "protective interest" grouped geographically, analysts in the Protective Intelligence Division can assemble descriptions and photographs for the teams of Secret Service agents who travel in advance of the Presidential party. A spokesman for the Service explained to the *New York Times* how the system works: "You take a waiter in a hotel dining room where the boss is going to speak. Let's say the computer turns up his name and we investigate and decide it would be better for him to be assigned to some other duties. No one has a constitutional right to wait on the President, you know. That's how it works."

Guided by a more sophisticated computer program, the same machine can also produce lists of individuals by their characteristics—such as all of the long-haired, skinny campus radicals in Walla Walla, Washington. No other government computer has this capability.

The data base now covers more than 50,000 persons. It is drawn from many sources, including the FBI, state and municipal police, military intelligence, the Internal Revenue Service, federal building guards, the White House, (which keeps a record of all abusive telephone calls and letters), and individual informants. Thus, to anyone concerned about the intimidating effect which this computer could have on the exercise of political rights, the criteria that determine who is worthy of space in the computer becomes critical.

The Secret Service contends that its analysts apply relatively sophisticated and realistic standards. But the guidelines it has issued to govern the reporting of information go far beyond the recommendations of the Warren Commission and leave much to be clarified. They call for:

- "Information pertaining to a threat, plan or attempt by an individual, a group or an organization to physically harm or embarrass the persons protected by the U. S. Secret Service, or any other high U. S. Government official at home or abroad.
- "Information pertaining to individuals, groups, or organizations who have plotted, attempted, or carried out assassinations of senior officials of domestic or foreign governments.
- "Information concerning the use of bodily harm or assassination as a political weapon. This should include training and techniques used to carry out the act.
- "Information on persons who insist upon personally contacting high Government officials for the purpose of redress of imaginary grievances, etc.
- "Information on any person who makes oral or written statements about high Government officials in the following categories: (1) threatening statements; (2) irrational statements, and (3) abusive statements.
- "Information on professional gate crashers.
- "Information pertaining to 'terrorist' bombings.
- "Information pertaining to the ownership or concealment by individuals or groups of caches of firearms, explosives, or other implements of war.
- "Information regarding anti-American or anti-U. S. Government demonstrations in the United States or overseas.
- "Information regarding civil disturbances."

The breadth and vagueness of these guidelines has prompted Senator Ervin to observe in a Senate speech: "Although I am not a 'professional gate crasher,' I am a 'malcontent' on many issues. I have written the President and other high officials complaining of grievances that some may consider 'imaginary.' And on occasion, I may also have 'embarrassed high government officials.'" Accordingly, he concluded, he was probably qualified for listing in the computer.

Private Organizations

Associate members of the domestic intelligence community today include a host of individuals and organizations in such fields as pre-employment reporting, industrial security, campus security, private detection, and retail credit.

One of the more chilling is a seemingly innocuous group called the Laymans Church League of America—a pre-employment firm based in Wheaton, Illinois. The sort of services it provides are described in a letter written in December 1968 by Andrew W. Hunter, a field director, to the president of one of the nation's leading department stores:

"American businessmen are faced with a grave problem . . . Our working forces include more than a few radicals, socialists, revolutionaries, communists, and troublemakers of all sorts. The colleges and schools are educating and training thousands more who will soon be seeking employment.

"The hiring and training costs to industry for individual workers runs into many thousands of dollars. Before they are employed, their educational and professional backgrounds are screened most carefully. On the other hand, little if anything is done to determine their philosophy of life. In many cases this is of paramount importance.

"The Church League of America is non-denominational, non-political, and tax exempt. For 32 years we have been intensively researching the activities of troublesome individuals, groups, and publications, about which management would be well advised to be aware. Our files are the most reliable, comprehensive and complete, and second only to those of the FBI which, of course, are not available to you.. . . .

"We can supply you with all the data regarding your people that you may deem advisable. . . . In return, we seek cooperation to the end that we may modernize and keep abreast of what appears to be an ever growing need.

"My office will be glad to send a representative, at your request, to go into this delicate matter at greater length."

Like pre-employment reporting, the industrial security business has drawn heavily upon the internal security agencies for policy guidance, training, and manpower. In fact, it is a common practice for lieutenant colonels who cannot make the grade in the combat arms to transfer to military intelligence about two years prior to retirement in the hope that the experience as commanders of stateside MI groups will qualify them for post-retirement jobs in industrial security.

Campus security, on the other hand, has been a haven for retired policemen and FBI agents. With the advent of student radicalism, many campus security chiefs have assembled extensive files on the political and social views of students. They also have hired photographers and recruited networks of informers. Some surveillance obviously makes sense, particularly where bombing, burning, and assault have been employed as expressions of dissent. But all too often, these departments have been insensitive to the rights of law-abiding students. Two years ago Yale University was shocked to discover that its security chief had amassed a huge file on the politics and associations of students, many of whom had never participated in campus demonstrations. As recently as last fall, security personnel at the University of Minnesota actively encouraged military and police agents to photograph demonstrations of all kinds on campus. They also helped to identify demonstrators in Army photographs and gave Army agents pictures they had taken.

The automation of civilian records has made banks, airlines, credit companies, hotels, car rental firms, and telephone companies, easy sources of information about the activities, habits, and associations of the government's critics. FBI inquiries into bank accounts, for example, have been widely publicized. Less well-known is the investigative use which military commands — including the Army Intelligence Command—have made of on-post credit unions.

The Impact of Political Surveillance

When most people hear of improper political surveillances, they think first of police states and military dictatorships. To start with this perception, however, may be to misperceive the problem.

The most immediate threats posed by political surveillance in the United States are more mundane. They exist in all data systems and involve such abuses as blackmail, defamation, release of information to unauthorized persons, blacklisting, and other forms of coercion and reprisal. These are the hard, tangible, everyday misuses of political data systems. Proof of their occurrence is irrefutable.

Less tangible, but no less real, is the "chilling effect" which knowledge of political surveillances can have upon the willingness of persons to participate in politics or otherwise exercise their Constitutional freedoms of expression and association, and their right to petition the government for redress of grievances. The chilling effect is easiest to demonstrate where police deliberately conduct harrassing surveillances in order to deter political expression and association. But it can also result from the creation of large political data centers. In *Anderson v. Sills,* a suit filed by the American Civil Liberties Union on behalf of Jersey City branch of the NAACP, the lower court held: "The secret files that would be maintained as a result of this [police] intelligence system are inherently dangerous, and by their very existence tend to restrict those who would advocate . . . social and political change."

The dynamics of the chilling effect are not well known, but research that has been done attributes great influence to the political tolerance level of society. My own experience confirms this finding. Thus far, most of the former intelligence agents whom I have asked to speak out against the Army's surveillance are less worried about official reprisals than they are about the reactions of their neighbors, friends, families and employers. While nearly all are convinced that the surveillance is wrong, many are hesitant to make their views public. Their most frequent explanations are: "I live in a conservative community. . . . The people here wouldn't understand. . . . I could lose my job." Some worry that their criticism of unauthorized intelligence activities could cost them clearances later in life, even though their criticism would in no way touch on classified matters.

Beyond the chilling effect, I believe, there is a real danger of the outright repression of unpopular political minorities by state and local police. We already have ample evidence of unwarranted and vindictive violence directed against Negroes and students by poorly trained and undisciplined policemen. However, this is nothing compared to the harrassment and brutality which could result if the disciplining of police departments does not keep pace with the growth of political intelligence about provocative dissenters. The record of local "red squads" has always been a shameful one, but it could become substantially worse if the new interstate and intrastate criminal intelligence systems become a vehicle for non-criminal information.

The unregulated spread of covert intelligence techniques to police investigations poses similar dangers. While it may make sense to allow the police limited covert powers (such as court-authorized wiretaps and informers) to deal with campus bombers and organized crime, it makes no sense whatever to permit the same tools to be used for the surveillance of non-violent protestors. Such techniques not only raise grave Constitutional problems; they also force moderates to either drop out of politics or to take sides and provoke extremists to resort to criminal means to express their dissent.

Finally, we must face the fact that police statism—especially at the local level—is now a clear, if not present danger. National and local members of the domestic intelligence community are no longer fragmented by narrow conceptions of jurisdiction, limited resources, or the boundaries of federalism. Computer and teletype technology has brought them together into a variety of regional and national galaxies, and it has made the political files of one the potential resource of others. Before we allow this process to go much further, we would do well to remind ourselves that a country may be able to survive the centralization of domestic intelligence without becoming authoritarian, but it almost certainly cannot become authoritarian without centralized domestic intelligence.

5

SUBVERSION OF DEMOCRACY

By Representative Abner J. Mikva

I first learned that I had been subjected to military surveillance in the winter of 1970 when John O'Brien overcame his understandable fears to retaliation and wrote to Senator Sam Ervin, informing him of the civilian spying activities being conducted by the 113th Military Intelligence Group in Illinois. I commend Mr. O'Brien for his courageous act; his is the true patriotism which will keep this nation free.

Upon learning that I had been spied upon by the Army, along with Senator Adlai Stevenson, Judge Otto Kerner, the Rev. Jesse Jackson, and a host of other public and private figures in my state, my first reaction was profound shock and outrage. In time those feelings gave way to a deeper sadness over the unavoidable message this brought as to the kind of society we have become.

I was elected by the people of the Second Congressional District of Illinois to be their representative in the Congress of the United States — to voice their concerns and desires regarding the policies of their country, and to try to steer America toward the goals they envisioned. In attempting to do this, I apparently did something which led some employee of our armed forces to decide that I ought to be watched. Was it because I proposed to cut military manpower by 10%? Was it because I co-sponsored H.R. 1000, the proposal to end the war in Vietnam? Is there any political activity, regardless of who is supported or opposed, which justifies the Army in spying on an elected representative of the people?

It should be unnecessary to have to enumerate the reasons why military surveillance of civilian politics is dangerous to a free society. But apparently there are those in government and in the military who do not understand the dangers. For their sakes, and for purposes of analysis of the problem we face, I would make four observations.

• First is the threat to the First Amendment rights of all citizens to privacy, free speech, and the right to petition their government for redress. The existence of arbitrary, widespread military surveillance of civilians—or even the popular belief that it exists—has a chilling effect on free speech. It discourages the kind of full, free and unrestrained exchange of ideas and viewpoints on which American democracy is based. More than any other, our guaranteed right to freely criticize our government and elected officials is what distinguishes us as a nation. It has long been the hallmark of totalitarian societies that only "approved" persons could participate and that only "acceptable" ideas could be heard. Military surveillance of civilian politics raises the spectre of such official "approval" and "acceptability" as some day being a requirement of American politics, as it has long been in the Communist countries we condemn.

Indeed, those military officials who would arrogate to themselves the duty to watch peaceful civilians' political activities are the true subversives in our society. It is they who, more than critics of the Vietnam war, pose a threat to the continued freedom of political expression and political action. If allowed to continue, they will end up creating a climate of fear and suspicion in this country the likes of which make Joseph McCarthy look like a civil libertarian. Are we to live in mutual distrust of our fellow citizens, ever suspicious of one another? If so, we will have destroyed the open society which justified the American Revolution and which we have fought for 200 years to protect—fear will become the watchword in America.

As a public official, I at least have a forum in which to defend my freedom and my reputation. I have a constituency to appear to for support. To whom shall the average citizen citizen look for help when the military invades his private life for misguided or mischievous purposes? I voiced earlier my appreciation for Mr. O'Brien's courage in coming forth with the details of the Army's civilian snooping. Why should it require an act of courage for a free American to inform his elected representatives of activities which he believes are wrong? Why should John O'Brien have to fear, as he has told us he does, that he and his family will now be subject to invasions of their privacy and retaliatory harassment by the Army? What kind of country is this? Who is in charge here?

• The second danger posed by the Army's spying is the very real possibility of intimidation and interference in the free decision-making process by government officials. Public officials are bound by oath to serve the public interest, and their decisions should be made on this basis alone.

It probably would be going too far to say that the wide acceptance of military programs by the Congress has been influenced by the fear of covert military surveillance. But who can say that in future months or future Congresses there will be none who will have second thoughts about a vote on military affairs? Who can be certain that his judgment will not be swayed, perhaps even unconsciously, by the belief that he is being watched? Even the possibility of surveillance raises the spectre of subtle political interference. The scenario might go something like this. Those who speak out strongly in opposition to the policies of those in power are subjected to precautionary surveillance by the military. Constituents learn that their elected representative is under Army surveillance. The inference is made, either explicitly or implicitly, that he must be doing something wrong, or at least questionable, and that suspicion will be evident in the next election results. After all, who wants to be represented by a man who is so disreputable that the Army feels that the national security requires that his activities be monitored.

Perhaps such a chain of events is unlikely. But it is entirely likely that some elected officials will exercise greater caution than they otherwise would in speaking their minds in order to be sure that their political future is not imperiled by a military spy. To protect the integrity of the decision-making process, we must protect public officials from the errant telescopes of overzealous protectors of the faith.

• Third is the threat to the important and fundamental policy of civilian control of the military. If civilian control means anything, it must mean that the military authorities have no responsibility, no reason, and no right to engage in surreptitious surveillance of the political process. To the extent that we allow these activities to go unchallenged, to the extent that we allow the men responsible for it to continue in positions of authority, we are putting in jeopardy the very freedom of our people and independence of our form of government.

• Finally, and most importantly, we must address the crisis of confidence which this whole sordid affair has aggravated. In the final event, the measure of a society's health is its ability to deal openly with its problems and to withstand—even encourage—public scrutiny. Lawyers have long understood the critical interrelationship between substance and procedure. Apparently our government, and especially the military establishment, has not yet come to understand that *what* you do is often overshadowed by *how* you do it. As a result, the feeling has grown up that the American people can be lied to and deceived without concern, so long as care is taken that overt actions are acceptable. The pattern is becoming a familiar one. Charges are levelled by the press or by public officials that we are engaged in prohibited activity (e.g. the use of prohibited defoliants in Vietnam). With great indignation, denials are issued. Then when uncontrovertible facts to the contrary are presented, there is sheepish acknowledgment that in fact the acts in question did occur but will be halted at once.

The military has a special penchant for such prevarication and obfuscation of the truth. My Lai was a disgraceful example. Another was the Pentagon's intervention in the grape and lettuce boycotts by increasing purchases from non-union growers. And now we have a third. The plain fact of the matter is that the American people have lost faith in the integrity of their military establishment and who can blame them. A poignant example, which should give pause to us all, the recent report in the press that almost 50% of the American people *did not believe* President's Nixon's solemn assertion that we had no ground troops in Laos. The government, and especially the military, has cried "wolf" once too often. We are now at the point where the people do not believe them even when they are telling the truth. How can a society stand strong when it is generally assumed that one cannot have any confidence in the veracity of the people who have been delegated to run the nation's affairs? We are reaping the harvest of this crisis in confidence, in the form of increased cynicism, alienation, and non-participation in the established institutions of our society. The military's greatest enemy is not the Vietcong, nor the critical young Americans who refuse to cooperate with it. Their greatest enemy is their own arrogant and un-American conviction that they are beyond scrutiny.

Are we to wait until West Point becomes another Sandhurst—that once-proud elite academy where England trained its finest soldiers and which now must advertise in the personal columns for applicants? Already we have witnessed a decline in enlistments and re-enlistments and an overwhelming breakdown in troop morale. Recently the Army announced a $3 million budget for commercial advertising aimed at attracting more enlistments. It is a shameful fact that great numbers of returning Vietnam veterans shun wearing the uniform because of the public's disrespect for the military establishment. There is growing respect for the growing number of young men who refuse to cooperate with the military in any way. The years of boondoggling in defense contracts and procurement have begun to catch up with the Army. Who was really surprised by the latest scandal involving the post exchanges? It is becoming clear that the cost of all this wheeling and dealing is that the military is doing what no enemy foreign or domestic has ever done—that is, destroy the military.

It is not the critics in the streets or in the Congress, but the cover-uppers in the Pentagon, who are bringing the public wrath down upon the military establishment.

Who believes that the intelligence files were really destroyed? Who believes that Secretary Laird or Secretary Resor or even the Joint Chiefs really know the full extent of the Army's domestic surveillance activities? The only way that the Pentagon can begin to restore public confidence in the military is by proving that the Army takes its mistakes as seriously as do its critics. There must be a complete purging of every command official who was responsible for establishing and operating this spy network. I, for one, would urge the resignation of every such command officer, in the interests of restoring America's credibility in its own military.

The important mission of these hearings is to restore America's confidence in its government by opening the windows and letting some fresh air into a closed room whose musty odor has despoiled our whole governmental house. Let us spy on the Army, now and ever more. Let us reinstate the fundamental right of the citizenry to know what their government is doing, and to control its activities. It is critical to our collective health as a nation that we do so.

I have tried to summarize what I see as the principal dangers presented by unchecked military spying on civilians. Let me conclude by suggesting some means of dealing with the problem.

First, it is essential that a full Congressional investigation go forward in order to reveal the full extent of the problem and who is responsible for it. In addition to the present actions of this subcommittee, I believe it would be most useful for the Government Operations Committee on the House side to conduct a parallel investigation into military surveillance. A resolution has already been introduced in the House calling on Chairman Chet Holifield to begin such an investigation.

Second, we should consider fashioning appropriate legislative remedies. The first and most obvious legislative remedy is a limitation in the Defense Department appropriations bill on the expenditure of any appropriated funds to finance military surveillance of the civilian population. I would hope that after looking into the present scope and nature of military spying on civilians, the Department of Defense Appropriations Subcommittee might write such a limitation into the next Defense Department appropriations bill. In any case, I plan to offer such a prohibition if it is not included in the committee's bill.

My prohibition would be worded approximately as follows:

"No part of the appropriations contained in this act shall be expended for salary of personnel, purchase or maintenance of equipment or premises, or support of operations which involve in whole or in part, surveillance, monitoring, information-gathering, reporting, record-keeping (whether on cards, mechanically by means of electronic data processing equipment, or otherwise), or any other intelligence activity by active-duty military personnel directed against any federal, state, or local public official, or candidate for public office, or against any citizen of the United States who is not on active military duty and is located within the United States."

As important as the passage of such a prohibition would be it is clearly not adequate by itself. After all, Representative George H. Mahon, Chairman of the Defense Appropriations Committee, has assured me that there never has been — to his knowledge — any appropriated money available for the kind of military spying which has lately been disclosed. Thus, it seems obvious that a mere limitation on expenditure of appropriations will by itself not guarantee against a recurrence of this activity and ease the mind of Americans.

Therefore, I propose a complete ban on all domestic surveillance by the military. I have with me a tentative draft of such a bill, prepared with the assistance of Mr. Christopher Pyle. The approach is simple and direct. It is declared a punishable offense for any member of the armed forces to order or conduct any surveillance activities within the United States. Private citizens are given standing to bring suit in federal court to enforce the provisions of the law, either by injunctive relief or by a civil suit for damages. The Army is not a law enforcement agency and it should not be acting like one. There is no reason at all why the Law Enforcement Assistance Administration budget for fiscal year 1971 should include a project calling for cooperation with the Defense Department in compiling domestic intelligence data. Domestic security problems are the proper province of civilian law enforcement agencies alone. The Army's sole function in relation to civil disturbance should be to supplement the peace-keeping capabilities of local and state agencies when they are unable to cope with a disturbance on their own. It is up to those civilian agencies to maintain the close contact with their communities which is necessary in order to anticipate trouble and to deal effectively with mass disorders. The role of the military in this area is properly restricted to providing additional manpower when the need arises.

It is simply not true, as Secretary of the Army Resor has recently asserted, that the Army is burdened with the Constitutional obligation to protect the states against domestic violence. The Constitution places upon Congress the responsibility to raise and support armies, to organize the militia, and to call forth the militia when necessary to "execute the Laws of the Union, suppress Insurrections and repel Invasions." (Article I, Sec. 8, Clauses 15, 16) As far as I can determine, Congress has never seen fit to authorize the United States Army to undertake the responsibility of preventing civil disorders.

Secretary Resor apparently relies on Sections 332 and 333 of Title 10 United States Code, for he quotes from Section 333 the phrase "domestic violence." Perhaps if the Secretary read those sections a bit more closely, he would see that neither one places upon the Army the responsibility of protecting the states against domestic violence. Rather, they authorize the President to call out the National Guard or the Armed Forces to supplement state and local law enforcement agencies in the event that he considers such drastic action necessary to enforce the laws of the United States or of a state. That power has been invoked by several Presidents, most recently by President John Kennedy in several civil rights disturbances in the South. On each occasion, it was the state militia, the National Guard, which was pressed into service, and an Executive Order was issued detailing the urgent need for assistance by the military. Regular Army troops have been needed to supplement the National Guard in only a handful of instances over the past 100 years. Not even Secretary Resor would claim that our nation is in such desperate straits as to require a continuing regular Army presence. In sum, there is no constitutional or legislative mandate such as Secretary Resor assumes, which imposes upon the Army an obligation to act as a domestic law enforcement agency. That responsibility falls on state and local law enforcement agencies. While in extreme emergencies, the state militia, the National Guard, and even the regular Army may be used to supplement such forces, that contingent responsibility in no way warrants an Army spy corps. If that is to be the justification for domestic snooping, the Army could similarly justify arresting and trying criminal suspects in order to relieve the crime problem threatening our urban areas.

The Army is not a national police force—yet. It must not be allowed to become one. The country either runs the Army, or the Army runs the country.

Similarly, there is no need for the military to undertake domestic spying in order to guarantee the security of military installations. The domestic security problems of the military should be treated no differently from those of any other branch of the federal government. If security problems arise or are anticipated in connection with a federal courthouse or any other federal property, it is the FBI, not the Army, which undertakes whatever security is necessary. Why should military installations be treated any differently? The only way we can be confident that the Army is out of the domestic snooping business is to require that all domestic intelligence activities be carried out by the FBI and the local low enforcemen agencies. Perhaps a law such as the one I have proposed, along with the removal of those responsible for military surveillance of civilians, will be a long first step in returning the Army to its proper position in our society.

Before I leave the subject of legislative solutions, I would like to call attention to a proposal offered by my distinguished colleague, Congressman Ed Koch of New York. Although my remarks have been primarily addressed to the constitutional issues raised by domestic military surveillance, I am deeply concerned over the problems of computer privacy.

I commend Congressman Koch's proposal. Under his bill every citizen would have the right upon request to have access to any dossiers kept on him by any federal agency. The names of informants would be deleted and other appropriate safeguards are provided for in the bill. The citizen would have the right to supplement his dossier with any additional information he deems relevant. Surely in a free society this is a minimum protection to the citizen given the fact that his government of necessity must collect information about him.

Conclusion

America has a great number of difficult problems to deal with today. Poverty, environmental pollution, revitalization of our urban centers, health care, education, and more. But before we can begin to deal effectively with these, we must decide what kind of society we intend to be. The fundamental character of our nation in turn depends on the relationship between the individual and society. Will we be an open, democratic country which welcomes critical scrutiny, or a defensive, suspicious people marked by fear and deception? It is time that those of us who believe in each other and in America take the reins of control away from men who so short-sighted in their self-righteousness as to believe that a secret society is a sound society.

6

THE EVOLUTION OF CIVILIAN SURVEILLANCE BY THE ARMED FORCES

By Morris Janowitz

The hallmark of a nation with domestic political institutions is the sharp separation of its military forces of national defense from its police and law enforcement agencies. Civilian control, civil liberties, due process and free and competitive political parties are strengthened by such an arrangement. It has been one of the persistent assumptions of the American political system that to allow the military, except in rare and extreme circumstances, to intervene in local police and law enforcement matters is to weaken the fabric of our domestic society. In turn to permit the armed forces to become emeshed in issues of domestic law and justice is to undermine their legitimacy to perform their essential duties.

This tradition does not mean that the military establishment should be isolated from civilian society. To the contrary, civilian control of the armed forces is based on their integration with civilian society. Reliance on short term enlistments, ROTC and OCS, a civilian based reserve, and the schooling of professional officers in civilian universities are illustrative of the wide range of devices for maintaining military-civilian contacts. But close contact with civilian life does not mean military surveillance or control of the civilian population.

In the historical traditions of the U.S., the military were not given continuing domestic intelligence duties. The main purpose of military intelligence as it evolved, concerned foreign and external military forces. In principle and in practice, the armed forces were to exercise surveillance over their own members only. However, during the last half century in the absence of clear directives to the contrary, from either the President of the United States or from the United States Congress, there has been a gradual, persistent and long term intrusion of military personnel into domestic surveillance and police work. The armed forces have sought to justify this trend as a response to new politico-military tactics of foreign adversaries. However, even within the ranks of the armed forces there is considerable doubt, resistance and even opposition to this development.

From an historical point of view, opposition to domestic surveillance by the military has been rooted in the very efforts that brought about the Revolutionary War. Armed revolt was based in part on opposition to the military intervention of the British in the domestic life of the colonists. During the years of the Revolutionary War, the independence movement had to guard itself against "Loyalist" sympathizers. When independence came, the founding fathers created a system of civilian control designed to contain the military in internal affairs.

The agonies of the Civil War presented the Union government with immediate problems of surveillance of civilian groups engaged in pro-Confederacy activities, both espionage and political. Military intelligence units were organized and expanded and President Lincoln was ultimately forced to engage private civilian groups including the Pinkertons to deal with his internal security problems. The involvement of military personnel in domestic law enforcement was conceived of as part of the immediate defense of the Union against presumed agents of the Confederacy. The extensive scope of military operations gravely strained the basic structure of civil liberties but with the termination of hostilities, long standing practices could be restored.

From the end of the Civil War to the outbreak of World War I, the ground and naval forces of the United States were excluded from any extensive domestic intelligence work since there was no justification and because of the vary limited numbers in the tiny military establishment. The outbreak of World War I produced an important transformation in the structure of military and naval intelligence work. The Imperial German Government launched a variety of efforts to penetrate the United States for purposes of espionage, sabotage and propaganda. The armed services felt justified in extending their surveillance activities to the civilian population. Military and naval intelligence units were quickly expanded and a variety of civilian contacts developed. War hysteria against German-American groups was extensive and there was considerable popular agitation and repression as well.

World War I intelligence included military surveillance of pacifist groups who opposed the war aims of the United States government. After the Russian revolution, the scope and intensity of surveillance over "left wing" persons and groups increased and persisted while the United States was engaged in military intervention in the Soviet Union. Military intelligence during the immediate post World War I period was involved in surveillance of racial groups as well. It was during these years that the Federal Bureau of Investigation was reorganized and expanded.

With the rapid reduction of the armed forces in the early 1920's, military surveillance of civilians was drastically curtailed. However, these new precedents were being established and not adequately challenged. The military had responsibility over their own personnel and their concerns extended outside military installations into civilian groups in a vague and diffuse fashion. However, the actual amount of civilian surveillance was limited since their meager resources were concentrated on overseas and foreign targets.

The role of intelligence operations by the armed forces had neither been debated nor legislated upon by Congress to any significant extent when the United States was attacked at Pearl Harbor. However, the federal executive and the military establishment in the 1930's had to face a new international environment. Modern warfare was being transformed into "total war." "Total war" meant (a) increased destructiveness because of the development of air power and (b) the extension of the concepts of war to include propaganda and subversion of the civilian population. The idea of a "Fifth Column" was partly a reality and partly an exaggerated myth.

The tactics of Nazi Germany and Imperial Japan supplied a new justification for military surveillance of civilians who might be actual or potential agents or supporters of foreign powers. Both civilian and military intelligence units were expanded with considerable confusion and overlap. Among other problems, they were concerned with the question of the reliability and loyalty of a wide range of political, ethnic and radical groups. In the case of the Japanese-Americans, the result was the tragic evacuation and internment of the loyal and the few disloyal alike. However, because of firm civilian political leadership, other minority groups, especially German-Americans and Italian-Americans were spared the indignities and hysteria that accompanied World War I.

Again, as after World War I, the termination of World War II saw a considerable reduction in surveillance of civilians by military authorities. However, the development of a cold war ideology after 1945, meant that these activities became continuous and permanent. The absence of clear directives resulted in a continued military surveillance of civiilans who might be alleged to be associated with the political warfare of the Soviet Union and subsequently Communist China, or who were opposed to United States foreign policies on the basis of "radical" ideology. The full extent and character of such surveillance has not been publicly documented. Much of it seems to have been sporadic and influenced by the decisions of local commanders who interpreted in their own fashion existing directives which were vague and diffuse.

With the build up of military operations in Indo China there was again an increase in personnel assigned to domestic military intelligence. As in the past, the primary mission was the surveillance of military personnel and civilians employed by the military, but the effort continued to spill over into a much more extensive and systematic coverage of civilian persons and groups. New directives were issued which included such vague terms as "subversive," which were interpreted by military intelligence personnel to include militant anti-war protestors and were explicitly political. These information collection efforts have come to require considerable numbers of personnel and appear to be of little or no interest to those civilian agencies officially charged with investigative responsibilities.

A further expansion of military surveillance took place after 1967 in response to racial violence. The armed forces were directed to increase their capacities for intervention in domestic unrest and accordingly expanded their surveillance of individuals and groups presumed to be potentially disruptive. These contemporary civilian surveillance activities which have received extensive attention in the mass media represent a continuation and extension of the military beyond its jurisdiction. In fact, these intelligence activities are completely irrelevant to the actual responsibiilty of the armed forces in domestic disorders. When actually employed, the army has operated with considerable restraint and with higher levels of performance than have local police forces, but such performance is unrelated to the operations of domestic military intelligence. Mass racial outbursts reflect underlying social and economic conditions and are not the result of individual agitation. The type of surveillance conducted by the military is not only at odds with civil-military traditions, but is also irrelevant to the underlying causes. Moreover, when United States military forces have been employed, these "background" investigations have not been and will not be used by troops dispatched to handle the tragedies of civil disorders. To the contrary, military surveillance of civilians only weakens the legitimacy of the armed services. Thus, in summary the present activities of military intelligence must be seen in an historical perspective of gradual extension of civilian surveillance.

Three points are essential: (1) It is essential that there be a fundamental and academic based research effort to document the rise and transformation of military intelligence activities over the last century. Such a research effort must be freed from immediate pressures and designed to give the United States Congress and the American public a dispassionate, balanced and penetrating analysis. (2) The United States Congress must quickly legislate to delimit clearly the responsibility of military intelligence and thereby relieve the armed forces of activities involving civilian surveillance which some of its best professional officers resist and which violate American traditions of civilian-military relations. (3) While recognizing the necessity for secrecy of military intelligence activities concerning foreign establishments, the education, career lines and organizational controls of military intelligence personnel must be transformed to bring them into the main stream of American Society. Much of our present difficulties derive not from anti-democratic goals of the military but from the mentality of an intelligence community which has become detached from the realities and traditions of American society.

7

MILITARY INTELLIGENCE OVERKILL

By Christopher H. Pyle

For at least five years, the U. S. Army has maintained a close watch over civilian political activity throughout the United States. Over 1,500 plain-clothes agents, working out of some 300 offices and scores of bases from coast to coast, have kept track of political protests of all kinds—from Klan rallies in North Carolina to anti-war speeches at Harvard. This aspect of their duties is unknown to most Americans, who know these soldier-agents, if at all, only as the personable young men who conduct background investigations of persons being considered for security clearances.

When this program began in the summer of 1965, its purpose was to provide early warning of civil disorders which the Army might be called upon to quell. In 1967, however, following the Newark and Detroit riots and the March on the Pentagon, its space was widened to include the political beliefs and actions of individuals and organizations active in the civil rights, white supremacy, black power, and anti-war movements. By January 1970 the Army had amassed a score of regional and national data banks on the membership, ideology, programs, and practices of virtually every activist political group in the country. These computer tapes, dossiers, card files, and microfilm described not only such violence prone organizations as the Minutemen and the Weathermen, but such non-violent groups as the Southern Christian Leadership Conference, Clergy and Laymen Concerned about Vietnam, Women Strike for Peace, and the National Association for the Advancement of Colored People. The Army's personality files and blacklists included not only Mark Rudd, Gus Hall, and Robert Shelton, but Brigadier General Hugh B. Hester and Rear Admiral Arnold E. True (war critics), Georgia State Representative Julian Bond, actress Jane Fonda, and folk singers Pete Seeger, Arlo Guthrie, Phil Ochs, Judy Collins, and Joan Baez.

Collection Methods

The Army obtained most of this political intelligence from overt sources. Its main sources of information were the files of municipal, state, and campus police, and the FBI, but it also had access to political data banks maintained by the Justice Department, the Secret Service, and the Civil Service Commission. In addition, Army intelligence units have subscribed to hundreds of community, campus, and "underground" newspapers and magazines, and to the major wire services. Recently, the Army Intelligence Command made inquiries concerning the feasibility of tying into the computerized state criminal records systems assembled by "Project Search."

Like other members of the domestic intelligence community, the Army has obtained only a fraction of its information on civilian politics from undercover operations. Nonetheless its agents:

• Infiltrated civilian organizations, such as the Southern Christian Leadership Conference and the National Mobilization Committee, which have no connection whatever with the armed forces.

• Sat among delegates on the floor of the 1968 Democratic National Convention.

• Operated on the floor of the Republican National Convention.

• Posed as press photographers and newsmen, sometimes with phony press credentials. One set of credentials used by the agents of the 116th MI Group in Washington, D. C., was made out in the name of Francis T. Naughton, *Richmond Times Dispatch.*

• Infiltrated the 1968 Poor Peoples Campaign and Resurrection City.

• Rode the buses and trains that carried demonstrators to the 1967 March on the Pentagon.

• Infiltrated a Yippie commune on DuPont Circle, Washington, D.C. during the 1969 Counter-Inaugural demonstration. The use of marijuana and liquor at government expense was authorized for this operation.

• Posed as students to monitor classes in the Black Studies program at New York University during the summer or fall of 1968.

• Were arrested at Howard University in 1969 by District of Columbia police while participating in a rock-throwing crowd.

• Posed as television newsmen interviewing demonstrators in Atlanta, Chicago, Washington, D.C., and Catonsville, Maryland.

• Infiltrated the Colorado Springs Young Adults Project (a coalition of church youth groups which operated a recreational center for emotionally disturbed young people), monitored an anti-war vigil in the Chapel of Colorado State College, maintained two full-time infiltrators in the local peace movement, and sent plainclothes agents to attend meetings of the Colorado Springs poverty board.

Army agents have even recruited civilians into their service—sometimes for pay, but more often through appeals to patriotism. For example, when Columbia University gave its students the option of closing their academic records to routine inspection by government investigators, the 108th Military Intelligence Group in Manhattan quietly persuaded an employee of the Registrar's Office to disclose information from the closed records surreptitously. At the University of Minnesota, agents from the 113th MI Group's Region V Office in Minneapolis frequently obtained the assistance of campus officials in identifying student demonstrators in photographs which the agents had taken.

Types of Information Sought

Most of the political information sought by the Army over the past five years has related not to the criminal acts of political fringe groups, but to the lawful and peaceful actions and expressions of civilians unassociated with the armed forces or civil disturbances. Typical of the hundreds of reports filed by Army agents each month are the following, taken from the unclassified intelligence summary for the week of March 18, 1968.

PHILADELPHIA, PA.: A. THE PHILADELPHIA CHAPTER OF THE WOMEN'S STRIKE FOR PEACE SPONSORED AN ANTI-DRAFT MEETING AT THE FIRST UNITARIAN CHURCH WHICH ATTRACTED AN AUDIENCE OF ABOUT 200 PERSONS. CONRAD LYNN, AN AUTHOR OF DRAFT EVASION LITERATURE, REPLACED YALE CHAPLAIN WILLIAM SLOANE COFFIN AS THE PRINCIPAL SPEAKER AT THE MEETING. FOLLOWING A QUESTION AND ANSWER PERIOD, ROBERT EDENBAUM OF THE CENTRAL COMMITTEE FOR CONSCIENTIOUS OBJECTORS STATED THAT MANY PHILADELPHIA LAWYERS WERE ACCEPTING DRAFT EVASION CASES. THE MEETING ENDED WITHOUT INCIDENT.

B. REV ALBERT CLEAGE, JR., THE FOUNDER OF THE BLACK CHRISTIAN NATIONALIST MOVEMENT IN DETROIT, SPOKE TO AN ESTIMATED 100 PERSONS AT THE EMMANUEL METHODIST CHURCH. CLEAGE SPOKE ON THE TOPIC OF BLACK UNITY AND THE PROBLEMS OF THE GHETTO. THE MEETING WAS PEACEFUL AND POLICE REPORTED NO INCIDENTS.

CHICAGO, ILL.: APPROXIMATELY 300 MEMBERS OF VETERANS FOR PEACE AND WOMEN FOR PEACE HELD A PEACEFUL DEMONSTRATION AT THE MUSEUM OF SCIENCE AND INDUSTRY PROTESTING AN EXHIBIT BY THE US ARMY. SEVERAL DEMONSTRATORS ENTERED THE

BUILDING IN SPITE OF WARNINGS BY MUSEUM OFFICIALS AND 6 WERE ARRESTED ON CHARGES OF DISORDERLY CONDUCT, RESISTING ARREST AND CRIMINAL TRESPASSING. FIVE OF THOSE ARRESTED WERE JUVENILES.

In addition to these incident reports, Army agents also assembled personality and organizational profiles. These reports, too frequently, had nothing to do with either the Army's civil disturbance function or its concern for the security of military installations, personnel, equipment, or supplies. Two such compilations which the Army has recently discontinued in response to Congressional criticism were the "Compendium" and "blacklist." The "Compendium" was a two-volume, yellow covered loose-leaf publication published by the domestic intelligence section of the Counterintelligence Analysis Branch (now Detachment) of the Office of the Assistant Chief of Staff for Intelligence. Begun after the Detroit riots of 1967, it was conceived of as a means for educating military intelligence units about a wide variety of individuals and organizations likely to be encountered at demonstrations. The "blacklist" was a large staplebound paperback booklet (eventually published in multiple volumes) put out by the U.S. Army Intelligence Command to described individuals and organizations who, in the words of one of its editors, "might cause trouble for the Army." More detailed than the "Compendium" it contained mug shots and vital statistics on controversial civilians, as well as descriptions of their beliefs and associations.

The Distribution System

Primary responsibility for collecting, distributing, and storing domestic intelligence has rested with the U.S. Army Intelligence Command (USAINTC), which has its headquarters in Baltimore, Maryland. Established in 1965, the Command directs the collection efforts of over 1,000 agents who work out of some 300 offices of eight stateside Military Intelligence Groups, seven of which were formerly assigned to the G-2 offices of the major stateside armies. The Command's principal function is not to collect political intelligence on Americans, but to protect the Army from espionage, sabotage, and subversion. Its main job is to investigate persons being considered for security clearances and to inspect military installations for adequate physical, wire-communications, and document security.

To assure prompt communication of its agents' reports, the Command set up a nationwide teletype network devoted exclusively to internal security information. Completed at great expense in the fall of 1967, this secret wire service has, until recently, given the Pentagon, and each major troop command and intelligence unit in the United States weekly, daily, and sometimes hourly reports on virtually all political protests wherever they have occurred. Courtesy copies of the reports were passed on to the FBI and to the Justice Department.

The clearing house for this information has been a wire mesh "cage" located inside a gray metal warehouse at Fort Holabird in southeast Baltimore. Until recently the sign on the door read "CONUS Intelligence Branch, Operations IV, U.S. Army Intelligence Command." (CONUS means Continental U.S.). Today the sign reads "Director of Investigations." Here reports from agents in the field were received, sorted, and sent out over a battery of teletype machines. Because the staff was small and the volume of reports large, there was no time to verify, edit, or interpret the information before it was passed on to "user organizations."

The principal consumer of this raw intelligence was the domestic intelligence section of the Counter Intelligence Analysis Detachment (CIAD) of the Office of the Army Assistant Chief of Staff for Intelligence (OACSI). Until recently, it was located in the Directorate for Civil Disturbance Planning and Operations (DCDPO). The name of this unit has recently been changed to the Directorate of Military Support (DOMS), the Army's mammoth, $2.7 million domestic war room under the Pentagon's mall parking lot. Now back with the CIAD's main offices in Alexandria, Virginia, the domestic intelligence section advises the Army brass on the likelihood of civil disorders and other threats to the military. Because of the emphasis given to its functions in recent years, the domestic intelligence section was until recently largfier than any of CIAD's foreign sections, including the section which monitors Southeast Asia.

Other recepients of CONUS intelligence reports have been the Army Material Command, the Military District of Washington, the Air Defense Command, and Army headquaters in Europe, Alaska, Hawaii, and Panama. Thus, contrary to the Army's protestations, distribution of domestic intelligence has not been limited to those units with a "need-to know."

Data Banks

Over the years the Army's records on civilian politics have accumulated in a score of local, regional, and national data banks. One of the largest was assembled by the Intelligence Command on an IBM

1401 computer. As reports came in they were transcribed onto IBM type cards, key-punched, and put on magnetic tape. Programmed to produce print-outs in 96 separate categories, this machine was fed both incident and personality information. The incident reports related, more or less, to the Army's role in civil disturbances and described such occurrences as bombings, mass violence, and arms thefts. The personality reports—extracted in most instances from incident reports—also were fed to the computer.

Thus the Intelligence Command's computerized data bank was unique. Unlike similar computers now in use at the FBI's National Crime Information Center and in numerous states, it was not restricted to the storage of case histories of persons arrested for or convicted of crimes. Rather it specialized in files devoted exclusively to descriptions of the *lawful* political activity of civilians. Typical was an IBM card prepared in 1967 for the computer file of Arlo Tatum, executive secretary of the Central Committee for Conscientious Objectors in Philadelphia. It contained a single notation—that Mr. Tatum once delivered a speech at the University of Oklahoma on the legal rights of conscientious objectors.

A second national data bank was assembled on microfilm by the Counterintelligence Analysis Detachment. Indexed by computer, this archive contained not only the Intelligence Command's teletype reports, but newspaper clippings and FBI reports.

Operating independently and competitively, the Continental Army Command assembled a large computerized file on dissident civilians at its headquaters at Fort Monroe, Virginia. This file was assembled not only from information received over the Intelligence Command's wire service, but from reports based upon the independent collection efforts of the G-2s (intelligence officers) of stateside military units and posts. The Continental Army Command, upset by the Pentagon's decision to centralize direction of riot control in its domestic war room, sought to develop its own domestic intelligence capacity in the hope that it might someday regain command of its riot troops.

In addition, each Military Intelligence Group has assembled extensive regional and local files at most of its metropolitan offices. These include dossiers on organizations and card files on individuals. Similarly, many Army posts and units have assembled files on local political activists. At Fort Hood, Texas, these were computerized for rapid recovery. In addition, all units have put together extensive photo collections.

Most of the Army's information, of course, has also been stored by the Justice Department in its huge civil disturbance computer.

Access to these data banks, despite Army promises, has not been kept on a strict "need to know" basis. The most extensive swapping of information has occurred at the field office level, where intelligence agents realized that they could not get information from civilian law enforcement authorities unless they gave something in return. Thus, during the fall of 1969, agents of the 113th Military Intelligence group continued to trade information with local FBI agents even after they had received an order from the Intelligence Command forbidding them to do so.

History of CONUS *Intelligence*

In their public and private pronouncements, Army spokesmen have contended repeatedly that the CONUS intelligence operation did not really get underway until after the Martin Luther King riots of April 1968. To understand why the Army undertook to monitor civilian politics, they have said, it is necessary to view the decision making in the light of a hundred burning cities.

I have no doubt that fear of growing racial violence was the primary impetus behind the decision to create a nationwide civil disturbance early warning system. But the claim that the Army's interest in the lawful beliefs, actions and associations of non-violent civilians also began at this time cannot be squared with the facts.

Army inteligence has, since its inception in 1917, aggressively sought information on civilian dissenters of all kinds. The categories of interest—subversion, disloyalty, threats against the Army, and civil disturbances—have not changed. Only the focus and size of the operations have fluctuated in response to the intensity of public fears and the availability of manpower and organization.

The intelligence apparatus is often dated from the Newark and Detroit riots of 1967. It could be traced just as easily to intelligence activities in support of troop alerts at the time of confrontation at the University of Mississippi in 1962, or the Birmingham, Alabama, riots of 1963. I have chosen to date it from 1965—the year of the Watts riots, the "black power" movement, and the establishment of the Army Intelligence Command.

The creation of the Intelligence command is significant for two reasons. First, it gave the Army a unified collection agency capable of absorbing the quantum leap in CONUS intelligence requirements that occurred in 1967. Second, it gave the Army a second CONUS intelligence collection agency. Loss of its stateside MI groups to the Intelligence

Command was a big blow to the Continental Army Command, but it still continued to monitor civilian political activity. When the former MI groups could not fulfill their informational requirements, CONARC commanders drew upon criminal investigators, regular military personnel, and conuterintelligence agents assigned to the MI detachments of stateside Army combat divisions.

The term "CONUS intelligence" was not adopted until 1966. Prior to that time the activity was called "domestic intelligence." Whatever the title, the 113th MI Group (then an INTC Group) was keeping files on civilians and civilian organizations in Minneapolis as early as 1962. Files recently destroyed at the Manhattan offices of the 108th MI Group date back to 1964, about the time that the Counterintelligence Analysis Branch set up its "North American" desk and began to keep files on right-wing and racial groups. During 1965, agents of the 112th MI Group in Oklahoma City regularly photographed and reported on tiny bands of anti-war protesters who picketed near the city's federal courthourse. The following summer, agents of the 111th MI Group rented an unmarked pick-up truck and followed James Meredith on his "walk against fear" through the Mississippi country side. About the same time the 112th MI Group in Texas was keeping files on State Senator Barbara Jordan, State Representative Curtis Graves, American Civil Liberties Union attorneys, anti-war activists, and the President of the Brotherhood of Railway Clerks.

Typical of the orders of the day are the teletype mesages of August 1966 issued by the 112th MI Group. The handbills, pamphlets, and brochures of anti-war groups were requested, according to one of the mesages, "for use by DA (Department of the Army) for analysis purposes."

The Ghetto Riots of 1967

Nonetheless, the Newark and Detroit riots of 1967 caught Army intelligence unprepared. No advance warning was given of either riot, and when Lt. Gen. John Throckmorton arrived in Detroit to take charge of a disorganized assemblage of National Guardsmen, he had only an oil company map to guide him.

On the Monday following the outbreak of violence in Newark, the Army Intelligence Command received orders to set up a nationwide civil disturbance early warning system. It immediately created the "CONUS Intelligence Section, Operations IV" to act as a clearing house for civil disturbance reports. To assure prompt reporting, a nationwide teletype network also was begun. Completed late in 1967, this network linked all region and headquarters offices of the MI groups to "Ops Four," and linked "Ops Four" to the Army Operations Center in the Pentagon and to all stand-by riot units.

When the Detroit riots broke out, analysts from the Counterintelligence Analysis Branch were assigned to augment the staff of the Army Operations Center. One of their first duties was to prepare a "Counterintelligence Estimate" of the situation. Although the document they compiled was little more than a history of the situation with a guess as to its outcome, it was an instant success. CIAB's domestic analysts were promptly given the task of preparing an expanded estimate for the remainder of the year. Along with their predictions they were told to include profiles of individuals and organizations who might either precipitate or foment trouble.

Shortly after the Detroit riots, Under Secretary of the Army David E. McGiffert convened a large conference to review the government's preparation for civil disorders. The meeting was attended by Deputy Attorney General Warren Christopher, White House Assistant Stephen Pollak, and representatives of the Army, the FBI, the Secret Service and local police departments. At the top of their agenda was the anti-war demonstration scheduled for October 21st.

The March on the Pentagon

The Army Intelligence Command went all out to infiltrate and monitor the October 1967 anti-war March on the Pentagon. Agents from every MI group in the country rode the buses and trains to Washington. Others joined FBI agents to question the managers of charter bus companies, interrogations which in some cases led companies to break their contracts with anti-war groups. Still others counted demonstrators and buses at armories in New York and from the overpasses on the Baltimore-Washington Expressway. Phoney draft cards were issued to agents from the 108th MI Group in New York to immunize them from prosecution should they be arrested in Washington. As an additional mark of identification, the same agents were instructed to wear ballpoint pens wrapped with elastic bands in their shirt pockets.

In Washington each agent had a telephone number to call to report any plans for violence he might have heard during the trip. Few called in, among other reasons, because telephones were hard to find. At the Pentagon, an aide to General William H. Blakefield, Commanding General of the Intelligence Command, was clubbed by the military police.

Despite these elaborate preparations, the Army underestimated the number of demonstrators that would show up, how long they would stay, and the degree of violence they would attempt. For these failures Major General William P. Yarborough, the Assistant Chief of Staff, caught what one of his assistants has described as "unshirted hell" from high civilian officials, apparently including President Johnson.

The results was a massive, Army-wide effort to keep track of individuals and groups suspected of inciting or precipitating violence. H. Rap Brown, Stokeley Carmichael, and David Dellinger were followered wherever they went. So too were the Reverends Martin Luther King and Ralph Abernathy. Teletype reports on their activities were distributed to the Pentagon, all MI group headquarters and region offices, and all stateside army commands on a daily and sometimes hourly basis.

Prominent civil rights, anti-war, and black power figures were not the only persons watched. At CIAB, investigations by the FBI into the backgrounds of over 400 demonstrators arrested at the Pentagon were recorded on microfilm. In Minneapolis, a card index keyed to files of clippings and reports took note of the non-violent political sentiments of a number of university professors and students. Even the director of the St. Paul Department of Human Rights was remembered in this file.

General Yarborough

The moving force behind the Army's decision to keep close track of political protest leaders was the Assistant Chief of Staff for Intelligence, Maj. Gen. William Yarborough. This flamboyant general, known as "Big Y" for the way he signed memorandums, could not comprehend either the spontaneity of ghetto riots or the disorganization characteristic of many anti-war groups. Much of his military career had been spent overseas in counterintelligence and psychological warfare where he had participated in, and tried to counter, genuine conspiracies to promote subversion and dissaffection. Accordingly, he found it difficult to believe that the huge outpouring of anti-war, anti-military sentiment expressed during the March on the Pentagon could have occurred without skillful, behind-the-scenes leadership by Communists, financed and directed from abroad. This conspiracy view of history led him repeatedly to demand evidence of plots when there were none, and to suspect David Dellinger and Gus Hall of being pivotal figures. To a lesser extent, these views were shared by his Deputy, Brig. Gen. Wesley M. Franklin, and his successor, Maj. Gen. Joseph A. McChristian.

The Blacklist

Sometime during the fall of 1967 the Army Intelligence Command hit upon the idea of mug books as a convenient way to disseminate its information on potential "troublemakers." Titled "The USAINTC Identification List" but referred to by its editors as the "blacklist," this document was first published as a glossy-covered paperback. It featured four pictures to a page and included identifying data and brief summaries of the political beliefs, activities, and associations of many civilians unassociated with the armed forces. During 1968 and 1969 it grew from one to six volumes. Four were complied by the Intelligence Command; two were borrowed from the Alabama state police.

The Compendium

At the Counterintelligence Analysis Branch a similar document was also undertaken during the fall of 1967. Although formally titled *Counterintelligence Research Project: Civil Disturbances and Dissidence: Cities and Organizations of Interest and Individuals of Interest,* it was better known as "The Compendium." The idea for this two-volume loose-leaf service originated with William L. Parkinson. Deputy Chief of CIAB. He envisioned it not as a potential round-up list, but as an encyclopedia to answer many of the questions that had tied up his telephone during the Detroit riots and the March on the Pentagon.

The descriptions were based mainly upon FBI reports, Army agent reports, and newspaper articles. Original sources were often unknown and no machinery existed to permit verifications. Whatever seemed credible to the analyists went in.

Organizations were divided into "left-wing," "right-wing," and "racial." Write-ups had to fit one of these categories. Information on each organization included its history, philosophy, current direction, leaders, location, and size of membership, when known. Groups profiled included not only the Students for a Democratic Society and the Congress of Racial Equality, but the Southern Christian Leadership Conference, the National Urban League, Young Americans for Freedom, and the John Birch Society.

The principal recipients of the Compendium were the MI group's headquarters and region office commanders, but copies were also sent to each of the major army commands, the FBI, the CIA, and the U.S. embassies in Canada and West Germany.

The Computers

The next step in the Army's response to civil disturbances was to decide how to store all of the information flooding in over the new teletypes. At the Intelligence Command, plans were laid during the winter of 1967-68 to computerize the storage of both incident and personality data. (It was the biographical file assembled on this computer which so surprised Army General Counsel Robert Jordan when he finally visited Fort Holabird in February 1970).

About the same time the Continental Army Command also decided to computerize its files. (When III Corps at Fort Hood, Texas, decided to put its civil disturbance records on tape is not known).

Of all the national records centers, only CIAB rejected computerization in favor of microfilm. However, CIAB did computerize the index to its archive.

The decision to computerize reveals something about each organization. At CIAB the analysts were concerned about the distortion and loss of information that occurs when detailed reports are compressed into key-punchable categories. But at CONARC and Fort Holabird, these considerations were rejected. Speed and volume were the criteria by which these collection agencies were evaluated. Problems of evaluation did not greatly concern them. They did very little evaluation anyway. Their job was not to find patterns of violence or test models of social change, but to regurgitate statistics and other summary data for briefings. Thus computers were for them little more than listing devices and adding machines.

Prediction Efforts

While the two domestic intelligence collection agencies planned their computers, analyists at CIAB studied standard metropolitan statistical areas in an effort to assess their potential need for Army troops. Four categories of cities were finally adopted. The first included those cities most likely to need federal troops in case of a riot. Typically these communities had a large number of black residents, a history of racial violence, and poorly equipped police and National Guard units. Category II applied to cities less likely to need federal troops, either because they had proportionately fewer blacks, less history of racial strife, or could expect substantial protection from the state National Guard.

Category III denoted cities with still less need for Army or National Guard assistance, either because their ghettos were relatively small or well off, or because their municipal and state police forces were substantial. In practice, it proved difficult to find cities which fit this description; where municipal police were strong, the state police were not, and vice-versa. Finally Category IV was reserved for cities in which there was little likelihood of violence. It mainly described those cities with few blacks and no history of racial violence.

The classification system was little more than crude guesswork. It was a useful way in which to survey the relative preparedness of local and state police and military forces, but it did little to indicate which citizes with sizable ghettos were likely to erupt first.

City Packets

The effort to collect tactical intelligence on potential riot areas began shortly after General Throckmorton's experience with the oil company map in Detroit. But it was not until after the classification of cities was completed that teams of military policemen and Army intelligence agents were sent out to actually reconnoiter the cities for up-to-date information on potential trouble areas, approach routes, bivouac sites, police and fire stations, gun shops, utility sub-stations, and other "areas of interest." Eventually this information was assembled into "city packets" for each of 150 cities deemed to have riot potential. Copies were distributed not only to the Army units assigned to provide back-up protection, but to the local MI group, municipal and state police, and the National Guard.

The city packets and the civil disturbance plans they contained contributed much to government planning at all levels. Unfortunately the packets also contained the names, addresses and political profiles of many local organizations and individuals whose past actions in no way indicated a propensity to foment disorder. The descriptions of them could not be of any practical use to riot troops; in the hands of state authorities, however, they might have encouraged the illegal round-up of political activists unsuspected of any crime.

Army Intelligence on the Eve of the April Riots

From this brief history it should be evident that the Army's interest in civilian politics developed well before the tragic riots of April 1968. The collection of personality and organizational data on political protesters actually preceded the assembling of city packets and the drafting of new civil disturbance plans. At each collection point, regionally and nationally, data banks on dissenters of all kinds were set up. The computers, card files, dossiers, identification lists, intelligence summaries, and photographic files were all begun *before* Dr. King's assassination. He himself was a major object of the surveillance. In fact, three days before his dealth, CIAB received and filed a scurrilous report on his personal life compiled from wiretaps and other sources by the Federal Bureau of Investigation.

The April Riots

The Army's files on Dr. King did not predict his murder; nor did the agents of the 111th MI Group in Memphis who watched his every public move. As they and scores of state and federal agents looked on, an escaped convict moved among them, fired the fatal shot, and fled.

Almost immediately rioting exploded in scores of cities. Before the month was over, 237 civil disorders had been reported. 68,915 soldiers were called to riot duty, 23,000 under federal control. Half of the federal troops were sent into Washington, D.C.; the remainder went to Baltimore and Chicago.

Like the rest of the government, Army intelligence had no advance warning of the disorders. But is was better prepared than it had been during the previous summer. Some city packets had been assembled and the new civil disturbance plans, published in December, had been supplemented in February with classified intelligence annexes. A revised edition of Field Manual 19-15, *Civil Disturbances and Disasters,* had been published in March. The Intelligence Command''s teletype network was in operation and new "emergency operations centers," crammed with radios and telephones, had been installed at MI group offices in a number of large cities. The operations centers were part of a contingency plan which envisioned MI agents as the eyes and ears of the Army Operations Center at the Pentagon.

Of all the MI groups that saw riot duty, probably none was better prepared than the 116th in Washington, D.C. Its deployment in time of riot was virtually guaranteed by the weakness of the D.C. National Guard, the availability of Army troops stationed nearby, and the fact that D.C. was both a federal city and the nation's Capital. Moreover, the 116th had been anticipating violence ever since Dr. King had announced his intention to lead a Poor People's Campaign into Washington and to set up an encampment near the Washington Monument. A week before the assassination, the unit staged a "field training exercise" to test its radios, surveillance teams, and operations center. The scenario was modeled after the October demonstrations. One message transmitted to the radio cars during the test read: "People are attacking the Pentagon."

On April 4, 1968, the news that Dr. King had died reach Washington about 8:30 p.m. Within an hour violence erupted. The 116th MI Group immediately called in all of its agents and began around-the-clock operations. Three-man teams were dispatched in unmarked radio cars to reconnoiter the city. Individual agents were sent to the precinct stations with instructions to report the names of all persons arrested. At the EOC others manned hot lines to the precincts, the Intelligence Command, the Army Operations Center, the 82nd Airborne Division, and the Military District of Washington. Information was posted on a large wall map illuminated with day-glo colors.

The white agents who cruised the ghettos that night in unmarked cars were deeply shaken by the experience. At least one team was stoned by rioters. The next night junior officers refused to go out unarmed and .38 caliber snub-nosed revolvers were issued to the leaders of each team.

Some Army agents went beyond their instructions and attempted to advise the police. Others kept to the fringes of the riot areas and reported only the observations of policemen and firemen. A few black agents mingled with the crowds. The Army Security Agency monitored citizen-band transmissions.

Opinions on the usefulness of this activity are mixed. One agent recalls that the Army agents were "the best behaved" of all the elements covering the riots, and were useful to troops because of their knowledge of the city. In addition, he says, the photographs they took were much in demand by other agencies.

The same individual, however, questions why his unit, which had assigned him to a precinct station, wanted him to report the names of all persons arrested by the police in connection with the riots. (As the number of persons arrested mounted, this order was rescinded). Other agents stress that they were not directed to work closely with troop units. As a consequence, they say, they did not contribute to the protection of lives or property.

At the Army Operations Center in the Pentagon dissatisfaction was voiced with the quality of some of the information received from agents in the streets. David E. McGiffert, then Under Secretary of the Army, has recalled: "I remember once during the King riots, I was in the war room and during the space of 30 to 40 minutes we got six reports on the whereabouts of Stokley Carmichael. The reports on him . . . were divided on whether he was a calming or a provocative influence . . . I believe two said he was in Georgetown, two or three said various parts of black neighborhoods, one said Baltimore, and one said Richmond."

The problem of Carmichael's whereabouts was solved several weeks later when the Army was deluged with FBI reports probing participation in the riots for signs of agitation or incitement by local black citizens or groups. The reports were put on microfilm at CIAB.

Planning for the Worst

Although the Army was better prepared to cope with the disorders in Washington, Baltimore, and Chicago in 1968 than it had been in Detroit in 1967, fear of a "long hot summer" of racial violence prompted another round of high level reviews. At the Pentagon on April 12 and again at the White House on April 15, Under Secretary of the Army McGiffert proposed that Army intelligence concentrate on civil disturbance warnings.

Out of those meetings also came a directive that the Army prepare to deploy 10,000 troops in any of 25 cities. Later that number was reduced to less than ten cities, after the Counter Intelligence Analysis Branch demonstrated that there weren't that many cities with indequate police and State National Guard units.

On April 26 the Pentagon announced the creation of a new 180-man staff exclusively devoted to coordinating the military's response to civil disorders. The Army Operations Center, with its world-wide responsibilties, could not effectively handle riots on top of everything else. The new command was to be called the "Directorate for Civil Disturbance Planning and Operations" (DCDPO). It was to be a joint Army-Air Force operation, headed by a three-star Army general. Its quarters were to be carved out of a storage area under the Pentagon's mall parking lot. To avoid having to pry funds out of a reluctant

Congress, the Joint Chiefs paid the $2.7 million construction bill out of their Contingency Fund.

On May 2 the Army issued its civil disturbance information plan which expanded still further the military's civil disturbance collection requirements. Brig. Gen. William H. Blakefield, head of the Army Intelligence Command, urged his MI groups to "beat the AP" in their reporting. At the Counter Intelligence Analysis Branch, analysts were instructed to call upon the Intelligence Command for any information they needed to keep track of the Poor People's Campaign, due to arrive in Washington in mid-to-late May.

Dr. King's Funeral

The funeral services for Martin Luther King, Jr., were held in Atlanta on April 9, 1968. They began at his father's church, the Ebenezer Baptist. An agent of the 111th MI Group in Atlanta described his unit's assignment for NBC News: "we had to cover every step of the funeral. We had to report on all dignitaries and personalities of any importance that were entering the area during the funeral, to include the Vice President of the United States. We were given no clear point for covering it, just that this was a black funeral and it was anticipated that there might be disorders and perhaps a racial problem because of the funeral itself."

The Army's instructions to its agents that day seemed to go beyond a desire for early warning of violence. Early warning was assured by the presence of Justice Department officials, FBI agents, and massive numbers of state and city policemen. In addition, the entire event was covered by three television networks and hundreds of newsmen and photographers. Nonetheless, an agent recalls:

"Two agent teams were assigned to march with the funeral procession itself throughout the whole course of the procession. We were told by our superiors that this had to be covered—that every fifteen minutes a report had to be telephoned via a hot line expressly established for this funeral back to Fort Holabird reporting the activities of the march itself, with emphasis on being ahead of AP and UPI wire services on all reporting information. They wanted to know exactly who was there, how many people were marching in the crowd, what the breakdown of the crowd was—did it look like a hostile crowd? Was it [a] . . . crowd of poor students in the crowd? Were there many militants in the area—just a complete breakdown of anything we might be able to give."

As the cortege moved through the streets of Atlanta, it was also followed by Army agents in unmarked radio cars. At one point an agent radioed from an unknown location: "Here comes the parade." He was quickly corrected by a black sergeant in another car: "It's not a parade!"

Hours before the procession began, a single agent had been staked out 100 yards from the grave-site.

All of the Army agents in Atlanta were kept on duty that night. Those not manning the emergency operations center roamed the streets collecting reports from storeowners that blacks had threatened to "burn them out" if they did not shut down out of respect for the slain civil rights leader.

Atlanta did not burn.

The Poor People's Campaign

Exactly one month later, on the evening of May 9, 1968, members of the Poor People's Campaign stopped at the Atlanta Civic Center on their way to Washington to commemorate Dr. King. Those present included the Supremes, the Rev. Ralph David Abernathy, Mrs. Corretta King, and an agent from Army intelligence. The agent recalls: "When Coretta King spoke, she told the audience how her husband had had a dream and now this dream was going to come true. When I called this in to the field office, I spoke to a captain . . . He wanted me to go back and find out what dream she was referring to."

The next day, many members of the bus caravan made a pilgrimage to Southview Cemetery where Dr. King was buried. Across the street from the cemetery, two agents in an unmarked car reported the license numbers of the cars that had brought people to the grave-site. Another mixed with the crowd and took notes on what the mourners were saying. A third agent remained near the grave to see if there was talk of more riots or demonstrations. He also made a list of the notables who came to the grave and reported that "King was eulogized."

Later that day, three MI radio cars followed the bus caravan to Social Circle, Georgia, where a march had been planned. At one point on the narrow, two-lane road, one of the MI cars drove recklessly alongside the procession in order to better collect license numbers. In addition, two undercover agents from the 111th MI Group rode all the way to Washington, D.C. on the busses.

The Poor People's mule train followed the busses by several weeks. Again, an agent who was there recalls: "That was probably one of the largest operations I have participated in in Army intelligence. The Atlanta Field Office established contact with the mule team when they entered Georgia . . .Approximately twelve agents met this caravan coming into the state. The mules were surveyed from that point on all the way through their trip into Georgia. They were constantly surveyed to include the number of mule trains, the number of people on the trains, and the number of mules, to differentiate between the number of horses since they couldn't supply enough mules. It was a very strong requirement of the Army to know the exact number of mules and the exact number of horses at all times."

When the procession passed through Douglasville, Ga., a humane society charged that the mules were being abused. Army agents were dispatched to photograph the rumps of the mules.

Resurrection City

The mules were followed every step of their way through Georgia by agents of the 111th MI Group. When they arrived by rail at the old Alexandria, Virginia, depot, a delegation from the 116th was on hand to greet them.

The Poor People who came to Washington with the mules also were closely watched. Army agents parked their cars on French Drive and observed the encampment in the company of the Metropolitan Police, the Park Police, and the FBI. They took down the license numbers of the Poor People's buses so that their ownership could be traced by the Intelligence Command. Overhead, a captain from the 116th flew aerial reconnaissance missions in helicopters and accumulated flight pay. From the top of the Washington Monument, a Signal Corps unit photographed the tent city for imagery interpreters at the Pentagon.

On the ground Army agents followed delegations of Poor People on their protest marches to Congress, the Department of Agriculture and Justice, and to the Bureau of Indian Affairs. Hundreds of feet of 35 mm black and white film was expended to record these events. While observing Resurrection City from just outside the snow fence, one of the teams from the 116th had its 35 mm Bessler Topcon camera taken away from them by a group of blacks.

Most of the Army surveillance of Poor People was overt. However, when a dispute broke out within the staff of the Southern Christian Leadership Conference, an agent was sent to cover a press conference in the basement of a building near the D.C. courthouses. He was instructed to pose as a newsman and was given a fake press pass made out to "Francis T. Naughton, *Richmond Times Dispatch.*" Another agent was directed to pretend that he was a newsman and to call a motel to "find out if Abernathy's motel bill had been paid." Still another agent, a black major, was temporarily taken off orders to Vietnam and sent into Resurrection City to live among its residents and to report on living conditions, attitudes, and leadership. He arrived about a week after the encampment opened and remained until it was closed by the Metropolitan Police.

The Republican National Convention

When Senator Robert F. Kennedy was assassinated on June 5, 1968, the fear of racial violence was compounded by a fear for the lives of all prominent public figures, in and out of office. The next day, Congress passed a joint resolution (Public Law 90-331, 90th Cong., 2d Sess., H.J.Res. 1292, June 6, 1968) which authorized the Secret-Service to borrow any personnel it needed from the armed forces in order to protect major Presidential and Vice-Presidential candidates. The law codified one aspect of the military's broader practice of loaning MI agents and military policemen to other federal agencies such as the State Department when extra manpower was urgently needed for the protection of dignitaries. In its haste, Congress did not stop to define or limit the meaning of the word "protection." As a result, military intelligence agents attended both the Republican and Democratic National Conventions that year.

In Miami, the 111th Group was assigned a room in the Convention Hall and had its own radio and telephone connections to the outside. According to an agent who was present, the unit's convention delegation was led by the group commander, a Colonel McBride, and seemed to operate independently of the Secret Service. The Army agents were isued blue lapel pins and were assigned to the floor of the convention by means of a duty roster. They generally remained on the perimeter and did not speak with delegates. The agent says that he did not have the slightest idea what was expected of him other than to keep his eyes and ears open. There was a hot line to the Miami field office and from there to Fort Holabird, but he never contributed any information and does not know what was included in the reports that were made. Col. McBride and his assistant, a Lt. Col. Raymond, seemed always to be on the floor.

The presence of Army agents on the floor of the Republican National Convention has been confirmed by Jack Warner, Public Information Officer for the Secret Service, and by Seymour Gelber, then Security Coordinator for the Miami Beach Police Department. According to Warner, the Secret Service borrowed personnel from all three services to assist with convention security. "Their presence related only to the security of candidates. They were under our control and filed no 'intelligence' reports to us." He added that the military agents had no time to "even take notes if they wanted to. They had their hands full with the security job." The agent who was present disagrees. According to Gelber:

". . . Army Intelligence basically contributed the knowledge that they had obtained through the years of their investigations concerning people who might be causing trouble in situations . . .

"Army Intelligence and Navy Intelligence resulted in taking still shots and then going downstairs and having another team examining each one of these still shots to determine any suspicious individuals whom they could recognize were present.

"The Army Intelligence as well as Navy Intelligence had rather complete files on people who might be trouble-prone and they also had contact with Washington and other parts of the country where they could get immediate information on any of these individuals, should that be necessary."

The Army also furnished about 30 men from its Criminal Investigations Division, but what role they played in convention security is not known. The Air Force was in charge of coordinating the Defense Department's contributions which included a Navy ship to house most of the federal personnel and Marine helicopters which circled overhead in case emergency evacuation of one or more candidates should prove necessary.

Ray C. Bliss, the Republican National Chairman, and Don Ross, his detail man for convention security, were unaware of the presence of military agents. Ross did know that the Secret Service had borrowed security personnel from other federal agencies, but assumed they were civilians.

The Democratic National Convention

The military's role in convention security grew still larger in anticipation of large-scale demonstrations at the Democratic National Convention in Chicago. Both the Attorney General and the analysts at CIAB were convinced that the Illinois National Guard was more than a match for the few thousand demonstrators planning to protest the Convention. But the President accepted the Pentagon's recommendations and several thousand Army troops were sent to Chicago just in case.

The 113th MI Group also was on hand. Agents were brought in from Minneapolis to take over personnel security investigations so that most of the Chicago-based agents could be freed for convention security. Again, the Army agents seemed to operate independently from the Secret Service. According to Richard Stahl, an agent with the Chicago field office, agents were assigned to monitor political figures from the time they arrived. The orders were vague, but it appears that their job was to alert the Army in case any trouble was directed against the politicians, or was precipitated by them. Stahl was assigned to the Georgia delegation and spent part of his time watching Governor Lester Maddox. Later he was assigned to a foot and vehicular surveillance of the Rev. Ralph David Abernathy, watched the Rev. Jesse Jackson, and tape-recorded a speech by Black Panther Chairman Bobby Seale.

Resourceful videotape cameramen from the 113th became famous when they succeeded in obtaining an exclusive interview with Abbie Hoffman on the night of the Chicago "police riot." The film was later made into an Army documentary and was requested by the prosecution in the Chicago Conspiracy case.

Navy agents were assigned similar tasks. Richard Schaller, a civilian analyst for the Naval Investigative Service, testified at the Conspiracy trial that he tape-recorded protest speeches by David Dellinger and others in Grant Park.

Military agents were also on the floor of the Convention. One agent from the staff of the Assistant Chief of Staff for Intelligence sat among the Illinois delegation.

In addition, the Army Security Agency shifted a company-sized electronic surveillance unit from Texas to Chicago where it worked out of storefronts and unmarked mobile vans. According to Ronald E. Weber, a visual aids specialist who assisted in briefings in the ASA war room before he deserted to Canada, the surveillance unit was sent to Chicago to monitor the transmissions of demonstrators. A former Secret Serviceman, on the other hand, has said: "The ASA was there to help the Secret Service protect against the use of electronic surveillance against the candidates." Jack Warner, the Secret Service public information officer, insists tha the ASA "did not assist us."

The Army General Counsel says that he knew nothing about the ASA operation.

Weber also has said that he heard a briefiing in which the ASA claimed credit for intercepting a telephone conservation between Senator Eugene McCarthy's Convention headquarters and "a known radical group." The conversation, he said, involved offers of medical assistance to demonstrators and bystanders injured by the Chicago police.

The presence of military intelligence agents at the Democratic National Convention was not disclosed to the Secretary of Defense, to the Attorney General, or to John Bailey, the Party Chairman. John Meeks, one of Bailey's coordinators, knew that military agents were involved in convention security, but did not know they would be on the floor. "If it had ever come up to me," he said, "I would have opposed it."

The Counter-Inaugural

By January 1969 the CONUS intelligence program was in high gear. The computers were in operation, multiple volumes of the Intelligence Command blacklist had been distributed, and the regional data banks were well established. CIAB and the Intelligence Command had become dumping grounds for FBI reports of all kinds and the civil disturbance wire service was disgorging spot reports at the rate of about 1,200 a month.

To handle the increased workload, special CONUS intelligence sections were set up in the headquarters and region offices of most MI groups. Because many agents had no stomach for watching lawful political protests, assignment to these sections was often made on a voluntary basis. At the 116th, the CONUS intelligence section was created by expanding an older Special Operations Section which, in simpler times, had contented itself with investigating possible cases of espionage and sabotage. In Evanston, Illinois, the Special Operational personel volunteered their services to the CONUS section in order to find something interesting to do.

The size of these sections was impressive. At the 116th, 20 agents were taken off personnel security investigations and assigned full-time to watch demonstrations, give warnings of violence, identify demonstrators, and keep files on individuals and organizations. At CIAB, the domestic section became the largest of all, even exceeding the section responsible for monitoring all counterintelligence emanating from Southeast Asia.

After Chicago, videotaping became the rage. Each MI group headquarters and region office had at least one of the $3,000 Sony cameras. To cover President Nixon's inauguration and the groups who planned to demonstrate at it, at least four teams were deployed. Two came from the 116th and one from the 902nd. The fourth was "Mid-West Video News"—specially flown in from Chicago for the occasion.

The 116th loaned a large number of its agents to the Secret Service which assigned them to work on mobile security teams under the direct command of Secret Servicemen. Others, however, deployed independently to monitor the demonstrators. Two grew beards and infiltrated the headquarters of the National Mobilization Committee. One actually moved into a "commune" of sorts on Dupont Circle where some of the leaders of the Counter-Inaugural and their Presidential "candidate" the pet pig "Pigasus," were staying. "Pigasus," like the Poor People's Mules, seemed to hold a special fascination for the Army Intelligence Command. Among the "EEI" (essential elements of information) issued were: Where is the pig? What are they going to do with the pig? Among the teletype reports issued that week is the following, republished by the Army Provost Marshal General for his criminal investigators throughout the country:

SUNDAY, 19 JANUARY - MONDAY, 20 JANUARY 1969
OUT-OF-TOWN DISSIDENTS CURRENTLY IN WASHINGTON ARE BEING HOUSED IN A "COMMUNE" AT 1728 S STREET NW ALONG WITH "PIGASUS" AND SEVERAL DOGS, WHO ARE PERMITTED TO MOVE AMONG THE PERSONS SLEEPING ON THE FLOOR BUT ARE NOT PERMITTED TO LEAVE THE BUILDING FOR FEAR OF BEING SEEN.

Agents of the 116th also were ordered to take down the license numbers of all cars belonging to the counter-inaugural demonstrators. Since determining which cars belonged to demonstrators and which did not was virtually impossible, the agents noted the numbers of all cars carrying college-age persons or displaying peace stickers. The license numbers were transmitted to the Intelligence Command by teletype and from there to MI groups in their respective states. With the assistance of state authorities, Army Intelligence eventually compiled a master list of about 400 cars and owners, a copy of which was forwarded to the FBI.

Some agents attended the Counter Inaugural Ball. Others were busy reporting bus arrivals and departures. At Dupont Circle the next morning a busload of demonstrators headed for Wilmington, Delaware, to protest the National Guard's six-month presence there, were detained for about an hour. The bus was delayed, according to the demonstrators who later filed suit, by military intelligence.

The McGiffert Memo

The demonstrators were not the only civilians who were becoming aware of the Army's domestic intelligence operations. Under Secretary of the Army David E. McGiffert and Army General Counsel Robert E. Jordan, III, were growing suspicious too.

McGiffert's doubts were aroused a few weeks after the Democratic National Convention when the Justice Department asked him for the Army's videotapes of Abbie Hoffman for possible use in the Chicago Conspiracy trial. Later he began to question where Army intelligence was getting some of the information that appeared in his morning briefings. He had always assumed that the materials were collected by liaison with civilian agencies. However, it was becoming increasingly clear to him that that was not the case and that someone was wasting a lot of money preparing reports that were neither useful nor discriminating.

As the change-over of Administrations, approached, McGiffert decided not to initiate an investigation he could not complete. Instead he wrote a memorandum to the Chief of Staff or Vice Chief of Staff. The memo, dated February 5, 1969, said in effect: Whatever is going on, let's knock it off. Let's get out of the business of watching civilians directly—if we are in it.

Robert Jordan's suspicions developed along with those of McGiffert. The briefings in late 1968, he later told Jared Stout of Newhouse News Services, "were the tip off. When we began to hear about rent strikes and clashes between police and Panthers, it seemed we were doing too much. It didn't seem too sinister to us at the time. The material could have been coming from the AP or UP tickers. It wasn't anything that had to be dug out by a shovel or investigative means. We weren't concerned about the sources."

In the same interview Jordan confirmed that the definition of Army intelligence needs had been left to the military and that whatever they decided to collect, or whomever they chose to watch, was not made known to him. Nor, he said, did he ask. "In retrospect, we may have been derelict. But this is a busy place where you deal with the problems before you. It wasn't a problem then."

The McGiffert memo has never been made public but, according to Jordan, it forbade all covert operations directed at civilian groups without the permission of the Under Secretary, and sought to reduce the direct observation of demonstrations to a minimum. "As far as we know," he said, "the order was obeyed."

Justice Says No

The memorandum appears to have been the first in a two-step Army plan. The second step was to try to dump the civil disturbance early warning system on the Justice Department.

Organizationally, the transfer of duties made sense. It had long been the Attorney General's duty to coordinate the federal government's response to civil disorders and, at least since the Oxford, Miss., crisis of 1962, Justice Department lawyers on the scene had been one of the government's principal sources of usable intelligence. Moreover, the Department had maintained its own civil disturbance information unit since 1966. Renamed the Interdivisional Information Unit (IDIU) in 1968, this operation first began to accumulate personality and organizational files just prior to the Democratic National Convention in Chicago. Despite Ramsey Clark's preference for relying on the Community Relations Service, the IDIU gradually established itself as the center of an information network which included not only the FBI and military intelligence services, but also U.S. attorneys, wire services, the Bureau of Narcotics and Dangerous Drugs, and Treasury Department agents.

Politically, however, the times were not auspicious. The new men at Justice were genuinely alarmed by the rhetoric and actions of the Weatherman, the Black Panthers, the New Mobe, and other dissidents. They also were convinced that the previous administration had been soft on crime and mass violence and lax in the collection of domestic intelligence. The use of military force to deal with civil disorders did not give them pause. During preparations for the inauguration of President Nixon, they had urged the overt show of military force as a deterrent to potential demonstrators.

A few weeks after the McGiffert memorandum was issued, Robert Jordan initiated discussions with the new Deputy Attorney General, Richard G. Kleindienst, in an effort to persuade him to assume full responsibility for gathering information on civil disturbances. The focus of the negotiations was a memorandum of understanding which Jordan hoped would more sharply draw the line between military and civilian functions in times of civil disorder. The Army, he argued, was willing to provide manpower during crises, but felt that advance investigations involving civilians should be conducted by a civilian agency.

The effort failed. In a meeting on April 1, 1969, Kleindienst refused to take over the early warning system on the ground that his department lacked the manpower to do the job. The Justice Department was equipped to analyze civil disturbance information, he said, but still needed the Army to collect it.

Kleindienst's argument became clearer in the weeks that followed. On April 12, the *New York Times* disclosed Administration plans to step up the FBI's surveillance of radical extremists and other left-wing groups and individuals. The decision came in the wake of a series of bombings and bomb scares which included the demolition of a Greenwich Village townhouse on March 6 and the bombing of three Manhattan office buildings on March 12. The Department also revealed plans to participate in a sweeping crackdown on campus rebels. Testifying in mid-May before the Senate Appropriations Committee, Jerrie Leonard, Assistant Attorney General in charge of civil rights, announced that a task force was being assembled to gather "military-like intelligence" for use in prosecuting campus disorders. Later, he reversed himself, but acknowledged that the Justice Department was sending teams to monitor all major disorders, including those on campuses. About the same time, the Attorney General ruled that the Black Panthers and the Weathermen were threats to national security and, as such, would be subject to FBI wiretapping without the benefit of court orders. Each of these new projects increased the drain on the Department's manpower and supported the Deputy Attorney General's contention that the Army's civil disturbance wire service should be kept going.

Civil Disobedience

Within Army intelligence, resistance to scaling down or transferring the CONUS intelligence program also was strong. To the military intelligence bureaucrat, an order he would rather not obey becomes little more than an invitation to negotiate. Evasions, deceptions, delays, and innocent misunderstandings are his defensive weapons—his special form of civil disobedience.

Thus the McGiffert memorandum was not self-executing. Indeed, it never reached the agents in the field. Encouraged by the harder line taken towards radicals and student rioters by the White House and Justice Department, the Intelligence Command strengthened the

CONUS intelligence sections at MI group and region headquarters. Spot reports continued to pour forth at the rate of about 1,200 a mouth despite a downturn in racial strife. CIAB went from a "Branch" to a "Division" and laid plans to up-date the Compendium. A memorandum which doubted the legality of many of the Army files was quietly shelved on the ground that the fewer persons who knew about the records, the better.

Most important, the autonomy of local intelligence commanders continued unrestrained. At Fort Carson, Colorado, the G-2 initiated a number of undercover operations which violated CONRAC directives and directly encroached upon the jurisdiction of the Colorado Springs office of the 113th MI Group. Knowing that the activities were beyond his authority, the G-2 instructed his agents to write their reports in the third person to make it appear that the information came from "walk-in" informers.

One operation conducted by the Fort Carson unit (the 5th Military Intelligence Detachment, 5th Mechanized Infantry Division), was to infiltrate a Colorado Springs youth group with both an agent and an informer. The agent was Oliver A. Peirce. The group was the Young Adults Project (YAP), a coalition of church youth groups and a ski club established to provide housing for transient youths. The surveillance was initiated because one of the founders of the group had led an anti-war demonstration outside the gates of Fort Carson. The surveillance was maintained for nearly six months despite repeated reports from Peirce that the group was both legitimate and innocuous. Other agents of the 5th MID infiltrated the local peace movement and attended meetings of the Colorado Springs poverty board.

The Moratoriums

By the time the fall anti-war demonstrations came, the McGiffert memorandum had been forgotten. On orders from the Pentagon, on-site surveillances were undertaken by MI agents throughout the country.

Oliver Peirce recalls his unit's operations in Colorado Springs in October: "Our office had at least a half a dozen agents covering the Moratorium. They had four or five agents inside the chapel [at Colorado State College] while people were speaking and they had a radio car outside the chapel. The agents would go in and take notes on who was speaking, what they said, if any military personnel took part, and they wanted to know everybody who took part. They wanted them all identified, including the clergymen and the people from the civilian community. And then they would come out to the radio car—or one of them would come out—and feed this information to Fort Carson by radio. I was at the other end of the radio recording the information as it came in. I would write down who spoke and a synopsis of what he said."

In Minneapolis, the Twin Cities and Region V offices of the 113th MI Group turned out in force to observe the local October Moratorium exercises. Two agents marched in the anti-war parade from the College of St. Thomas to Macalester College where they were joined by several others, including the Region V commander, Lt. Col. Donald E. Mattson. The agents then followed the crowd to the Macalester Field House where they monitored a number of speakers, including Georgia State Representatives Julian Bond and Senator Walter F. Mondale (D-Minn.). When special agent George A. Lewis was first informed by his captain that he would have to attend the Macalester rally in an official capacity, he exclaimed: "You're kidding me!" "No," the captain replied, "you will be there."

On October 15, Col. John W. Downie, Director of Counterintelligence, Office of the Assistant Chief of Staff for Intelligence, reported to the Pentagon's brass:

"*Washington, D.C.* VMC (Vietnam Moratorium Committee activities began on the evening of 14 October when members of the House of Representatives kept the House in session until 2317 hours. A short, peaceful, impromptu demonstration by several hundred local college students followed on the steps of the Capitol. Approximately 800 students from Georgetown University staged a procession through the Georgetown section of Washington late last evening. There were no incidents. Today's most significant activity appears to be the planned rally at the Sylvan Theater at 1800 hours, where Mrs. Martin Luther King and Dr. Benjamin Spock will address a rally and lead a march to the White House. No violence at the rally or during the march is expected. Tomas Reeves, the Executive Secretary of the National Committee to Repeal the Draft, announced plans to demonstrate peacefully tonight at the Sheraton Park Hotel, Washington, D. C. The hotel is the meeting site for the Association of the U. S. Army . . . Attempts may be made to discuss the war with military personnel in attendance."

Throughout the country millions of Americans joined in the protest against the Vietnam War. There was little violence.

Preparations for the November 15 Moratorium were the most elaborate ever. An analyst at CIAD recalls:

"We were uptight for the 15 October demonstrations and fantastically involved in the 13-15 November march. We had bus counts, plane counts, train counts, people on the helicopters counting—a big operation.

"That night at Dupont Circle [Nov. 14] there were more Army people than Carter has pills. Half of CIAB attended (in an unofficial capacity), plus half of the Army General Counsel's office, the AGC himself, the 902nd, the 116th, etc.

"On the big day, the center [the new Directorate for Civil Disturbance Planning and Operations] was in full operation. LTG McCaffrey, head of the DCDPO, expected the White House to be "sacked' (quote un-quote) . . . . The Army had closed circuit TV piped into the center to watch the festivities, to take care of crowd counts, etc."

Television coverage, as before, was furnished by the 116th and 902nd MI Groups, with the assistance of the roving reporters from "Mid-West News" in Chicago.

Impressed by the extravagance of these operations, former Attorney General Ramsey Clark has written: "The Army, for all its protestations, loves war games. It came to riot control with alacrity. It has spent millions in establishing military command capabilities, riot potential intelligence, liaison and training with local law enforcement. Never doubt that the Pentagon will seek riot control duty if the opportunity arises. That it can do so in the posture of saving life and property makes its interest nearly irresistible. The assignment of a lieutenant general to full-time riot control command, and his presence among civilian law enforcement and Justice Department officials on a regular basis beginning in October and November 1969, shows how quickly and thoroughly the military can become involved."

Disclosure and Denial

I first disclosed the existence of this blanket surveillance in the January 1970 issue of *The Washington Monthly.* Since then the CONUS intelligence program has gradually been cut back. Helped by the cumulative pressure of Congressional inquiries, lawsuits, and the disclosures of former intelligence agents, the Army's civilian superiors have finally asserted some measure of control. However, the reluctance with which they have approached this task, and the resistance they have met are instructive in explaining both how the program could exist without their knowledge, and how it can continue despite their promises.

When *The Washington Monthly* reached the newsstands on January 9, the Pentagon's Office of Public Information refused to comment. Reporters were told to submit their questions in writing. From its headquarters at Fort Holabird in Baltimore, the Army Intelligence Command wired orders to each of its intelligence groups limiting the collection of domestic intelligence to "essential elements of information." Agents were forbidden to discuss any aspect of the program with newsmen and were warned that any who did would be prosecuted for breach of national security. From his office on the second floor of the Pentagon, Robert E. Jordan III, Army General Counsel and Special Assistant to the Secretary for Civil Functions, suspended all replies to Congressional inquiries. In violation of its own regulations, the Army even refused to acknowledge receipt of them.

By the end of the month, however, the rising tide of criticism could not be ignored. Recognizing this, the Army issued, on January 26, the first in a series of partial admissions. In jargon of the spy trade, such admissions are known as "plausible denials," because they are invested with just enough truth to mask an essential falsehood. Thus the Army confirmed the existence of the nationwide intelligence apparatus (true), but said that it collected political intelligence only "in connection with Army civil disturbance responsibilities" (false). "Civil disturbance incident reports are transmitted over (an) . . . automatic voice network teletype system to the U. S. Army Intelligence Command headquarters" (true) and "information on incidents by types and geographical location is placed in the data bank from keypunched cards" (also true). But: "This is incident information only and does not include individual biographies or personality data" (false).

The statement also acknowledged that the Army "does publish an identification list, sometimes with photos, of persons who have been active in past civil disturbance activity" (true), but failed to mention that the list (actually a booklet) also contained detailed descriptions of persons and organizations never involved in civil disturbances.

Finally, the Army admitted in a backhanded way that its agents had infiltrated civilian political groups: "For some time there has been a special prohibition against military persons undertaking such activities as undercover operations in the civilian community." Of course, it did not say when the order was issued, or whether it had been obeyed.

The "plausible denials" satisfied no one. Inquiries directed to the Secretary of the Army, Stanley R. Resor, poured forth from both Houses of Congress. Legislators of such diverse persuasions as Senators Williams of Delaware, Hart of Michigan, Dole of Kansas, Brooke of Massachusetts, Percy of Illinois, Fulbright of Arkansas, and Cook of Kentucky demanded to know if the charges were true and, of so, by what authority and for what purpose the Army was spying on law-abiding citizens.

Congressman Cornelius E. Gallagher (D-N.J.), Chairman of the House Invasion of Privacy Subcommittee, and Senator Sam J. Ervin, Jr. (D-N.C.), Chairman of the Senate Subcommittee on Constitutional Rights, led the attack. Gallagher wrote to Secretary Resor on January 26: "I am deeply concerned about the implications of collecting dossiers on Americans who are pursuing constitutionally protected activities, especially when they are to be imbedded in immediately available form in a computerized data system."

Senator Ervin, a member of the Armed Services Committee and a former judge, was more forceful. "The Army," he said in a Senate speech on February 2, "has no business operating data banks for the surveillance of private citizens; nor do they have any business in domestic politics."

When the Army continued to avoid inquiries during the month of February, however, members of Congress expressed annoyance at being ignored. Congressman Gallagher, usually a staunch friend of the military, was especially annoyed. After waiting over two weeks for the Army to acknowledge his letter, he threatened to hold hearings.

Still the Army stalled for time. It had good reason. Like Congress and the public, its civilian hierarchy first learned of the Intelligence Command's unbridled curiosity from the press. Unable to learn more from the Assistant Chief of Staff for Intelligence, who greatly downplayed the CONUS system's capabilities, the civilians resolved to conduct their own inquiry. This reached a point of revelation sometime in mid-February when Army General Counsel Jordan went to Fort Holabird and watched as the computer bank on dissidents disgorged a lengthy print-out on Mrs. Martin Luther King, Jr.

On February 25, Jordan dispatched the Army's first reply to more than 30 Congressional critics. Each received the same letter, regardless of the questions he had asked. It opened with a lengthy defense of the Intelligence Command's library of security clearance dossiers—never at issue—and closed with a brief confession: "There have been some activities which have been undertaken in the civil disturbance field which, on review, have been determined to be beyond the Army's mission requirements."

"For example, the Intelligence Command published . . . an identification list which included the names and descriptions of individuals who might become involved in civil disturbance situations." And: "The Intelligence Command has operated a computer data bank . . . which included information about political incidents and individuals involved in potential civil disturbance incidents."

Jordan assured members of Congress that both the identification list and the data bank had been ordered destroyed. "Thus," he concluded, "The Army does not currently maintain the identification list referred to above. No computer data bank of civil disturbance information is being maintained . . . ."

Again, the denials were both plausible and deceptive. Jordan's seemingly candid letter failed to mention that in addition to the Fort Holabird computer (an IBM 1401) and the Intelligence Command's identification list (published in over 330 copies), the Army also maintained:

- Over 375 copies of a two-volume, loose-leaf encyclopedia on dissent entitled *Counterintelligence Research Project,* but probably known as "the Compendium" compiled by the domestic intelligence section of the Counter-Intelligence Analysis Division (CIAD) a Pentagon-based unit responsible for briefiing high Army officials like Jordan on protest politics, the Compendium contained descriptions of hundreds of organizations and individuals, including the John Birch Society, the Urban League, the Fifth Avenue Peace Parade Committee, Negro playwright LeRoi Jones, and the late Rev. Martin Luther King, Jr.

- A computer-indexed, microfilm archive of intelligence reports, newspaper clippings, and other records of political protests and civil disturbances at CIAD headquarters in Alexandria, Virginia. The index to this data bank was a computer print-out, 50 lines to a page, a foot-and-a-half thick. It catalogued microfilmed documents relating to such groups as Young Americans for Freedom, the Southern Christian Leadership Conference, and the Center of the Study of Democratic Institutions. Individuals listed include Rear Admiral Arnold E. True and Brigadier General Hugh B. Hester (war critics), Georgia State Representative Julian Bond, and folk singers, Joan Baez, Phil Ochs, and Arlo Guthrie.

- A computerized data bank on civil disturbances, political protests, and "resistance in the Army (RITA)" at the Continental Army Command headquarters, Fort Monroe, Virginia. The civil disturbance-political protest side of this data bank was developed because the Continental Army Command hoped to recapture supervision of its riot control troops from the Pentagon's special 180-man Directorate for Civil Disturbance Planning and Operations.

• A computerized data bank similar to the Continental Army Command's at Fort Hood, Texas.

• Non-computerized regional data banks at each stateside Army command and at many military installations. In addition to the usual agent reports, incident reports, and newspaper clippings, these records include booklet-size "CONUS intelligence summaries" published each month by the 1st, 3rd, 4th, 5th, and 6th Armies, and the Military District of Washington.

• Non-computerized files at most of the Intelligence Command's 300 stateside intelligence group offices. These records on local political groups and individuals were similar to, but more detailed than, the records at Fort Holabird which the Army promised to destroy. The political files of the 108th Military Intelligence Group's Manhattan offices, for example, filled five four-drawer file cabinets and required a full-time custodian. (Card files and dossiers maintained by the 116th MI Group in Washington, D.C. covered more than 1000 persons and 75 groups).

Congressional reactions to Jordan's admissions, omissions, and denials were mixed. Congressman Gallagher—although fully aware of the omissions—seemed pleased. Without withdrawing his threat of hearings, he announced to the press that the Army would no longer keep tabs on peaceful demonstrations or publish a list of individuals who might be involved in a riot. His announcement, repeated in interviews over the weekend, became the basis of widespread and erroneous newspaper reports. The *New York Times* of February 27 was typical: "Army Ends Watch on Civil Protests."

Other members of Congress were slower to react. Before they did Morton Kondracke of the *Chicago Sun-Times* reported on February 28: "The Army acknowledged yesterday that it maintains files on the political activities of civilians other than the computerized political data bank it told Congressmen it was closing down." Kondracke, a thorough reporter, listed them all.

The following Monday, Senator Ervin expressed his dissatisfaction with Jordan's letter. In a letter to the Secretary of the Army he reiterated his demand for a complete report to Congress, and in a

Senate floor speech denounced the surveillance as a "usurpation of authority." "The business of the Army in [civil disturbances] . . . situations is to know about the conditions of highways, bridges, and facilities. It is not to predict trends and reactions by keeping track of the thoughts and actions of Americans exercising first amendment freedoms."

"If there ever were a case of military overkill," he added, "this is it. . . . I suggest the Army regroup and define its strategic objectives, lower its sights, and reidentify its enemy. Under our Constitution that enemy is not the American citizen."

The Army Regroups

Within the Army, much regrouping was already going on. A letter received by Congressman Gallagher from sources close to the 116th Military Intelligence Group at Fort McNair in Washington, D. C., described what was happening at the lower echelons:

"On the morning after news reports about the dismantling of the CONUS system first appeared in the Washington papers . . . members of the 116th were . . . informed that their unit and its operations would be unaffected . . . . They were told that the only major effect of the Congressional and press criticism would be destruction of the national data bank and related files that were kept at Fort Holabird. Files kept by the regional MI groups (which were the basis for the Fort Holabird file and contained more information) would remain intact, and members of the MI Groups would continue their operations of surveillance, infiltration, and reporting as previously.

"In addition, all files and operations of the 116th were to be classified to prevent the release of any information about them; disclosure of such information would subject people who released that information to court-martial or prosecution in civilian court for violation of national security.

"At the present time, the files of the 116th MI Group consist of a 5x7 card file on several thousand persons in the Washington area. On these cards are a picture of each person, his name, and address, occupation, background, a record of political groups with which he has been affiliated, notes on political meetings, rallies, and demonstrations which he has attended, and summaries of his views on political issues.

"To gather such information, the 116th routinely assigns some 20 of its men as full-time undercover agents to infiltrate political groups and observe politically active persons . . . Some of these officers have grown beards and long hair to pass as students on local college campuses. In addition, other members pose as members of the working press to obtain pictures of those involved in political activities; concealed tape recorders are also commonly used to record speeches and conversations at political events."

Higher up the chain of command, officials at Fort Holabird also balked at carrying out the new policy. Questioned by Joseph Hanlon of *Computerworld* on March 10, an Intelligence Command spokesman refused to say whether the computer tapes there had actually been erased or merely placed in storage. He admitted, however, that the "input" to the data bank (presumably the keypunch cards) had not been destroyed.

Higher still, the civilians supposedly in charge of the Army struggled to find out what their military subordinates were doing. Robert Jordan, surprised by the *Washington Monthly* article and by his pilgrimage to the Fort Holabird computer, was taken aback once more on February 27 during a conference with Congressman Gallagher. Asked why his letter made no mention of the microfilm archives at CIAD, he replied: "I'll have to check into that."

To help Jordan out, Secretary Resor wrote to the Army Chief of Staff, General William C. Westmoreland, on March 5: "I would appreciate your asking all commanders in CONUS, Alaska, and Hawaii down to the installation level to report whether their command has any form of computerized data bank relating to civilians or civilian activities, other than data banks dealing with routine dealing with routine administrative matters."

Undersecretary Beal Replies

On March 20, before the results of this canvass were known, Under Secretary of the Army Thaddeus R. Beal wrote long letters to both Ervin and Gallagher. He claimed: "The only other 'intelligence files' concerning civilians maintained by the Army consist of the files maintained by the Counterintelligence Analysis Division."

No reference was made in either letter to: the Continental Army Command's computer files at Fort Monroe, about which Gallagher had made specific inquiries; the regional data banks kept by most of the 300 offices of the Army Intelligence Command; or similar records maintained by the G-2s (intelligence officers) of each stateside Army command and of many Army posts, including the Fort Hood computer.

The microfilm archives at CIAD, Beal went on to say, contain only "limited files concerning political activity" in keeping with that unit's responsibility "for identifying factors which affect civil disturbance potential. . . ." He did not mention that these files took up over 200 rolls of microfilm, at 500 frames a roll. Nor did he acknowledge that the unit's domestic intelligence section, which was larger than any of its foreign intelligence sections, had charged its "left wing," "right wing," and "racial" desks with maintaining detailed card files on dissident individuals and groups. These files were in addition to mounds of current FBI and Army reports and newspaper clippings which were kept for about a month before being coded on key-coded on key-punch cards(for the computerized index) and recorded on microfilm.

The Under Secretary's claim that the archive was used only in connection with civil disturbance planning was similarly misleading. According to former CIAD employees, one of the principal uses of this file—if not the main reason for its existence—had been to satisfy the curiosity of the Pentagon's brass. A not unusual assignment carried out by one domestic intelligence expert was to write an unclassified report on SDS for a general to send to his daughter at an exclusive Eastern women's college.

In addition to these "plausible denials," Beal also admitted that CIAD had compiled "an identification list . . . on individuals and organizations associated with civil disturbances. This list was last updated in late 1969 [true] and is available to a limited number of Department of the Army organizations with civil disturbance responsibilities" [false]. According to persons who helped compile it, the Compendium went out to over 150 Army intelligence and troop units, plus the FBI, the Justice Department, Naval and Air Force Intelligence, the CIA, and U.S. embassies in West Germany and Canada.

More important, Beal conceded that "the lists are now out of date, are not considered necessary. . . . [and] are being . . . destroyed. . . ." In addition he promised that the Army would: 1) henceforth limit its curiosity to "incidents where there is a high potential for violence or disaster growing beyond the capability of state and local police and the National Guard to control;" and 2) destroy all existing *computerized* data banks on civilian politics.

No new computerized data banks, he said, would be established without the approval of both the Secretary of the Army and the Chief of Staff after "consultations with concerned committees of Congress."

The concessions were substantial. To Congressman Gallagher, they were sufficient. "In view of the Army's commendable action in reversing its former policy," he announced, "I see no further need for a Congressional hearing at this time."

To Senator Ervin, on the other hand, Beal's assurances were plainly inadequate. The investigation of the Subcommittee on Constitutional Rights continued.

The Civil Liberties Union Goes to Court

While Congressmen and Senators struggled with the Army's evasions and deceptions, the civilian intelligence program was being attacked in the courts. On February 17 the American Civil Liberties Union filed suit in Federal District Court in Washington, D. C., against the Secretary of Defense, the Secretary of the Army, and the Army Chief of Staff, and the Commanding General of the Intelligence Command. The suit charged that the surveillance, data banks, and blacklists violated the Bill of Rights by reason of the chilling effect which knowledge of their existence can have upon the willingness of citizens to exercise their freedoms of speech, press, and association and their right to petition the government for redress of grievances.

The plaintiffs were 13 individuals and organizations whose nonviolent, lawful politics had been the subject of widely distributed Army reports. The first was Arlo Tatum, executive director of the Quaker-sponsored Central Committee for Conscientious Objectors in Philadelphia. An IBM card prepared for his computer file at Fort Holabird showed only that he had once delivered a speech at the University of Oklahoma on the legal rights of conscientious objectors. Other plaintiffs included Women's Strike for Peace, Veterans for Peace, Conrad Lynn, and the Reverend Albert Cleage, Jr.

Even before filing suit, the ACLU was aware that a cover-up might be attempted at the lower, as well as higher echelons of the Army. This suspicion was confirmed by the letter describing the activities of the 116th MI Group and by former intelligence agents who warned that many units would hide copies of blacklists and personality files, regardless of what their civilian supervisors told them to do.

In an effort to prevent this, the ACLU asked the District Court on March 12 for a preliminary injunction ordering the Army to cease its destruction of the records and to deliver them (along with inventories, receipts, and certificates of destruction) to the court for safekeeping, pending the outcome of the suit. Then, if the plaintiffs were successful, the court would be in a position to assure complete destruction of the records.

A hearing on this request, and an opposing motion by the Army which asked that the entire suit be thrown out for failure to show that the program violated anyone's constitutional rights, was convened in Washington on April 22 before U. S. District Court Judge George L. Hart, Jr.

Judge Hart, a graduate of Virginia Military Institute and a battlefield colonel during World War II, was openly hostile to the ACLU's contentions. He began the proceedings with an announcement that he would not hear testimony.

In effect, this announcement meant that Judge Hart had prejudged the ACLU's claims. Few, if any, judges would consider issuing an injunction against the government on the basis of affidavits (written statements by persons not present to testify). To do so would deny the government the opportunity to cross-examine the witnesses against it and would be universally regarded as an abuse of judicial discretion.

Judge Hart's reasons became clearer as the hearing progressed. For example, when Frank Askin, the ACLU's chief counsel of the hearing, argued that it would be all right for members of Army Intelligence to follow accounts of protest politics in the newspapers, but that they should not be permitted to maintain computerized files on the political activities of specific individuals, the judge scoffed: "It's all right if they remember it, but they can't take note of it. . . . Isn't that ridiculous?"

Nor could he understand why citizens should fear the military's surveillance any more than they should fear reporting of political activities by the news services. "Newspapers don't have guns and don't have jails," Askin responded. ". . . nobody is afraid that one of these days the newsmen are all going to sweep into town and come to arrest the troublemakers."

But the judge was unimpressed: "There is no threat that the Army is going to come in and arrest you. . . . If it does," he added, "We still sit here with the writ of habeas corpus."

"But, your Honor, then why are they keeping these lists of people, that's the issue at stake. . . . They have no need for this. . . ."

"It may help them to know what persons are likely to cause trouble [in civil disturbances] and thereby keep an eye on them,"

Hart replied, forgetting that the Army had agreed to withdraw the lists precisely because they were not needed for that or any other purpose.

The ACLU's other contentions—that the surveillance had exceeded the Army's civil disturbance responsibilities, that riot control troops do not need blacklists to enforce curfews or clear streets, that the CONUS intelligence operations encroached upon the authority of civilian law enforcement agencies— were also rejected. Even Askin's offer to present a former intelligence agent who had infiltrated a coalition of church groups was brushed aside with the question: "Did they have a sign saying 'No Military Personnel Are Admitted?"

"What . . . the plaintiffs are complaining of here," Judge Hart decided, "is that the Army is keeping the type of information that is available to the news media in this country and which is in the morgues of the newspapers . . . and magazines. . . . They show no unconstitutional action on the part of the Army; they show no threat to their rights." Accordingly, he refused to confiscate the records. Instead, he dismissed the suit.

The ACLU's attorneys promptly announced their intention to appeal. At a press conference following the hearing they introduced two witnesses whose testimony Judge Hart had refused to hear. One was Ralph Stein, 26, who ran the Left Wing Desk at the Counterintelligence Analysis Branch (now Detachment) from August 1967 to October 1968. He described the microfilm archive, its computerized index, and the "Compendium," which he helped to write.

Another witness for the ACLU was Oliver Peirce, 25, who served as an agent with the 5th Military Intelligence Detachment at Fort Carson, Colorado, during the summer and fall of 1969. Although the 5th MID belonged to a mechanized infantry division and not to the Army Intelligence Command, it also maintained a close watch over political activists in the Colorado Springs area.

One of Peirce's assignments was to infiltrate a group called the Young Adults Project (YAP), which was established by a coalition of local church groups, the Young Democrats, and a ski club to operate a recreation center for emotionally disturbed young people. Although the project was entirely non-political, Pierce said, he and a soldier informant were directed to make detailed reports on its meetings because one of the group's founders had attended anti-war demonstrations outside the fort and had once been a member of SDS.

In addition to watching YAP, the 5th MID also assigned five

undercover agents to monitor an anti-war vigil in the chapel of Colorado State College, maintained two full-time infiltrators within the local peace movement, and sent others to observe meetings of the Colorado Springs poverty board.

Operations such as these, Peirce said, were carried out even though they often duplicated political surveillances conducted by the FBI, state and local police, and the Colorado Springs office of the 113th Military Intelligence Group (part of the Army Intelligence Command).

Reforms

While the Justice Department's attorneys were vigorously defending the surveillance in court, the Army General Counsel was attacking it within the bureacuracy. His strategy was two-fold: first, to bar future excesses by promulgating a new Army-wide policy, and second, to dump responsibility for the civil disturbance early warning system squarely on the FBI and the Justice Department, where it belonged in the first place.

During April and May representatives of the General Counsel's Office and Pentagon intelligence officers hammered out a new set of ground rules to cover the "collection, reporting, processing, and storage of civil disturbance information." These were promulgated on June 9, 1970, without notice to interested committees of Congress, in the form of a letter signed by Col. Robert E. Lynch, the Army's Acting Adjutant General.

"Henceforth," Lynch's letter said, "Army intelligence resources will not be used for collection of civil disturbance information until the Director for Civil Disturbance Planning and Operations . . . has made a determination that there is a distinct threat of civil disturbance beyond the capability of local and State authorities to control." A "civil disturbance," of course, was generously defined as any "situation in which a civil jurisdiction is required to apply a greater than usual degree of police enforcement in order to insure the maintenance of law and order."

"Covert agent operations," the letter continued, "will not be used to obtain civil disturbance information on individuals or organizations without the concurrence of the Federal Bureau of Investigation and the specific approval of each operation by the Under Secretary of the Army." What constituted a "covert operation" was not spelled out, but the letter seemed to say that Army agents should restrict their curiosity to reading the newspapers and talking with civilian authorities.

Other provisions declared that "Army elements will maintain the capability of reporting civil disturbance information," and "will be prepared to store civil disturbance information during a period in which there is a distinct threat of, or an actual, civil disturbance. . . ." No criteria, such as a governor's request for federal troops, were set forth to guide the Army's brass in determining when a "distinct threat" might be deemed to exist.

The ban on computerized civil disturbance data banks was reiterated but the disposition of photographic collections, microfilm archives, dossiers, and card files, remained in doubt. "Army elements" should be prepared ". . . on order . . . to destroy accumulated files or forward them . . . for release to the Department of Justice."

Finally, the letter concluded with the classic escape clause: "Collection requirements related to direct threats to Army personnel, installations, or material are not affected by this letter."

It was the old shell-game—now you see it, now you don't. On July 27 the Chairman of the Subcommittee on Constitutional Rights again wrote to the Secretary of the Army: "I confess that the exceptions, qualifications, and lack of criteria in your policy letter could lead the average citizen—which I consider myself—to wonder just how much of a change it represents in government policy." Describing the Lynch letter to the Senate on July 29, he observed: "In some cases the last half of his sentences seem to cancel out the first half of his sentences."

The Shift to the Justice Department

But even though the order left much to be desired, it represented a crucial turning point. The Army had decided to give up its early warning system, and relinquish that responsibility and many Army records to the Department of Justice.

Actually, both the Army and the Department of Justice had been running parallel operations for over a year. The Civil Disturbance Group and Interdivisional Intelligence Unit at Justice had their own analysts, war room, and computer. The FBI had been collecting information on individuals, organizations, and incidents relating to protest politics since its inception. Army reports regularly went to both the Department and the Bureau, thereby relieving FBI agents of the drugery of having to clip many newspapers or attend petty demonstrations. Accordingly, the civilians were happy to keep the

Army in the business. The Army's intelligence chiefs agreed, and described the Justice Department as inadequate to the task of running an early warning system. As late as February 27, the Army General Counsel's Office agreed. As one of his assistants explained to a reporter: "We've been pushing for a long time to get Justice and the FBI to take over this responsibility completely." But, "Justice does not have the capability, in our minds, to do the job. We have to have an answer if we're asked 'Will there be violence.' Until we are satisfied that Justice can answer the question satisfactorily, we have to do it ourselves."

A week later, James T. Devine, chief of the Justice Department's Civil Disturbance Group, told the same reporter: "We are ready. . . . We are quite capable. We are qualified to do everything as far as advising the President is concerned."

The Lynch letter thus indicates that by May 1970 the Army had decided to take the Justice Department at its word, and that the Justice Department, like it or not, would have to get along without the Army's wire service.

Records Destruction

During late June, early July, the Army's incinerators for classified trash burned overtime. Former agents have reported the destruction of CONUS intelligence records at such widely dispersed locations as Fort McPherson, Trenton, Minneapolis, Boston, and New York City.

Where "in-and-outers" opposed to the surveillance were in charge, the destruction was relatively complete. This also seems to have been the case where the records were kept by career officers indifferent to the program but wary of inspections. Resistance to the directive was greatest at the region and headquarters levels. There the bulk of the CONUS intelligence records were maintained under the supervision of "intelligence civilian career personnel" (ICCPS).

No one felt the need to watch civilian politics more strongly than the ICCPS who ran many of the CONUS intelligence and special operations sections of the stateside MI groups. Their conviction was grounded on both ideology and experience; many were conservative former undercover operatives home on "repatriation" tours. Having been intimately involved in uncovering conspiracies against governments overseas, they assumed the existence of conspiracies at home. Thus they believed in the need for personality files, organizational files, and blacklists on American citizens.

Emotionally, the ICPPS were as repelled by the order to destroy files as most scholars would be by an order to burn books. The files were the stock and symbol of their profession, as well as the chief product of their labors. In addition, if the CONUS intelligence operations were actually abolished in the midst of the economy drive then going on, many ICCPS would be in danger of losing their jobs.

Thus, as soon as the Lynch letter was received, the search for loopholes began. They were not difficult to find. Personality files were poured into organizational files, which in turn became "local intelligence studies" of "subversive" elements in the surrounding community. (See AR 381-130), Para 34). Files on anti-war groups were redesignated for inclusion in the RITA program, even in the absence of evidence indicating that the groups had ever sought to undermine military discipline or unlawfully obstruct recruitment. Within CONARC, the policy letter was distributed along with a note instructing intelligence officers to continue to clip newspapers. Since the commanding general still wanted civil disturbance reports from his own units, CONARC's system continued to run—on clippings and paste!

Where loopholes could not be found, personality and organizational files were hidden or disguised. The Counterintelligence Analysis Detachment (formerly Branch) obeyed the order to destroy its copy of the Compendium—but not until after it had put both volumes on microfilm. As a clerk in that office recalled: "The tendency was to keep the information while obeying the order. . . . The order didn't say destroy the information, just destroy the Compendium." Deceptions were encouraged by rumors that the controversy would soon blow over, and when it did , those who saved records would be rewarded for their foresight.

Preparations for Senate Hearings

On July 29, 1970, Senator Ervin formally announced that his subcommittee would hold hearings in the Fall. To help clarify the issue, he dispatched detailed questionnaires to all federal agencies known to have accumulated large data banks. Among those polled were the Departments of Army, Navy, Air Force, and Defense. Senator Ervin also invited the Secretary of the Army to testify about CONUS intelligence operations.

The prospect of hearings did much to intensify the Army's enforcement of the new policy. The Army Counsel's staff actually got out into the field to test compliance. So too did Col John W. Downie, Director of Counterintellgence in the Office of the Assistant Chief of Staff for Intelligence. Violations of the directives were found.

The questionnaires also assisted the Pentagon's civilian chiefs in their effort to gain control over a bureaucracy long accustomed to immunity from scrutiny by elected or appointed officials. But responsive answers were hard to come by. Like their superiors, the intelligence bureacrats had a tactical sense of the truth when dealing with inquiries from outsiders. To them, both the Army General Counsel and the Secretary of Defense were outsiders. As the former clerk of the task group set up by Col. Downie to answer Jordan's inquiries recalls: "They (the task group) were afraid that if they told Jordan anything, he would pass it on to the press."

New Disclosures

The hearings scheduled for October 6, 7, and 8 were caught in the Senate's rush to recess for the fall elections. The postponement gave the Army's civilian authorities more time to discover the answers to the Subcommittee's questions. They apparently needed it. The Army's answers to the questionnaire of July 27 were not returned until November 27.

During the same four months, NBC News enjoyed greater success with its own investigation. Tom Pettit and Bill Hill, a prize-winning investigative news team, criss-crossed the country in search of former intelligence agents willing to tell how they watched law-abiding citizens for the Army. The result was an hour-long documentary entitled "The Man From Uncle (Sam)." It was shown on "First Tuesday," December 1, 1970.

Among other things, NBC disclosed that Army intelligence:

• Followed the Poor People's Campaign and their mules all the way to Washington, D.C.

• Infiltrated undercover agents into Resurrection City.

• Maintained a command post inside the Republican National Convention at Miami in 1968.

• Had an agent from the Office of the Assistant Chief of Staff for Intelligence on the floor of the 1968 Democratic National Convention in Chicago.

• Kept card files, dossiers, and photographs on students and faculty at the University of Minnesota.

• Infiltrated the headquarters of the National Mobilization Committee during the Counter-Inaugural demonstrations of January 1969.

• Infiltrated Moratorium Day exercises inside the chapel of Colorado State College in October 1969.

About the same time Jared Stout, an investigative reporter for Newhouse News Services, uncovered still more information about the military's involvement at the 1968 national party conventions. His revelations included the presence of agents of Naval and Air Force intelligence on the floors of both conventions, the deployment in Chicago of a large electronic surveillance unit from the Army Security Agency to monitor convention demonstrations from storefronts and unmarked vans, and an ASA report of a wiretap of a telephone call from the Convention headquarters of Senator Eugene McCarthy.

Stout also revealed that most of the Army's domestic intelligence operations had been carried out without notice to or permission from high Defense and Army officials. On December 4th Army General Counsel Robert Jordan admitted to him that the commanding general of the Intelligence Command, Brig. Gen. William H. Blakefield, had actually denied the existence of computerized records when first asked. "But I don't think he lied to me," Jordan added. "I don't think he knew about them."

Similarly, former Attorney General Ramsey Clark and convention officials of both parties told Stout that they were unaware of the presence of military intelligence agents at the conventions, or of the deployment of the ASA electronic surveillance unit in Chicago. A spokesman for the Secret Service, which had responsibility for convention security, likewise disclaimed knowledge of the ASA operation. In an interview with Morton Kondracke of the *Chicago Sun-Times,* former Secretary of Defense Clark Clifford admitted that "these were matters that never came to the attention of the Secretary." The individual services, he said, "conducted their intelligence activities independent of the Secretary's office."

Monitoring Elected Officials

These new disclosures reawakened public interest in the domestic operations of Army intelligence. They also prompted still other former agents to come forward with their stories. None was more shocking than John M. O'Brien, formerly of the Special Operations Section, Region I, of the 113th MI Group in Evanston, Illinois.

O'Brien revealed to Senator Ervin and to Jared Stout that his office had kept records on over 800 civilians unassociated with the armed forces, including Senator Adlai E. Stevenson, III, Congressman Abner J. Mikva, and federal circuit court judge Otto Kerner.

It was the designation of Stevenson as an object of surveillance in

September 1969 that triggered O'Brien's disenchantment with the CONUS intelligence program. At that time the Senator was Treasurer of the State of Illinois and had staged a picnic at his family farm in Libertyville as a prelude to his Senate candidacy. Guests at the picnic included Chicago Mayor Richard Daley and Negro leader Rev. Jesse Jackson. During the course of the picnic a photograph was taken that showed Jackson in Stevenson's car. This picture was later interpreted, O'Brien said, to indicate a "new relationship" between Jackson and Stevenson. After that, "military inteligence agents of the 113th covered every appearance of Stevenson in Chicago, at least up to June, 1970."

Jesse Jackson was "targeted," O'Brien disclosed, because of his role as head of "Operation Breadbasket," the economic arm of the Southern Christian Leadership Conference. Stevenson also was watched, he said, because of his anti-war views. Mikva came under scrutiny "because of his outspoken criticism of [Vietnam] war policy and because he aided draft resisters." As far as he knew, Judge Kerner was not the object of direct surveillance, but "we just started keeping files on him after the (Kerner) Commission report." Judge Kerner was chairman of the National Advisory Commission on Civil Disorders which found no evidence of conspiracy in the government's intelligence on 23 urban riots that occurred in 1967.

O'Brien estimated that "approximately 50 percent of all collection activities targeted against civilian (s) . . . were initiated at the local level. The remaining 50 percent of such activities were levied . . . from the command center at Fort Holabird, Maryland."

When he questioned the collection of information on non-military organizations and individuals, O'Brien said, "my superiors justified the collection . . . to me by stating that it was the responsibility of the Army to maintain watch over potentially dangerous organizations and individuals. My Group operations officer . . . informed me that civilian agencies such as the FBI and Secret Service did not have the availability of personnel as did the Army; and therefore the Army was better staffed to conduct large-scale collection operations targeted against the civilian population. In response to my question of what value the information concerning civilians would have to the mission of the Army, my team chief stated: "What does it matter, the information all ends up in the same place."

Reaction to O'Brien's Disclosures

With the disclosure that the Army had been watching elected officials, the threshold of public shock was finally reached. In Congress, Representative George H. Mahon (D-Tex.), Chairman of the House Appropriations Committee, called the surveillance "an outrage" and promised that his Defense Appropriations Subcommittee would investigate.

Representative Chet Holifield (D-Cal.), Chairman of the House Committee on Government Operations and its Subcommittee on Military Operations, also promised an investigation. Senator Edward M. Kennedy (D-Mass.) called for legislation and Representative Abner J. Mikva urged the Secretary of Defense to "separate from the service every person at a command level who condoned or supported such spying activities." The Chairman of the House Internal Security Committee, Richard H. Ichord (D-Mo.), agreed that "Army intelligence has no business spying on civilians."

Protests also came from Senator Jacob Javits (R-N.Y.), and Representatives Roman C. Pucinski (D-Ill.), Richard Poff (R-Va.), Phillip Burton (D-Cal.), Ogden R. Reid (R-N.Y.), Thomas S. Foley (D-Wash.), William R. Anderson (D-Tenn.), Samuel Stratton (D-N.Y.), Edward J. Derwinski (R-Ill.), Charles H. Whalen, Jr. (R-Ohio), Sidney R. Yates (D-Ill.), Edward I. Koch (D-N.Y.), Morris K. Udall (D-Ariz.), Jonanthan B. Bingham (D-N.Y.), Paul Findley (R-Ill.), Henry B. Gonzalez (D-Tex.), John N. Erlenborn (R-Ill), John Conyers, Jr. (D-Mich.), James Scheuer (D-N.Y.), Don Edwards (D-Cal.), and David Pryor (D-Ark.).

President Nixon, in a statement released through White House Press Secretary Ron Ziegler, said that he was "totally, completely, and unequivocally" opposed to spying by the military on political figures. He added: "It will not be done under this administration."

Army's Denial of O'Brien's Charges

On December 17, the Army issued an emphatic denial to O'Brien's charges. "On the basis of information I have received," Secretary Resor announced, "I can state that neither Senator Stevenson, Representative Mikva, nor Governor Kerner are or ever have been the subject of military intelligence or investigations related to political activities. Allegations to the contrary are without foundation in fact."

"I want to emphasize," he continued, "that had any such alleged activities been conducted, they would have been in violation of Army policies."

Resor did not appear for questioning on his statement, which he said was based on a "preliminary check" of O'Brien's charges. According to Representatives Cornelius Gallagher (D- N.J.), Chairman of the House Invasion of Privacy Inquiry, Resor based his denial on a conference with Col. Joseph Walker, Jr., commander of the 113th MI Group.

The statement did not deny that the Army had watched the Rev. Jesse Jackson, or any of the 800 other Illinois citizens referred to by O'Brien. Nor did it make clear whether Stevenson, Mikva, or Kerner might have been monitored as part of an intelligence effort that focused on other individuals or organizations. O'Brien's charge that Region I's files in Evanston contained information on the three officials also was not denied, but Resor did say that Judge Kerner, a former National Guard general, had been the subject of a background investigation in connection with his military duties. "The last entry" in this file, he offered, "was in 1952."

Congressman Mikva was not persuaded by the denial. "I am no spy," he said in a House floor speech on December 18, "but it did not ever seem likely that these alleged spies would put their snooping results in my Army personnel files, or in Senator Stevenson's Marine Corps file." In Chicago, O'Brien said: "I stick by what I've said. The [Resor] statement is strictly a matter of semantics."

A Second Lawsuit Is Filed

The Illinois Division of the American Civil Liberties Union also was unimpressed by Resor's denial. The Union and its director, Jay Miller, had both been mentioned by O'Brien as objects of Army scrutiny. On December 21, the ACLU filed suit in U.S. District Court in Chicago to enjoin the surveillance.

Plaintiffs in the class action includes the ACLU and its director, two Chicago alderman, a businessman, a newspaper reporter, and the Reverend Jesse Jackson. All, according to O'Brien, had been the subject of Army files. Defendants named were Gen. William C. Westmoreland; Maj. Gen. Joseph A. McChristian, Assistant Chief of Staff for Intelligence; Brig. Gen. Jack Matthews, Commanding General of the Army Intelligence Command; and Col. Joseph Walker, Jr., commanding officer of the 113th MI Group, Fort Sheridan, Illinois.

At the outset of the suit, U.S. District Court Judge Richard B. Austin accepted the assurance of U.S. Attorney Wiliam J. Bauer that no Army records would be removed or destroyed pending the litigation. Accordingly, he denied a motion by ACLU attorney Alexander Polikoff that the Army be required to surrender its records to the court.

The hearing was scheduled to begin on Monday December 28 with John M. O'Brien as the ACLU's chief witness.

General Wickham's Letter

In the midst of the controversy surrounding O'Brien's disclosures the the Army quietly issued a supplement to Colonel Lynch's letter of June 9. The supplement, signed by Maj. Gen. Kenneth G. Wickham, Army Adjutant General, represented a careful rethinking of the Army's domestic intelligence needs. Unlike the letter of June 9, it reached beyond the civil disturbance program to regulate all "Counterintelligence Activities Concerning Civilians Not Affiliated with the Department of Defense."

Situations warranting the collection of information on civilians by any and all means, including infiltration, were henceforth to be limited to:

• Attempts to subvert loyalty, discipline, or morale of Department of Defense military or civilian personnel by actively encouraging desertion, disobedience of lawful orders or regulations, or disruption of military activities.

• Theft of arms, ammunition, or equipment, or destruction or sabotage of facilities, equipment, or records belonging to Army units or installations.

• Threats to the security of Army elements or operations or to classified defense information through espionage on behalf of any recipient, foreign or domestic.

• Unauthorized demonstrations on active duty or reserve Army installations or through demonstrations immediately adjacent to them which are of such a size or character that they are likely to interfere with the conduct of military activities.

• Threats of physical violence to Department of Defense military or civilian personnel in connection with their official activities.

• Threats to the physical safety of government officials who have been authorized protection by Army resources.

• Threats of sabotage or espionage directed against Federal installations for which the Army has been delegated Department of Defense security responsibility.

In addition to more precisely defining the Army's needs for information on unaffiliated individuals and organizations, the Wickham letter went on to forbid Army units to summarize or store any information in any form if that information was not warranted for collection under the enumerated categories. In particular, it banned the preparation of biographical sketches of civilians, or statements describing the nature and intent of civilian organizations except when necessary to determine the existence of a situation warranting collection, or to assist Army officials in evaluating requests for speakers, drill teams, bands, or other forms of civic support.

While reasonable men might argue over the meaning of certain phrases, the Wickham letter constituted a major advance in the Army's formulation of its domestic intelligence needs.

Reorganization Announced

The Wickham letter, although revolutionary in content, went quietly into effect without notice to interested members of Congress or to the public. In contrast, extensive publicity was given to Secretary Laird's anouncement on December 23rd that concern for Constitutional rights had led him to order a reorganization of the entire military intelligence structure.

"I want to be certain," Laird's memorandum began, "that Department of Defense intelligence and counterintelligence activities are completely consistent with constitutional rights, all other legal provisions, and national security needs. These activities must be conducted in a manner which recognizes and preserves individual human rights. Policy determinations governing such activities must be retained under civilian cognizance and control.

"One matter of particular concern to me is the one related to intelligence and counterintelligence activities involving the use of investigative and counterintelligence personnel. Actions have been taken to eliminate some past abuses incident to such activities, but further corrective actions are necessary as a matter of urgent priority."

Among the "corrective actions" announced were: (1) the Director of the Defense Intelligence Agency (Gen. Bennett) henceforth would report directly to the Secretary of Defense rather than to the Joint Chiefs of Staff. (2) the Joint Chiefs were forbidden to establish their own intelligence staff to replace DIA, but would have to continue to rely upon it for all their intelligence. (3) the Director of DIA was put in charge of "all direct intelligence collection by human resources and counterintelligence investigative functions throughout the Department of Defense."

How these changes would enhance the protection of human rights was not clear on the face of the memorandum. The reorganization would clearly strengthen the Secretary of Defense in policy disputes with the Joint Chiefs by giving him first call on DIA's intelligence. This would enhance civilian control over the military in the formulation of defense and foreign policy, but would seem to do little to affect the conduct of domestic intelligence. The reorganization also would exclude the service secretaries and their staffs from the chain of command inside the intelligence establishment at the very moment when the Army's civilian hierarchy was getting a grip on domestic operations. Moreover, it would insert still another layer of military bureaucracy—DIA—between responsible civilians and domestic intelligence operatives.

At the same time, the centralization mandated by the reorganization opened the possibility that the Army's recent enlightment might be transferred by DOD directive to the Air Force and Navy as well. Whether this short-term gain would be worth the long-term loss of civilian control by the service secretaries remained to be seen. For civil libertarians, the immediate trade-off would depend upon the capacities and intentions of Laird's Special Assistant for Intelligence, Robert F. Froehlke. An announcement from him on the details of the reorganization was scheduled for early February.

ACLU *v. Westmoreland*

The hearing in the ACLU's second lawsuit against Army intelligence lasted four days. It began with a protracted sparring match as the ACLU's attorney, Alexander Polikoff, struggled to persuade a skeptical judge to deny the Army's motion to dismiss and hear the plaintiff's evidence.

Judge Austin was in a wry and acerbic mood. "Maybe I'm dense today," he said during Polikoff's opening argument, "but I don't see why it is wrong for the Army to sit down with all the other spies." "It's not related to the needs of the Army," the attorney replied. "It's unlawful for the Army to do it because it doesn't have the same law enforcement powers as the other agencies."

Austin was unpersuaded, but finally agreed to hear the evidence anyway. John M. O'Brien was the ACLU's chief witness. Among other things, he disclosed:

• As late as November 1969, ten months after Under Secretary of the Army McGiffert had ordered a cutback in CONUS intelligence, his unit was told to step up its surveillance activities. The order came from Brig. Gen. William H. Blakefield, Commanding General of the Army Intelligence Command, during a visit which he paid to the 113th MI Group.

• In November 1970, five months after the Lynch letter ordered and end to routing CONUS intelligence operations, he paid a personal visit to his former office and saw that it was still maintaining files on civilians.

• In addition to the plaintiffs, Region I of the 113th Group maintained files on: Seymour Gale, board president of the Ned Trier High School District 203; Leroy Wolins, an official of Veterans for Peace; George Hiscott, "an Evanston Cadillac dealer believed to be a network commander of the right-wing Minuteman organization;" Jack Speigal, "associated with the Communist party;" Danny Queen, "alleged to be a Communist and seen at two or three meetings;" Father James Groppi, a militant Milwaukee priest; the Rev. Ralph David Abernathy, leader of the Southern Christian Leadership Conference; Marvin Schibrough, a Northwestern University mathematics professor; Michael Marcus, "a Northwestern University professor during 1968-69."

• He and other agents staked out the suburban Willmette home of Seymour Gale, the school board president, when a meeting was held there which included members of the Student Mobilization Committee and Veterans for Peace. The agents took down the auto license numbers of Gale's guests and later, as a prank, sent an order of pizza C.O.D. to his door.

The government's chief rebuttal witness was Thomas L. Filkins, the civilian career agent (ICCP) who was O'Brien's superior as head of the Special Operations Section at Region I. He swore that he had "never told O'Brien to monitor or survey or keep files" on Senator Stevenson. The charges to the contrary, he said, were "wholly untrue." However, under cross-examination Filkins admitted:

• The 113th did "monitor" the speeches of both Senator Stevenson and Representative Mikva. "This was used by us as a yardstick," he explained; his unit reported speeches not likely to be followed by violence along with those that were. For the same reasons, he said, the Army followed the public appearances of such men as Mayor Daley and Governor Oglivie.

• He accompanied O'Brien to a rally in August 1969 commemorating the 24th anniversary of the bombing of Hiroshima. (Representative Mikva appeared at that rally.)

• He also attended a debate at Lake Forest College to monitor speeches by members of the American Nazi Party and accompanied police who raided an Evanston church that had opened its doors to young radicals during the October 1969 street violence by the Weatherman faction of SDS.

• The 113th kept a file on the Daughters of the American Revolution because the Fifth Army chief of staff had wanted to make sure that it was not an extremist group before he accepted an invitation to address its local chapter.

• Files were maintained on two black Chicago aldermen, William Cousins and A. A. Rayner because of their connections with Veterans for Peace.

• Files were kept on other Illinois citizens until June 1970 when they were burned in the incinerator at the Great Lakes Naval Base. The burning was ordered by the Department of the Army, he said, because the persons were not considered subversive.

• The only files not destroyed or forwarded to the Army Intellimence Command were those on members of Students for a Democratic Society. These, he said, were sent to the Chicago Police Department. (Transfer of Army files to municipal police departments was not authorized by the Lynch letter of June 9, 1970).

• O'Brien's claim that the stake-out team sent school board president Seymour Gale unordered pizzas as a prank was untrue. It was "fried chicken," Filkins said.

The ACLU's chief rebuttal witness was Richard G. Stahl of Peoria, Illinois, formerly an agent with the Chicago Field Office of Region I of the 113th MI Group. He testified that during the 1968 Democratic Convention he was ordered to conduct foot surveillances of the Rev. Ralph David Abernathy, head of the Southern Christian Leadership Conference, and Governor Lester Maddox of Georgia, a convention delegate.

Other convention assignments Stahl said he carried out included watching the Rev. Jesse Jackson and tape-recording a speech in Lincoln Park by Bobby Seale, chairman of the Black Panther Party. After the Convention, he told the court, he was assigned to cover disturbances at several high schools in Chicago, including Waller High School.

The presentation of evidence took three and a half days and filled 1,172 pages of transcript. When it was done, Judge Austin dismissed the suit. In his oral opinion, the judge held that the Army had been far too inept in its surveillance of civilian politics to inhibit anyone from exercising his First Amendment rights:

"If anything was disclosed by the evidence here, it is that there will be no 'Seven Days in May' for this country. Army activities, as disclosed in this hearing, are typical of the gigantic Washington boondoggle. The military intelligence is the Army's WPA, . . . leaf-raking, shovel-wielding and paper-shuffling presided over by too many Col. Throttlebottoms."

"From this threatening assemblage of Keystone Cops, the chief beneficiary . . . has been newspaper circulation. The chief menace has been an increase in air pollution from the burning of newspapers. . . . I hope those who swore their civil liberties have been chilled have been warmed by the revelations of this hearing."

The ACLU announced that it would appeal.

CONUS *Intelligence Today*

It remains to be seen how complete and permanent the Army's retreat from civilian surveillance will be. But from what various Army spokesmen have said, and from the observations of former agents and other persons who cannot now be identified, it is possible to draw these conclusions:

• Despite its evasiveness with Congress and the public, the Army's civilian hierarchy has demonstrated a genuine intention to achieve substantial reforms. The Wickham directive, in particular, demonstrates that the Army General Counsel and his staff now know what the military's legitimate domestic intelligence needs are, and have been able to formulate that knowledge into a binding directive.

• To assure compliance with destruction orders, persons on the staff of the Secretary of the Army and in the Office of the Assistant Chief of Staff for Intelligence have actually left Washington to inspect files. So far, however, the inspections have been limited to a few headquarters and region offices. Thus, the Army's assurances that the program has stopped continue to be based on insufficient knowledge.

• Information received from agents recently discharged from Army intelligence indicate that many records on civilians and civilian organizations unaffiliated with the armed forces have been destroyed. Records destruction appears to have occurred in waves: after the Lynch letter, just prior to announced inspections, and immediately after the disclosures by John O'Brien.

- The CONUS intelligence program has not been abolished. Instead the name has been changed to "Current Intelligence" and the positions assigned to career intelligence agents. The classification of formerly unclassified files on civilians and civilian organizations and the invocation of the doctrine of executive privilege also suggest an intent to continue. There are some indications that old CONUS intelligence functions may find new homes within the Continental Army Command and the Criminal Investigations Division.
- The evasions and deceptions perpetrated on the Army's civilian hierarchy and on the Congress during the post 13 months demonstrate the difficulties involved in re-educating the military intelligence bureacurecy. Resistance to the new policies remains particularly strong among the ICCPS (intelligence civilian career personnel) whose jobs depend upon the continuation of some form of domestic intelligence.

Beyond the Limits

Intentionally or not, the Army went far beyond the limits of its needs and authority in collecting domestic political information. It created an activity which, by its existence alone, jeopardized individual rights, democratic political processes, and even the national security it sought to protect.

There is no question that the Army must have domestic intelligence. In order to assist civilian authorities, it needs maps and descriptions of potential riot or disaster areas, as well as early warnings of incidents likely to provoke mass violence. Before trusting its employees with military secrets, it has to look into their past behavior for evidence of disloyalty or unsuitability. The Army also must investigate train wrecks, fires, and other disasters which may disrupt its lines of supply. And where ultra-militant groups seek to attack military installations, destroy files, or solicit soldiers to commit crimes, it has the right and obligation to keep informed about the groups' specific objectives, plans and techniques.

The Army needs this kind of information so that it can fulfill long-established, legitimate responsibilities. But must it also distribute and store detailed reports on the political beliefs and actions of individuals and groups?

Army Intelligence officials believed they must. Without detailed knowledge of community "infactucture," they have argued, riot-control troops would not be able to enforce curfews or quell violence. To support this contention, they have cited the usefulness of personality files and blacklists in breaking up guerrilla organizations in Malaya and South Vietnam. One early proponent of this view was the Army's Assistant Chief of Staff for Intelligence during 1967-68, Maj. Gen. William P. Yarborough. At the height of the Detroit riots of 1967 he instructed his staff in the domestic war room; "Men, get out your counter-insurgency manuals. We have an insurgency on our hands."

Of course, there was no insurgency. As one war room officer who attempted to carry out the General's order later observed: "There we were, plotting power plants, radio stations, and armories on the situation maps when we should have been locating the liquor and color-television stores instead." A year later the National Advisory Commission on Civil Disorders reached a similar conclusion about the motives of ghetto rioters. "The urban disorders of the summer of 1967," it declared unequivocally, "were not caused by, nor were they the consequences of, any organized plan or 'conspiracy.'" After reviewing all of the federal government's intelligence reports on 23 riots, it found "no evidence that all or any of the disorders or the incidents that led to them were planned or directed by any organizations or groups, international, national, or local."

Intensive investigations subsequently conducted by local police departments, grand juries, city and state committees, and private organizations have concurred. One of the more recent, a study of 1968 "urban guerrilla" activities by the Lemberg Center for the Study of Violence at Brandeis University, is typical. It found that press and police accounts of shooting incidents were grossly exaggerated. While acknowledging that there had been "a few shoot-outs with the police" some of which "may have been planned," the Center concluded that there was "no wave of uprisings and no set pattern of murderous conflict" from which one could predict organized violence even remotely resembling guerrilla warfare.

But even if there were grounds for making such a prediction, the Army's case for personality files and blacklists would remain weak. The purpose of these records, according to counterinsurgency manuals, is to facilitate the selective arrest of guerrillas and insurgents. However, within the United States the Army has no authority to round up suspects the moment civilians take up arms. The seizure of civilians on suspicion of conspiring or attempting to overthrow the government by unlawful means or of inciting people to crime is, and continues to be, the responsibility of local and state police and the FBI. The President may order Army units to help state or federalized National Guard troops keep the peace or fight guerrillas, but the Army does not acquire authority to arrest civilians unless and until civilian law enforcement has broken down and a declaration of martial law puts all governmental authority in the area of conflict in the hands of the military. In that highly remote circumstance, the Army units might have some need for personality files and blacklists on criminally inclined, politically motivated civilians. By then, however, it certainly would have full access to the more extensive and up-to-date files of the civilian agencies and thus would not have had to prepare its own.

The Army's need to keep its own dossiers on the politics of law-abiding citizens and groups makes even less sense. So long as there is a possibility that peaceful protests may get out of hand, some surveillance undoubtedly is in order. But must the Army conduct it? Are its agents and record keepers more competent than those of the FBI or of the police departments of the cities in which large demonstrations typically occur? Are the civilian law enforcement agencies so uncooperative that the Army must substantially duplicate their efforts?

More extraordinary still is why the Intelligence Command each week alerted military headquarters in Alaska, Hawaii, Panama, and Europe to stateside non-events like the following:

MIAMI, FLA.: A SPOKESMAN FOR THE SOUTHERN STUDENTS ORGANIZING COMMITTEE ANNOUNCED PLANS FOR A DEMONSTRATION TO BE HELD ON THE CAMPUS OF THE UNIVERSITY OF MIAMI IN THE MORNING. ACCORDING TO THE SPOKESMAN, A GROUP OF ANTI-WAR/DRAFT SUPPORTERS WILL PARTICIATE IN THE DEMONSTRATION.

PHILADELPHIA, PA: MEMBERS OF THE VIETNAM WEEK COMMITTEE COMPOSED OF PROFESSORS AND STUDENTS OF THE UNIVERSITY OF PENNSYLVANIA, WILL CONDUCT A "SLEEP-IN" TO PROTEST THE SCHEDULED APPEARANCE OF DOW CHEMICAL COMPANY RECRUITERS ON CAMPUS. THE NEXT DAY, 19 MARCH, THE SAME ORGANIZATION WILL SPONSOR A PROTEST RALLY ON COMPUS.

Perhaps the best answer to all of these questions is that much of the CONUS intelligence program served no military need at all. But if this is so, then where did the Army get the authority to run it?

The Army's Authority

According to the Nixon Administration, authority for this kind of program comes from the Constitution. So, at least, the Justice Department claimed in June 1969 in a brief defending the FBI's failure to obtain search warrants before tapping telephone calls of what were then the "Chicago Eight." The Justice Department argued that Article Two of the Constitution authorizes the President and his agents to engage in whatever "intelligence-gathering operations he believes are necessary to protect the security of the nation" and that this authority "is not dependent upon any grant of legislative authority from Congress, but rather is an inherent power of the President, derived from the Constitution itself." Thus, the Department contended, "Congress cannot tell the President what means he may employ to obtain information he needs to determine the proper deployment of his forces."

If this is so, then Army agents have the authority to undertake any surveillance that does not run afoul of the Constitution and the courts; indeed, they can investigate anything that is normally investigated by the federal government's civilian agencies! Moreover, they do not have to obey laws like the Omnibus Crime Control Act of 1968, which forbids most wiretapping and electronic eavesdropping without prior judicial authorization in the form of a warrant.

Fortunately, the "inherent powers doctrine," as the theory is called, has few supporters. The courts have never accepted the proposition that Congress is powerless to prescribe how the President shall exercise his executive powers. The leading precedent is *Youngstown Sheet & Tube Co. v. Sawyer,* a 1952 decision of the Supreme Court which rejected President Truman's claim to inherent power to seize the nation's steel mills to avert a strike which threatened the flow of equipment to American troops fighting in Korea. If there were not inherent Presidential power to meet that emergency, it seems likely that none exists to authorize the intelligence powers which the government claims today.

Indeed, federal district court judges in Los Angeles and Detroit have recently ruled in separate cases that there is no inherent Presidential power authorizing the government to wiretap without a warrant in cases not involving the operations of foreign intelligence agencies.

Thus it would seem that the courts ultimately must rule that the Army's authority to collect domestic intelligence is limited by, and can only be inferred from, those laws which traditionally mark off the Army's responsibility for law enforcement from that of other agencies. These include not only the statutes which restrict the Army to a back-up function in times of riot, but the laws and inter-agency agreements which assign federal authority to watch unlawful political activity within the United States to the FBI and the Secret Service. Other sources of the Army's authority include the Uniform Code of Military Justice, which permits investigation of unlawful political activity within the armed services, and those laws and federal-state agreements under which the Army governs many of its installations. These rules, and not the vague provisions of Article Two, are the legitimate sources of the military's domestic intelligence powers.

Yet even if the current Administration's claim to an inherent constitutional power to watch lawful political activity were to be accepted by the courts, the surveillance itself should be forbidden by the Bill of Rights. The reason is the chilling effect which knowledge of surveillance can have upon the willingness of citizens to exercise their freedoms of speech, press, and association, and their right to petition the government for redress of grievances.

Ten years ago the federal courts would not have accepted this contention. Then the courts were hesitant even to accept constitutional challenges to the government's collection of political information when the plaintiffs could prove that the investigators had no other purpose than to deter them from exercising their rights under the First Amendment. Recently, however, some courts have begun to accept the proposition that vague and overbroad laws and administrative actions are unconstitutional if they inhibit the exercise of these rights, regardless of whether that effect was intended.

Typical of this growing body of constitutional interpretation is the 1965 case of *Lamont v. Postmaster General.* There the Supreme Court struck down a federal statute which authorized the Post Office to suspend delivery of unsolicited mail which the government agents regarded as "Communist political propaganda" until the addressee returned a reply post-card declaring that he wished to receive the mail. The Court, in a unanimous opinion, held that the effect of this practice, whatever the government's purpose, was to abridge freedom of speech by inhibiting the right to read.

If people are likely to be deterred in the exercise of their rights by the fear of being labeled "Communist" then it follows that they should be inhibited by knowledge that reports of individual participation in public demonstrations data bank at Fort Holabird. Thus, even if the Army's collection of personality files and blacklists is not proscribed by legislation, it still may be unlawful.

The Program's Impact

Beyond the Army's need for the present CONUS intelligence program and its authority to pursue it lies the matter of the program's impact upon the public interest. In particular, there is its effect upon the rights of individuals, the democratic process, and the nation's security.

The impact which the program can have upon the exercise of political rights needs no further explication. The threat it poses to job rights and privacy, however, may not be so apparent.

Like the freedom from inhibitory surveillances, the job rights threatened are rights in the making. As yet no one has established a legal right to a job that requires a security clearance or to a security clearance essential to a job. Nevertheless, in recent years the courts have begun to recognize that those who already hold federal jobs and security clearances have a right not to be deprived of either without just cause, or at the very least, without the rudiments of fairness. The filing of CONUS intelligence spot reports in security clearance dossiers, if continued, would have nullified even this protection, by making unverified, erroneous, and irrelevant reports available to the "adjudicators" who decide who should and who should not receive security clearances.

If the men and women who adjudicate security clearances were competent to evaluate such unreliable information, its inclusion in security files might be less cause for concern. Unfortunately, they are not. The most highly trained adjudicators—civilians employed by the stateside army commands—receive only nine days of job instruction on loyalty determinations at the Army Intelligence School. Moreover, this training does not even touch upon the subject of suitability, although almost 98 per cent of all clearances denied today are rejected ostensibly on that ground. The least trained adjudicators—intelligence officers assigned to field commands—receive exactly two classroom hours on loyalty and two on suitability while being trained to become investigators. Because of this extremely brief training, it is not unusual for an adjudicator to conclude that a person arrested in connection with a political protest is not suited for a security clearance, regardless of the circumstances of his arrest, the legality of his detention, or his innocence of the charges.

The adjudicators' lack of training is compounded by security regulations which permit—indeed, seem to require—the denial of clearance on less evidence than would support a magistrate's finding of "probable cause." In other words, it is not a question of whether reliable evidence indicates that the individual cannot be trusted with state secrets, but of whether the granting of the clearance would be "clearly consistent with the interests of national security." No one really knows what this ambiguous phrase means, but in practice it frequently is used to justify findings of guilt by association. For example, soldiers and civilian employees of the Army with foreign-born spouses are virtually blocked from jobs requiring access to especially sensitive intelligence. Their association with a spouse who once "associated with foreigners" is taken as proof of their vulnerability to recruitment by foreign agents. Moreover, in nearly all other cases, adjudicators usually have to make their decisions without knowing the source of the evidence, without hearing the accused confront his accusers, or without hearing the accused defend himself with knowledge of their identity.

Given the tenuousness of the right to due process under these conditions, the influx of CONUS intelligence reports would have made the system even more unjust than it is now. At the present time, little information on political activity is developed in the course of most background investigations. Army investigations, in particular, tend to be superficial; in some sections of the country shortages of personnel, caused by the war in Vietnam, have forced the Intelligence Command to abandon interviews of character references in favor of questionnaires-by-mail as its main means of inquiry. But if questionnaires had continued to be supplemented by CONUS political reports, the number of clearances unjustly denied would have sky-rocketed. These injustices would have occurred not only within the military; they would have reverberated throughout all federal agencies with access to the Fort Holabird data bank.

The Army's domestic intelligence program also imperiled numerous expectations of privacy, some of which enjoy the status of legal rights. It did so by exposing Americans to governmental scrutiny, and the fear of scrutiny, to an extent to which they have never been exposed before. Even the Budget Bureau's ill-starred proposal to consolidate the federal government's statistical records into a National Data Center would not have brought together so much information about individual beliefs and actions.

The privacy of politically active citizens was especially threatened by the Army's practice of watching political protests, large and small, throughout the United States. To the potential protester, it is one thing to expect local press and police coverage; it is quite another to expect a military surveillance which specializes in keeping permanent records of lawful political activity.

What effect awareness of the CONUS intelligence program will have on the vast majority of people who are *not* politically active is more difficult to predict. By itself, news that the Army has been watching civilian politics is not likely to cause most people to worry personally about their privacy. But it is one more increment in a growing pattern of governmental intrusiveness that could have a significant cumulative impact.

Such a pattern is now well established. Among the more widely publicized activities in recent years have been the CIA's surreptitious financing of student groups, labor unions, and foundations (despite the territorial limits of that agency's mandate), the Post Office's use of peepholes in restroom walls, and the Defense Department's misuse of lie detectors. Others include countless illegal wiretaps by the FBI, the Internal Revenue Service, and the Department of the Interior. More recently, the publication of confidential FBI wiretap information by *Life* and *Newsweek* which linked Jets' quarterback Joe Namath to Mafia figures suggests that the FBI has now assumed responsibility for enforcing professional football's code of conduct.

The cumulative impact of such abuses of power and privacy eventually must convince even the most anonymous of individuals that the United States is moving towards a society in which no one has control over what others know about him. Public awareness of the Army's activities cannot but hasten this conviction.

Even as it is being dismantled, the CONUS intelligence machinery threatens the country's political health. It does so by giving rise to fears which, if not allayed, can seriously inhibit political participation and enhance the potential clout of demagogues and others predisposed to misusing security files for partisan or personal purposes.

The most immediate risk posed, of course, is to political participation. Once citizens come to fear that government agencies will misuse information concerning their political activities, their withdrawal from politics can be expected. This withdrawal can occur in a variety of ways. Some people may decline to become involved in potentially controversial community organizations and projects. Others may go further and avoid all persons who support unpopular ideas or who criticize the government. Some may refuse to object to the abuse of government authority, especially when the abuse is committed in the name of national security. Others may stop reading political publications, out of fear that the government might learn of their reading habits and disapprove. Indeed, an adjudicator of security clearances once asked me if she could lose her clearance if she allowed her daughter to subscribe to *The National Observer!*

Inhibitions generated by awareness of extensive domestic surveillance are likely to be strongest at the local level. This is where most citizens participate in politics if they become involved at all. The withdrawal can be expected to occur all across the political spectrum, although the strongest objections to surveillance will undoubtedly come from the left. Those most likely to be deterred, however, are not the extremists of the right or left, whose sense of commitment runs deep, but the moderates, who normally hold the balance of power. Depletion of their ranks would, of course, strengthen the influence of the extremists, polarize debate, increase animosities, and decrease tolerance. As political positions rigidify, compromise and flexibility would become harder to achieve. And the capacity of government to renew itself and promote responsible progress would also suffer.

A less immediate but no less serious danger continues to lie in the potential for misuse inherent in the Army's remaining files on individuals and groups. It is frightening to imagine what could happen if a demagogue in the Martin Dies-Joseph McCarthy tradition were to gain access to the CONUS intelligence files, or if an Otto Otepka in uniform were to leak a copy of the Intelligence Command's so-called "blacklist" to friends in Congress, or if a General Edwin Walker were to take charge of the Intelligence Command.

Such speculation assumes, of course, that the Army cannot guarantee the inviolability of its files. The assumption, unfortunately, has some validity. In 1969, information from the Army's confidential service record on New Orleans District Attorney Jim Garrison was leaked to the press. Officers at the Investigative Records Repository at Fort Holabird (which functions as the Army's lending library for such files) suspected that the leak came from a civilian agency in Washington. They were helpless to do anything about it, however, because they had no system of records accountability by which they could fix responsibility. When asked why such a system did not exist, one officer told me: "We probably couldn't stop it [the leaks] if we tried."

Finally, if the CONUS intelligence apparatus is allowed to continue (or to reestablish itself) it could have the paradoxical effect of undermining the very security it has sought to protect. It could do so in at least two ways. First by increasing the "cost" of lawful political activity, it would tend to force extremist groups to go underground, there to act out their us-versus-them view of politics by criminal means. Second, but intruding too closely into the lives of government employees (or prospective employees), it would tend to inhibit them from applying for jobs requiring security clearance or from exercising initiative and imagination in those jobs. A good intelligence officer must be able to analyze and report accurately, and to do so he must feel free to immerse himself in the ideas and culture of the people he studies. A good scientist must have freedom to pursue his curiosities, or he is not likely to work for the government, which rarely pays as much as private industry. The direct consequences of programs which deny this freedom is to impair the quality of secret work and the caliber of the men who do it. As John Stuart Mill warned over a century ago: "A state which dwarfs its men, in order that they may be more docile instruments in its hands, even for beneficial purposes, will find that with small men no great thing can really be accomplished . . . ."

What Can Be Done?

If the Army has exceeded the limits of its needs and authority to establish a domestic intelligence program, what steps should be taken to curb its excesses and to assure that they do not occur again?

An obvious first step—a court challenge—has already been taken. A declaratory judgment, with or without an injunction, which confines the scope of the Army's curiosity to matters directly affecting the deployment of riot troops or the security of military personnel, installations, equipment, and supplies would go far towards redressing the balance. For one thing, it would give support to the civilian authorities in the Departments of Defense and Army who are now trying to persuade their subordinates not to evade and confound their orders.

Unfortunately, it will be many months at best before a final judgment is rendered. Meanwhile, as the delays multiply and Army security restrictions tighten, the ACLU will find it increasingly difficult to keep its evidence up-to-date. Moreover, a favorable decision could be—and probably would be—ignored and evaded for many more years. Thus while the symbolic value of such a decision would justify the time and the expense, an effective challenge of the intelligence program will require special emphasis on the development of legislative and administrative remedies.

A Framework for Analysis

Whoever attempts to devise legislative or administrative remedies must be prepared to undertake subtle analyses of competing interests and values, for while the excesses of the program must be permanently curbed, the Army's ability to fulfill its legitimate responsibilities must not be impaired

The analysis should proceed from the assumption that the powers of intelligence agencies in general, and the Army in particular, must be construed strictly, in accordance with such established principles as civilian control of the military, Presidential control of the bureaucracies, state and civilian primacy in law enforcement, compartmentalization and decentralization of intelligence duties, and obedience to law.

Justification for each alleged intelligence need should be demanded in terms of the federal statutes, executive orders, and Department of the Army regulations which define the Army's stateside missions. Vague claims to an "inherent power" to spy on civilians derived somehow from the President's duties as Commander-in-Chief or chief executive should be flatly rejected.

Each need for which authority exists (or should exist) ought next to be weighed against the threats it may pose to the rights of individuals, to the vitality of the political process, and to the security of the nation. Where the threats are clear and the need doubtful, authority should be denied. Where both the threat and the need can be demonstrated, less hazardous alternatives should be considered. In this circumstance, the capacity of politically responsible officials to control the alternatives should be weighed. Where reliable controls cannot be devised, the intelligence effort should not be authorized—even though the denial of authority may deprive the government of useful knowledge of the domestic political scene. Whatever risk results from imposition of these restraints must be accepted as a price worth paying for individual liberties and truly free society.

Making use of this approach, the Senate Subcommittee on Constitutional Rights might profitably ask Defense Department witnesses what specific military need was (or is) served by:

- The maintenance of local and regional card files, dossiers, photgraphs, and other records on civilians and civilian organizations unaffiliated with the armed forces?

• The maintenance of computerized records on civilian dissenters at Fort Holabird, Fort Monroe, and Fort Hood?

• The publication of the Intelligence Command's blacklist and CIAD's Compendium?

• The publication of weekly and monthly "CONUS Intelligence Summaries" by CONUS, the Intelligence Command, and all stateside armies?

• The publication of CONUS intelligence newsletters by some MI Groups such as the 108th MI Group's office in Manhattan?

• The publication by the Air Force of "Significant Counterintelligence Briefs" containing information about Huey Newton's speaking campaign and other matters unrelated to the mission of the Office of Special Investigations?

• The publication by the Navy of domestic political information in its "Trends" reports?

• The distribution of CONUS intelligence summaries and publications to Army units in Europe Alaska, and Panama?

Is it true, as former intelligence agents have claimed, that Army intelligence:

• Directed agents to conceal their military affiliations and purposes and infiltrate: the 1967 March on the Pentagon, the Poor People's Campaign, Resurrection City, the Black Studies program at New York University, the National Mobilization Committee's Counter-Inaugural headquarters, and the Young Adults Project, Colorado Springs, Colorado?

• Ordered agents to conduct foot surveillances of prominent black leaders including the Rev. Ralph David Abernathy, and the Rev. Jesse Jackson?

• Kept files, other than personnel security files, on elected and appointed officials of federal and state governments, including: Georgia State Representative Julian Bond, Chicago Aldermen A. A. Rayner and William Cousins Jr., United States Senators Adlai Stevenson III, J. William Fulbright, and Eugene McCarthy, Representative Abner J. Mikva, U.S. Circuit Court Judge and former Governor of Illinois, Otto Kerner, New Trier, Illinois, School Board President Seymour Gale, and former Washington, D. C., school board member Julius Hobson?

• Assigned agents to the floors of both the Republican and Democratic National Conventions in 1968?

• Kept files on professors Marvin Schibrough, Michael Marcus, and

Jon R. Waltz of Northwestern University, and Professors Grover Maxwell, David Noble, Allen Spear, and Mulford Sibley of the University of Minnesota?

• Kept files on Young Americans for Freedom, the American Friends Service Committee, Women's Strike for Peace, the Urban League, the National Association for the Advancement for Colored People, SANE, the American Civil Liberties Union, the Center for the Study of Democratic Institutions, and the John Birch Society?

• Assigned agents to impersonate newsmen and television camera crews for the purpose of interviewing, observing, and/or photographing civilian political activities?

• Placed unverified CONUS intelligence reports in security clearance dossiers at the Investigate Records Repository, Fort Holabird, Maryland?

• Who authorized these activities? Under what authority? For what purpose?

• Are personality or organizational data on civilians needed in order for troops to clear streets, detain rioters, or enforce curfew? Have riot control units ever been issued copies of the Intelligence Command's "identification list" before going into riot areas? If so, why?

Did the personality, organizational, or incident files serve any useful purpose that could in any way justify the expense of collecting them or the risks to civil liberties inherent in them?

Does the Defense Department believe that personnel security units should maintain a search file on all civilians for use in checking out those civilians who might apply for a job requiring a security clearance? Should raw intelligence reports, like the CONUS intelligence spot reports, be filed in the dossiers of persons who have already been granted a security clearance?

When, if at all, in the continuum of events leading up to the use of federal troops to put down a riot must of the Army Intelligence Command be called upon? For what purpose? Is there anything they can do which riot control units, military police, National Guard units, and civilian police cannot do?

Drawing the Lines

If this line of inquiry is pursued, the Subcommittee should find that the Defense Department cannot demonstrate a substantial military need for:

• A civil disturbance early warning system of its own. To the extent that such systems are required, civilian authorities ought to run them.

• Most of its personality and organization files on individuals and groups not affiliated with the armed forces.

• Identification lists describing civilian political activities of any kind.

• Plainclothes agents to monitor civil disturbances not occurring on or within close proximity to military installations.

• Undercover agents and informants to infiltrate anti-war, anti-draft, or anti-poverty groups, or college classrooms.

• The computerized data banks the Army has promised to destroy.

• CIAD's microfilm archive on civilian political activity.

• Sending agents of the U. S. Army Intelligence Command into the streets during a civil disturbance to supplement the intelligence gathering efforts of riot control units, military police, National Guard, or civilian police.

At the same time the Defense Department should be able to establish some need for:

• Descriptive information, such as maps, bridge loads, potential bivouac and helicopter landing sites, pertaining to cities which have a substantial potential for race riots. This information, along with the names, addresses, and telephone numbers of appropriate municipal and state authorities, has properly been collected by the Army in "city books" for approximately 150 cities.

• Similar information on areas in which mass demonstrations like the Selma March, Resurrection City, and the March on the Pentagon are planned.

• Standby communications systems linking military intelligence offices in potential riot areas to the Pentagon's domestic war room which can be activated the moment troops are ordered out.

• Information from civilian law enforcement authorities alerting it to acts of espionage, sabotage, or solicitations to crime affecting military personnel, installations, equipment or supplies.

• Information from civilian authorities—and by direct on-site surveillance by Army agents—of disasters (such as airplane crashes and train wrecks), bombings (such as the Army Mathematics Center at the University of Wisconsin), and demonstrations (such as attempts to block troop trains) which might directly and immediately affect military operations.

• The means to investigate violations of the Uniform Code of Military Justice.

• The means to investigate persons being considered for security clearances. (However, any need which the Department might claim for a clipping file on the possibly "disloyal" statements or actions of civilians on the ground that they someday might apply for security clearance should be rejected as violative of the First Amendment).

Necessary Reforms

Once the lines between legitimate and illegitimate surveillance have been drawn, it should not be difficult to devise new rules to govern military intelligence agents. These rules should:

• Limit the maintenance of civil disturbances early warning systems within the military to incidents occurring within units or on posts.

• Forbid any infiltration of civilian political groups by military intelligence agents except insofar as that infiltration is for the purpose of countering the activities of foreign intelligence agencies or otherwise enforcing federal laws governing treason, espionage, sabotage, or the solicitation of military personnel to commit crimes. In each of these limited instances, the specific authorization of the Under Secretary of the military service and the concurrence of Director of the Federal Bureau of Investigation should be required.

• Forbid the Director of Military Support (formerly Civil Disturbance Planning and Operations) to order the off-post surveillance of any civil disturbance until such time as a governor or the President has called out the troops.

• Limit surveillances in support of riot troops to the collection of "order of battle" information by military police, intelligence personnel who are part of riot control units, and by riot control troops themselves. Intelligence Command personnel who operate independently of riot control units should not be called out to double as tactical intelligence personnel.

• Forbid the maintenance of personality files, organization files, and identification lists which do not directly relate to violations of the Uniform Code of Military Justice or of federal laws relating to military security.

• Forbid the conversion of incident reports filed during riots into personality reports, except where the activity reported relates to criminal activity by persons subject to military law or employed by the military.

• Require the destruction of incident reports filed by intelligence units on riot duty within sixty days of the restoration of civilian law enforcement.

- Establish effective legal, technological, and administrative safeguards against the abuse of individual rights in the process of collecting, reporting, storing, and disseminating domestic intelligence or personnel security information. For example, the Army's current intelligence and personnel security headquarters should be located on separate posts (they now share the same room and some of the same personnel) in order to reduce the danger of informal leakage of current intelligence material into the hands of security clearance adjudicators.
- Improve the professional quality of Intelligence Command personnel and security clearance adjudicators.
- Provide for the assignment of a substantial percentage of noncareer intelligence agents to local "current intelligence" and "special operations" sections as the only effective way of guaranteeing eventual disclosures of wrong-doing.

Congressional Action

Since the Army has conceded the need for many of these reforms and expressed the intention to carry them out, is further action from Congress necessary? I submit that it is.

Bureaucracies are ill-equipped to stop or diminish what they are doing without help from outside. As Richard Halloran observed recently in the *New York Times*: "Bureaucracies seem to follow the laws of physics—a bureaucracy at rest tends to stay at rest; a bureaucracy in motion tends to remain in motion."

During the past year we have seen ample evidence of these laws in action. Despite their public evasions and deceptions, the civilian authorities within the Army have tried to put the brakes on the domestic intelligence machine. But as crisis managers, they have been repeatedly distracted by other events which have demanded their attention. Only the persistence of this Subcommittee, assisted by the revelations of former intelligence agents, has brought them back to the task. Even so, they have a difficult time trying to find out what has been happening below decks. Their subordinates repeatedly have misled them—even lied to them—about the scope and direction of domestic intelligence activities.

The Subcommittee should see for itself just how weak and sporadic civilian control of military intelligence is and has been by asking the government's witnesses the following questions:

Did the Secretary or Under Secretary of the Army authorize: Any of the infiltration mentioned? Any of the civil disturbance computerized data banks? The Intelligence Command identification list? The CIAD Compendium?

Who decided that Army Intelligence, rather than the Justice Department and FBI, should run the civil disturbance early warning system? The President? The FBI? The Secretary of Defense? The Secretary of the Army? Or Army Intelligence? Why wasn't this function shifted from the Army to those agencies earlier than 1970

Is it true that the entire CONUS intelligence program was established without the promulgation of specific regulations defining its mission and restricting its scope? If not, what directives specified its mission? Did any directives come from the Internal Security Committee of the National Security Council?

Didn't "The Delimitations Agreement of 1949" (AR 381-115) assign all investigations of civilians to the Federal Bureau of Investigation?

The Army has admitted to maintaining computerized data banks on civilian political activity at Fort Holabird, Fort Monroe, and Fort Hood. Have others been discovered in the Army? Navy? Marines? Air Force?

What has happened to each of these computerized data banks? When was each discontinued? When were the computer tapes, keypunch cards, computer programs, and print-outs actually destroyed? Where were they destroyed? Who can personally attest to their destruction? Do any remnants of these banks remain today?

What has happened to the Compendium? Were the documents withdrawn to the issuing authority and destroyed there, or were they ordered to be destroyed in the field? Were all copies accounted for? If not, how many copies are "wild?"

On March 20, 1970, Under Secretary of the Army Thaddeus R. Beal informed Representative Cornelius E. Gallagher (D-N.J.) that "The Assistant Chief of Staff for Intelligence of the Department of the Army directed on 18 February 1970 that all copies of this [Intelligence Command] identification list be returned from Army field agencies to the Intelligence Command where they will be destroyed." Was that order carried out, or was it countermanded to permit destruction of the lists in the field? Who countermanded it? Without recall of actual documents, how can the Department be certain that they all have been destroyed?

How many inspections of the 300 Intelligence Command offices have been made by inspectors from Washington? When? How many inspections have ben conducted at the field office and residence office level by inspectors from Washington? How many inspections have been made of CONARS units?

What records, if any, have been turned over to other federal agencies? To state agencies? Which records to which agencies, and why?

What has been done to sanitize security clearance dossiers contaminated by the insertion of CONUS intelligence "spot reports?" When, and by whom?

What has been done to render harmless CIAD's microfilm archive on domestic politics? When, and by whom?

What efforts have been taken to determine the extent to which the Navy, Marines, and Air Force have been collecting, processing, distributing, and storing information on civilians and civilian organizations unaffiliated with the armed forces?

Are the Secretaries of Defense, Army, Navy, and Air Force satisfied that their counterintelligence units have been sufficiently sensitive to the First Amendment rights of the persons they investigate? If not, what steps have been taken—other than by restructuring—to apprise counterintelligence personnel as to what those rights are and how they should go about respecting them?

Are the Secretaries satisfied that they have been adequately informed about domestic intelligence activities by their subordinates? If not, what steps have or will be taken to correct this sitution? Are any disciplinary actions contemplated for subordinates who have been less than candid?

Are any disciplinary actions contemplated against any of the persons responsible for the "abuses" mentioned by Secretary Laird in his announcement of December 23, 1970?

The answers to these questions—or the Department's inability to answer them—should confirm that the civilians who are supposed to be in control of military intelligence:

- Had little to do with the creation of the domestic intelligence apparatus.
- Have had a difficult time finding out about it.
- Have seen their orders to dismantle that apparatus evaded and disobeyed.
- Have not conducted enough inspections personally to know the extent to which compliance has been achieved.
- Have reason to believe that their orders will continue to be evaded and disobeyed.
- Need the help of Congress to do what they say they want to do.

Ultimately the task is one of persuasion—those who oppose military surveillance of civilians must persuade those that want to do it that they shouldn't either because it is unconstitutional, illegal, immoral, unnecessary, or politically too dangerous. The most effective way to drive the message home, and to make sure that it is heard by future generations of intelligence agents, is to put it in the form of a statute. How such a statute might be worded is suggested by the draft bill included as an appendix to my testimony.

The draft bill is based on a very simple historical precedent. In 1878 Congress passed the *posse comitatus* act (18 U.S.C. Sec. 1385) to make it a crime for a local military commander to order his troops to serve in a sheriff's posse or otherwise usurp enforcement of civilian law. Like the laws governing the use of federal troops to assist civilian authorities put down riots or enforce court orders (10 U.S.C. Sec. 331, 332, 333) the *posse comitatus* act intended federal troops to serve as a back-up force under the direct control of the President.

The law I propose would merely extend the *posse comitatus* act to military intelligence. It would provide that just as troops may not ride in the sheriff's posse without the President's permission, military intelligence agents may not ride with his intelligence squad.

Nothing in the law would in any way deprive military intelligence of the information it needs to do its job, as defined in General Wickham's letter of December 15, 1970. On the contrary, the law would assist the Army by preserving its neutrality in domestic politics. With such a statute on the books, political protesters can be assured that when the Army is called out, its soldiers will come without institutionally conceived notions of who is right and who is wrong, but only to protect lives, preserve property, and restore order.

8

EXPANSION OF COUNTERINTELLIGENCE

By Ralph M. Stein

I served in the U.S. Army from October 22, 1965 to October 21, 1968 and was honorably discharged as a sergeant. After basic training I attended the U.S. Army Intelligence School at Fort Holabird, Baltimore, and graduated from the military intelligence specialist course in April 1966. I served as a special agent in the Investigations Section, Company B, 502d Military Intelligence Battalion, Republic of Korea, from May 1966 to June 1967. After returning from Korea I was assigned to the Counterintelligence Analysis Branch, Counterintelligence Division, Directorate of Security, Office of the Assistant Chief of Staff for Intelligence (ACSI), from July 1967 until my discharge, serving for all but the first few days of my assignment in the Domestic Intelligence Section of CIAB. I received a certificate of commendation from the Assistant Chief of Staff for Intelligence at the time of my discharge. I was cited for excellence in domestic intelligence analysis work at CIAB.

I have been conducting a study of the activities of the U.S. Army Intelligence Command and other Army organizations engaged in domestic surveillance and data compilation for the past 13 months, working in association with Mr. Christopher Pyle. My investigation, which is still in progress, has taken me from coast to coast, to large cities in California and small Midwest towns. I have interviewed concerned Americans with information on the Army's activities on college campuses in New England and at business firms in the South. Students, professionals, military personnel and civil servants, white and black, have discussed with me their concern about the Army's domestic surveillance. I will divide my remarks into three areas for the sake of preserving clarity. I will first describe my own activities and observations while serving in Army Intelligence. I will then summarize the results of my investigation and I will conclude by explaining my views and respectfully proposing measures by which we will be able to protect ourselves from future wholesale surveillance by the military while still safeguarding America's legitimate internal security interests.

I must make one subjective clarification at this point. I am not against the existence of the military intelligence establishment nor do I harbor any ill feelings or grudges against any of my former superiors or associates, some of whom are still close friends of mine today. Personally, I respect most of the career civilians and officers with and for whom I worked. I do feel, however, that these individuals are, as I shall later explain, by training and experience peculiarly disqualified to engage in domestic intelligence work, an activity the military should not be undertaking in the first place.

In July of 1967 I reported to CIAB which was then located in a warehouse building in the 1400 block of South Eads Street in Arlington, Virginia. After an initial assignment of a few day's duration with CIAB's Eurasian Section, I was dispatched to the Army Operations Center (AOC) in the Pentagon to assist in preparing intelligence analyses of the then raging Detroit riot. Teams, each consisting of two analysts, were sent by CIAB to the Army Operations Center to make sense out of the mass of reports, sometimes conflicting, emanating from Detroit. During this chaotic period, we attempted to keep the generals in the AOC abreast of developments by preparing hourly reports and delivering briefings on request.

The information provided by members of the 113th Military Intelligence Group in Detroit encompassed every conceivable activity occuring on the streets of that troubled city from sniper reports to arrests for domestic quarreling. We were instructed to request every bit of information they could obtain and they complied. Whatever the value this information might have been to the commanders in Detroit, it was purely superfluous and confusing in Washington. The reports from General Throckmorton on the progress of his troops were of far more importance in determining the extent of the riot at any given time. It was both my expectation and my impression that the data compilation by the 113th was strictly *ad hoc.*

While Captain Perry Cole and I worked our four p.m. to midnight shift, other members of CIAB prepared and rapidly published a new document, a counter-intelligence Estimate of Civil Disturbances. This report, which evaluated the potentiality for future civil disturbances, using Army and FBI sources, was well received by its military recipients and it later became a standard CIAB project.

Expansion of Domestic Intelligence Section

Immediately after returning to CIAB from the Pentagon assignment, I was summoned by the new branch chief, Lieut. Col. Robert J. Brown. He informed me that CIAB was to begin a new, sophisticated and somewhat all-encompassing domestic intelligence effort and I was directed to start and maintain a left wing desk. My responsibilities would include being thoroughly familiar and conversant with all aspects of New Left and traditional left wing activities as well as with anti-war activities so as to be able to prepare summaries, reports and briefings when requested. I was instructed to monitor the activities of both individuals and organizations and I was told that I would be under the direction of the deputy branch chief, William L. Parkinson, and under the specific direction of Captain Byron E. Wicks, the officer in charge of CIAB's Domestic Section. Col. Brown concluded by stating that the Domestic Section would be receiving more manpower and that I was now "Mr. New Left" as far as he was concerned.

My first step was to ascertain what had been done in the past. In May 1966, while assigned to a work detail at Fort Holabird, I was startled to discover that the Army Intelligence Command maintained a very large library of classified reports on civilian organizations and personalities. This library was under the direction of a civilian employee, Millie Adkins. At the time, I assumed the library was for reference purposes, but I really gave it little thought as I was preoccupied with preparing to go overseas.

Inquiring at CIAB as to past activities, I discovered that CIAB had been engaged in domestic intelligence since at least 1965. At that time a WAC captain had started a North American desk. She spent her time gathering information primarily on right wing groups such as the Minutemen, John Birch Society, American Nazi Party, and Ku Klux Klan. I was told that CIAB had tried to provide information for the Pentagon during the Watts disturbance, but had lacked the resources.

At this point I began to organize my desk and two other agent-analysts (also known as action officers) instituted Racial and Right Wing desks. While I received no written orders, my verbal instructions, which were constantly being added to and updated, were broad. I was to cover literally all aspects of left wing activity in the United States. I was also to be sufficiently acquainted with racial activities so as to be competent to again participate in Army Operations Center activities during civil unrest. When I specifically inquired as to the need for relevance with regard to civil disturbances, I was told that all groups and all prominent personalities of the Old Left, New Left and anti-war area were to be monitored; right wing and racial analysts received similar directions. I was unable to ascertain the originating authority for this policy.

From the day I assumed responsibility for the left wing desk until my departure, I received thousands of FBI reports and a great number of military intelligence reports on groups and persons engaged in dissident activity. The amount of information received seemed to increase monthly. I retained much of the information, placing the material into the CIAB microfilm data bank or into a hard copy file. The microfilm data bank, incidentally, was being used as a depository for domestic intelligence information before my assignment to CIAB.

Some of the information was used to write reports or briefings. Most of the information received did not concern violence nor did it concern any situation involving the United States Army. As I will show later, the monitoring of civilian political activities did not in any way enhance or improve the Army's ability to perform its legitimate civil disturbance activity. In fact, this screening was counterproductive to the accomplishment of the Army's overall mission because of the drain in manpower and time spent.

Because of the great volume of information kept by CIAB and other military units on civilian activities, I will break down military monitoring and data retention efforts as best I can to illustrate how deeply the military became involved in civilian affairs, violating a tradition of non-involvement dating back to our Revolution.

Organizations Covered

It is no exaggeration to state that CIAB's files covered virtually every group engaged in dissent in the U.S. From memory, I present a very incomplete list. (See page 152).

Most of the organizations I have listed are nationally known. Some have little popular support and have engaged in activities generally deserving of widespread disapprobation. A few of the groups did sponsor activities designed to hamper the Army in the accomplishment of its lawful mission and information on such activities, when obtained by the FBI, was appropriate for the Army to receive. Most of the information collected, however, which included organizational philosophy and beliefs, membership, programs, funding, publications, liaison with other groups and future plans, was not of any value in determining the possibility of civil disturbances and the collection of

Right Wing

American Nazi Party (later National Socialist White People's Party)
National Renaissance Party
Ku Klux Klan
United Klans of America
John Birch Society
The Minutemen
Numerous anti-semitic fringe groups

Left Wing and Anti-War

Workers World Party
Communist Party, USA
Communist Party, Marxist-Leninist
Socialist Workers Party
Progressive Labor Party
Students for a Democratic Society
Southern Students Organizing Committee
Spartacist League
Young Socialist Alliance
National Mobilization Committee to End the War in Vietnam
Student Mobilization to End the War in Vietnam
SANE
Fifth Avenue Vietnam Peace Parade Committee
Business Executives Move to End the War in Vietnam
Clergy and Laymen Concerned About the War
National Lawyers Guild
Emergency Civil Liberties Committee
The Resistance
The Revolutionary Contingent
Yiddisher Kultur Farband
National Conference for New Politics
Women's Strike for Peace
Women's International League for Peace and Freedom
Peace and Freedom Party
Urban League
Youth International Party

Racial

Congress of Racial Equality
National Association for the Advancement of Colored People
Student Non-Violent Coordinating Committee
Revolutionary Action Movement
Southern Christian Leadership Conference
Many local groups opposed to discrimination.

such information constituted complete monitoring of political affairs, in most cases lawful and fully protected by the First Amendment.

It is natural that I can most easily recall the names of the organizations that are well known and often reported on by the news media. I must emphasize here that the Army collected and received information on many purely local groups which engaged entirely in constitutionally protected activity. Examples include black groups devoted solely to securing better housing, vigil groups in New England which met regularly to light candles and pray for peace, and student organizations interested in increasing the relevancy of their education.

Reports on individuals were also kept by CIAB. Again, virtually every prominent leader of a group—racial, right wing, or left wing—

was included as were many, many members. The reports, which often reflected information obtained covertly by either FBI informants or, less frequently, by Army Intelligence special agents, contained information which did not help CIAB analysts prepare the Army for riot duty, but which did bare the individual's life and secrets. Financial information, sexual activities (especially illicit or unconventional), personal beliefs and associations were all reported in great detail. It is again very important to emphasize that while many of the persons recorded in the CIAB file are or were famous, the greater majority are anonymous Americans whose political and social lives were observed, often surreptitiously, with the results being sent to CIAB analysts other Army intelligence units, Federal agencies, and local law enforcement authorities.

Among the better known persons in CIAB's files are:

Dr. Martin Luther King
H. Rap Brown
Whitney Young
Julius Hobson, Sr.
Herbert Aptheker
Bettina Aptheker Kurzweil
Albert Cleage
Stokely Carmichael
David Dellinger
Abbie Hoffman
Thomas Hayden
Rennie Davis
Cora Weiss
Dagmar Wilson
Joan Baez
Arlo Guthrie
Julian Bond
Arlo Tatum
Roy Wilkins
Gus Hall
Conrad Lynn
George Lincoln Rockwell
Bernadine Dohrn
Rear Adm. Arnold E. True, USN, Ret.
Brig. Gen. Hugh B. Hester, USA, Ret.
Brig. Gen. Herbert Holdridge, USA, Ret.
Maj. Gen. Edwin Walker, USA, Ret.
Rev. Ralph David Abernathy
Rev. Jesse Jackson
Hosea Williams
Rev. Walter Fauntroy
Rufus Mayfield
Jerry Rubin
Dr. Benjamin Spock
Rev. William S. Coffin
Rev. James Groppi
A. J. Muste
A. Philip Randolph

It is instructive to relate the process of placing names in CIAB's microfilm data bank, a procedure called coding. Using a special Intelligence Subject Code, the analysts would use various number combinations which indicated a person's status and beliefs. For instance, 134.295 indicated that a person was a non-Communist while 135.295 indicated Communist Party membership or advocacy of communism. While no problem ever existed with a self-proclaimed communist, the individual analyst would have to choose a designation arbitrarily in many doubtful cases or where identifying information was lacking. The result? Many persons who are not communists have been so listed in CIAB's data bank.

At the time of my departure from CIAB, the microfilm data bank contained thousands of names of individuals and hundreds of organizations. Many of the individuals listed were students who merely participated in a meeting or rally sponsored by an organization under surveillance.

The Compendium

In late October 1967, the deputy chief of CIAB, Mr. Parkinson, summoned me to his office and outlined his concept for a new CIAB publication which would serve as an encyclopedic reference book of dissenters and their organizations. This was the beginning of the Counterintelligence Research Project, Persons and Organizations of Civil Disturbance Interest, commonly known as the Compendium. It was originally planned to update this book, published in looseleaf format, regularly. On practical grounds I opposed this project from the onset as I doubted the book could be kept relevant. Later on it became obvious that the information had no intrinsic relevancy to the Army's lawful civil disturbance mission.

The Compendium was published, in early 1968, I believe, with about 375 copies being printed and bound in yellow, three hole looseleaf binders. The classification of this document was secret. The Compendium was published in two volumes. Organizations and personalities were divided into left wing, right wing and racial categories. At a later date, a cities section was added and this constituted the only part of the Compendium which was relevant to the Army's mission.

Each organization and personality was represented by, on the average, one page of text, which summarized the person's or organization's beliefs and activities. Distribution of the Compendium was restricted to military intelligence units and federal internal security agencies.

It was originally Mr. Parkinson's intention, which he stated to me several times, that this Compendium would provide instant information to agents in the field and obviate the need for requesting information from Washington or Fort Holabird. There was no subsequent decrease in requests for information. Actually, requests for data from both the U.S. Army Intelligence Command Investigative Records Repository and from CIAB continued to climb throughout my service.

The information contained in the Compendium, before the section on cities was added, was pure domestic intelligence of political activities. Because it sought to summarize and was updated very infrequently, it had no bearing whatsoever on the execution of the Army's civil disturbance function.

The information in the Compendium was largely obtained from FBI sources, about which more will be said later. I found and still believe that much of the information used in writing the Compendium was either factually inaccurate or misleading. These faults were greatly magnified when the information was utilized to write sketchy, classified summaries which did not indicate sources consulted.

Sources of Information

I would estimate that approximately 80% of the classified information received by CIAB came from the FBI. During my period of service, the FBI obviously made no attempt to screen reports for relevance to the Army mission and so CIAB daily received a veritable flood of information, the major part of which related to totally civilian political activities in which the Army should have had no interest. Reports included information on fund raising by blacks, anti-war protests and speeches in all our cities, detailed background investigations on anti-war protestors arrested for misdemeanor offenses by local police, political activities such as the National Conference for New Politics, Ku Klux Klan meetings, and many reports on the political activities of individuals.

Occasionally the FBI reports forwarded by Mr. Patrick Putnam, the FBI liaison agent to CIAB, would be amusing. An example was their detailed investigation of a mental hospital patient who asserted his claim to the throne of Spain. More often, however, there would be little to laugh at as we read reports which indicated the depth and scope of FBI surveillance of constitutionally protected activity. Many of these reports contained information of such a nature as to indicate that covert means were used to obtain the information.

The FBI reports, which were also furnished to Operations IV at the U.S. Army Intelligence Command, Fort Holabird, were studied by the analysts and many reports were coded. The result of this effort to study FBI reports and incorporate them into the CIAB and Operations IV data banks was to give military intelligence a vast library of unevaluated information which did not contribute to the Army's civil disturbance mission. Never were we able to use the data in the microfilm library to advantage with regard to helping the Army anticipate or control a riot. In fact, a major CIAB study, *Threshholds of Violence,* undertaken in early 1968 by Sergeant George A. Koopman and Mr. Kenneth Zima, stated that there were no indicators available to intelligence which would give advance warning of a civil disturbance.

In addition to providing a daily deluge of reports from all parts of the U.S., the FBI sent regular status reports on various organizations and individuals. This information, which added to the Army's surveillance of civilians, was even less useful than the rest of the information submitted by the Bureau. Two examples will suffice. Every three months the FBI prepares a detailed summary of the activities of the Communist Party, U.S.A. These summaries are regional in nature and there are many of them, at least 25. Generally based on the reports of informers, these reports detail the finances, programs, activities, meetings and other ascertained information on the Communist Party in a particular region. These reports, which suggested to all who read them that the CPUSA had become a moribund group, were put in the microfilm data bank. It is possible that there may be some substantial reason why the FBI is still collecting such information so intensively, but there is no reason why the Army should receive such reports. They told us nothing about civil disturbances; they told us everything about the political activities of CPUSA members.

The FBI also put out status reports on the New Left. Again, although these reports purported to warn about possible violence, the language and analyses were so general in nature that they made no contribution to Army Intelligence other than to provide still more information on the activities of civilians. The same comment can be validly made with reference to FBI reports on the Ku Klux Klan.

Approximately 600 persons were arrested at the October 21, 1967 Pentagon anti-war protest. Most of these arrests on a Federal, not a military, reservation were for misdemeanor offenses and most of those so charged were young demonstrators. The FBI conducted a background investigation on each of the individuals taken into custody and provided the Army with reports that not only listed the details of the offense but also revealed the individual's background, education, schooling, membership in groups, associations, travels and often contained information on other members of the subject's family as well. I doubt whether probation officers receive as detailed a history of their charges as we received on these people.

FBI reports were not the only source of information for CIAB. Reports from the field special agents of the U.S. Army Intelligence Command comprised a major source of information. Some of these reports were unclassified and were on-site reporting of demonstrations and meetings. It often seemed to us, as we watched the teletypwriter print one of these spot reports after another, that virtually every public protest meeting was monitored by Army agents, with the results being immediately forwarded to Washington through Baltimore. These reports came in around-the-clock. During civil disturbance, these reports, which were then occasionally useful, indicated the agent's perception of the situation. During more normal times, however, such reports concerned labor negotiations, vigils for peace, pro-Vietnam rallies, anti-war activities far removed from military installations and purely criminal occurrences, especially in inner cities.

Agent Reports, form DA-341, were utilized to report classified information or to transmit enclosures, Such reports contained information on penetration operations by military intelligence special agents into black and student groups. Agent Reports were sent from the field to the Operations IV section at Fort Holabird which was administered by Mr. Andrew Havre, a civilian career intelligence officer. Many of these reports were the sent to CIAB; all were available at Operations IV for CIAB researchers and I used the facilities several times. These reports reflected activities on campus, particularly with regard to coordination and planning for nationwide antiwar protests.

The enclosures sent with agent reports usually consisted of handbills, flyers, newspaper articles, "underground" newspapers, and similar material. The information reported was generally of local interest only and of legitimate Army interest virtually never (the exception being when the articles or flyers suggested direct action against the Army). Again, this mass of material was carefully catalogued, especially at Operations IV.

Another source of information for CIAB was publications which were received either openly at our office or at a cover location. We received each morning the *New York Times*, the *Washington Post* and the *Wall Street Journal* and each week such publications as the *National Observer*. These publications came right to our office. Analysts scanned the papers for articles relating to their desk and then clipped the articles and either had them microfilmed or put into the files. Several persons, including a Federal judge, have characterized this activity as being both harmless in essence and constituting the major part of domestic intelligence surveillance. I emphatically state that it was neither. The overwhelming bulk of material in CIAB's files was classified. Newspaper articles were used to help complete the picture and were often retained so that unclassified responses could be made with the authority cited. The maintenance of files which included newspaper files allowed the Army to have a domestic surveillance instrument that, in scope, covered every conceivable activity, legal and illegal.

When CIAB desired a publication but did not want the publishers to know that Army Intelligence was interested in them, a cover address was used. This was R. Allan Lee Associates, Box 922, Alexandria, Virginia 22333. Publications as diverse as the *Berkely Barb* and the newsletter of SANE were received regularly.

I have talked about the input into CIAB and about the Compendium. On a daily basis, however, the information collected was put to two main uses: the preparation of briefings and the written responses to requests for information, commonly called "actions."

Briefings were delivered on request to the Assistant Chief of Staff for Intelligence, other members of the General Staff and to personnel in the Army Operations Center during riots, commitment of Federal troops, and at less appropriate times such as during the monitoring of the Poor People's Campaign. The AOC briefings generally constituted a legitimate function and were often relevant to the crisis at hand. The briefings for the ACSI, however, were often a different story. These briefings were called "desktop" briefings, were generally by request, and dealt almost exclusively with civilian groups and personalities.

Sometime after the Pentagon demonstration, the ACSI, Maj. Gen. William P. Yarborough, requested a weekly briefing on a group engaged in dissident, either left wing or racial. Choice of groups to be briefed was left to CIAB. As a matter of convenience, we alternated with the Racial Desk presenting one week and my Left Wing Desk the next. These briefings went on for quite a few months. Often, Gen. Yarborough would be absent and the briefing would be delivered before the Deputy ACSI, Maj. Gen. Wesley M. Franklin or Brig. Gen. Vasco Finelli. The connection between the Army's role in civil disturbances and the material covered in these briefings was highly tenuous or wholly absent. In effect, the ACSI was receiving a weekly political intelligence briefing which stressed the activities of the group of the week and its membership. I personally briefed on the Young Socialist Alliance, the Students for a Democratic Society, the Fifth Avenue Vietnam Peace Parade Committee and the National Mobilization Committee to End the War in Vietnam to name a few. My colleagues on the Racial Desk briefed on the Southern Christian

Leadership Conference, RAM, and on a number of local black self-help groups.

Briefings on individuals also were frequent. For reasons still unclear to me, there was a great preoccupation on the part of many General Staff members with the background and activities of David Dellinger. There seemed to be a belief that he controlled so vast a segment of dissenters that he could initiate violence at his pleasure. I prepared a briefing on Mr. Dellinger, drawing heavily from classified files, which reflected his life's work, philosophy, travels, and future plans as well as present activities and associations. It was evident to my co-workers, as it was to me, that whatever opinion one might personally hold of Mr. Dellinger, and mine was negative, he was not behind any riot anywhere at any time nor did he ever plan to cause a riot. Yet requests to be briefed on Mr. Dellinger were numerous. I last briefed on this subject in the summer of 1968 before Lieut. Gen. George Mather, then chief of what was called the Directorate of Civil Disturbance Plans and Operations. An Air Force major general also attended the briefing. The fascination and interest by these generals, as well as by many others in the Pentagon, is indicative of the counterproductive paradigm, verbalized by the general staff, that key men were behind disturbances and agitators started urban riots.

I wish to relate one further briefing before discussing written responses because, more than any other briefing, this one still disturbs me today. I went to the Central Intelligence Agency at McLean, Virginia, in the company of then Captain Darrell R. Johnson, my immediate supervisor at the time (I believe it was late in 1967) to deliver a briefing on "underground" and student protest newspapers. Mr. Jim Ludlum of the CIA had requested the briefing several days before and he was present with three other men whose names I no longer recall. Although the ostensible purpose of my briefing was to acquaint them with the financing for the purpose of determining if there was any foreign support (there wasn't—most of the papers were going broke), the questions asked suggested a deep interest in the beliefs of the students who published these papers. I think an inquiry into the CIA's involvement in domestic intelligence is needed. I made a number of remarks at CIAB after the briefing regarding the type of information requested by the CIA and my confusion about their interest and I was then told by Mr. Parkinson that I would not have to deal with Mr. Ludlum in the future. I saw Mr. Ludlum at CIAB on several subsequent occasions.

This was not the first time I had been asked to analyze, in detail, publications and their sponsors. At one point I prepared a very complete study of *Ramparts* magazine which included an analysis of the editorial policy of that publication as well as complete background summaries on its leading editors and writers. This report was given to Mr. Merrill Kelly of the Directorate of Security.

Written responses to requests for information entailed either a quick response or an involved study which might take weeks. In most instances the request for information came from the Pentagon, often from the ACSI itself.

I would like to relate two examples of unnecessary requests for information before discussing more serious examples of domestic intelligence. In late 1967 or early 1968, a brigadier general assigned to the Pentagon, whose name may have been Deane, requested a report, of an unclassified nature, on the Students for a Democratic Society. He stated that his daughter was then attending Briarcliff College in New York State and that she was quite concerned about the increased interest in SDS among the student body and wished to have facts at her fingertips so she could combat the SDS. I accordingly prepared a history of SDS and a summary of its activities from the *New York Times, Time, Newsweek* and publicly available SDS publications. This report, which took several hours of Army time to produce, was sent to the general for mailing to his daughter at her school. This unclassified report was placed in the CIAB reading file. It was still there in April 1970 when I first disclosed this incident. The Army feels the need to downgrade my account and Colonel John Downie, the Director of Security at ACSI, has stated that the request was only for a list of schools at which SDS chapters were known to exist. Such a list, incidentally, was maintained at CIAB, but was classified because SDS never published a list of member chapters.

Perhaps the strangest request came from ACSI on December 1st of 1967 when General Yarborough received a marketing research questionnaire which asked if he preferred *Newsweek, Time* or *U.S. News and World Report.* The researchers attached a new quarter to the form. General Yarborough penned the following note to the Director of Security: "What kind of an outfit is this? Why do they give quarters away? Y." The Director of Security logged the memo, assigning it number 370 and sent it to CIAB where is was given to me for response. I made a formal response, in writing, in which I explained the psychology of making a token payment in the hope of insuring a response.

Far more indicative of the scope of domestic intelligence were the many requirements for reports on individuals active in the anti-war movement or in racial affairs. CIAB prepared many reports on the activities of Dr. Benjamin Spock, Stokely Carmichael, Thomas Hayden, Dr. Martin Luther King, Rev. Ralph David Abernathy, and on many others. Even military heroes were not exempt and reports on the travels of much decorated retired Rear Admiral Arnold E. True were frequent. I spent much time preparing a complete background report on a retired reserve brigadier general, a WW II Silver Star recipient, who spoke out publicly against the Vietnam war on Memorial Day, 1967, in the Midwest. Very often, the request for information would follow a widely reported public appearance by the person in question and there would be no relevance whatsoever to civil disturbances and would not be related in any way to plans to deploy troops.

Liaison With Field Units

Towards the end of 1967, increasing dissatisfaction was voiced by supervisors at CIAB about the quality and quantity of information being provided by Intelligence Command units in the field. After several liaison conferences, authority was granted for CIAB to dispatch analysts to the field to initiate liaison with the working special agents. In February 1968, I went on the first liaison trip which afforded me the opportunity to perceive the depth of field office involvement in domestic intelligence. While I had many friends and acquaintances who were keeping me up to date on their surveillance activities and I realized how deep the Army's involvement was from my Washington office, this trip was still quite a revelation.

Our trip, which covered the First Army area, began at G-2, First U.S. Army, Fort George G. Meade, Maryland, At a conference attended by representative of the 109th Military Intelligence Group, it was stated that the collection of information on dissident groups, particularly blacks and anti-war demonstrators, had to be increased. A Col. Brinley outlined the needs of the First Army which, to me, seemed both all inclusive and irrelevant to the Army's proper role.

We then traveled to Boston and held a conference with the officers of the 108th Military Intelligence Group at the Boston Field Office. We explained to them that an increase in CONUS Intelligence has been mandated and they indicated that while they were behind in carrying out their primary mission, Personnel Security Investigations, they would try to increase their domestic surveillance, especially of colleges in the Boston area.

From Boston we flew to New York City where Lt. Col. Luther Morris, the 108th's region commander, informed us that he considered domestic intelligence collection to be a challenge which his unit would meet. Actually, the 108th in New York City had more material than any other place I had visited previously or would visit subsequently. Under the direction of a woman employee, a black who was supposedly well connected with black militants, a large filing system had been established on dissident groups, student activists and campus goings-on. This woman informed me that she frequently went out on nighttime intelligence gathering operations with the knowledge and tacit approval of her supervisor. Capt. Alfred Diaz, of 108th MI Group headquarters, acquainted us with the 108th plan for future collection which indicated even wider parameters for domestic surveillance. Incidentally, it was this office which infiltrated an agent into a black studies course at New York University.

A visit to Philadelphia followed and a lecture by the commander there indicated that that office was well aware of domestic intelligence requirements and was seeking to meet them. The chief complaint in Philadelphia, voiced I believe by a Capt. White, was that too many agents were shipped off to Vietnam before they could get familiar enough with the city to effectively engage in domestic intelligence. The Philadelphia office maintained, as did all offices visited by myself and other team members, effective ongoing liaison with the local police.

Our last job on this trip was to a region headquarters of the 109th in Columbus, Ohio. The main topic of interest to this office was Ohio State University. Their files reflected much on student activity and virtually nothing of relevance to mlitary requirements with regard to civil disturbances.

When comparing notes with other CIAB personnel on their trips, both during my service and since, the verdict was always the same: A great deal of collection of information on activities that were either lawful or were of only local law enforcement interest with a noticeable consequent weakening of the unit's ability to perform its vital task of insuring that persons requiring security clearances from the Army receive thorough and professional background investigations.

I would point out here that while only a few of the Army's more than 1,000 agents in the U.S. spent most of their time collecting information on civilian activities, all spent all of their time when an event occurred which the Intelligence Command wished followed. An example of this was the Poor People's Campaign.

The April 1968 Riots

I spent quite a bit of time in the Army Operations Center during the April 1968 riots. The information we had been collecting for so long was useless when the rioting actually occurred. Some generals, however, were obsessed with the idea that individuals were behind the rioting and we were required to brief these officers on the whereabouts of certain "key agitators." Stokely Carmichael was allegedly a key conspirator and we enjoyed one of the few amusing episodes of that tragic week as we reported, all within the space of one hour, that Mr. Carmichael had been "accurately" reported to be in (1) NW Washington, (2) Baltimore, (3) Atlanta and (4) Salt Lake City doing one of two things (a) telling people to get guns and fight or (b) telling everyone to "cool it" and go home. The last time I reported the location of the incredibly peripatetic Mr. Carmichael, a somewhat unhappy Gen. Johnson, the Chief of Staff, stated he wanted the name and organization of each person calling in further reports on Mr. Carmichael.

Poor People's Campaign

Army Intelligence monitored the progress of the PPC as it had never monitored anything before. Agents followed every march, attended every rally, took scores of photos, and filed hundreds of reports. This monitoring continued throughout the life of the PPC and Resurrection City. While the Army certainly had a right to know how many people would be camping in Washington, this information was easily obtained from local sources. The blanket coverage of the PPC was the largest coordinated surveillance operation during or since my service.

Up to this point I have discussed the input and output of CIAB without discussing the personnel involved. I wish to indicate here briefly, the background of some of the analysts who were preparing and delivering briefings and writing responses to questions. Bear in mind the complexity of the issues of black militancy, urban decay, and youth alienation.

The right wing analyst had a B.A. in American studies with his major interest being political developments in the 1870s and 1880s. He had no experience working with black communities or with right wing groups.

The first Racial Desk analyst had no experiential or educational background or training in racial problems and yet he briefed generals on the Black mood in America. He was highly conscientious and tried to learn, but his reports understandably reflected his lack of knowledge of Negro affairs.

The officer who took charge of my desk in January 1968 had just graduated the basic intelligence officer's course after transferring from Armor. He had a B.S. in chemistry and no background in domestic and political affairs. He had been out of the country the previous year serving in Vietnam where he commanded a tank unit.

A West Point graduate with an infantry background and straight from Vietnam took over the racial desk from the original analyst. An exceptionally perceptive officer, he learned quickly and contributed much to balance the picture.

The officer who daily prepared a summary known as the Black Book which recounted domestic disturbances throughout the country for the previous 24 hours and who read this brifing to Undersecretary McGiffert each morning, made no secret of his strong right wing, anti-black attitude. Despite pressure from several domestic analysts at CIAB, he continued to present misleading reports to Mr. McGiffert. It is my understanding that Mr. McGiffert considered this officer's morning briefings to be worthless and irrelevant.

I came to CIAB straight from Korea with an academic background in Asian and American social history and political science. Of course I was out of contact with many trends in America and I had to learn quite fast.

The civilians who worked in domestic intelligence were highly conscientious men who were trained for espionage and counter-intelligence operations overseas. Their mentality, with regard to subversive threats, was unfortunately too often based on 1950's challenges and problems. These men had spent the major part of their adult lives overseas, had raised their families there, and were assigned to duties in the U. S. for what was derisively termed "a repatriation tour." Every one of these men was eager to return overseas and each made frequent efforts to secure an overseas transfer and some succeeded. Their concepts and thought processes were not geared to evaluating sociological and political data, even if the military was justified in collecting such data. These men usually supervised—Mr. Parkinson was the branch deputy chief—and often delivered the more important briefings. Several had retired from active duty in intelligence, had gone straight to work for the Army, and were civilian in name only.

To briefly summarize, CIAB, during my period of service, had substantially invested itself in domestic intelligence of a political and social nature. Files and the microfilm data bank contained much information not only on well-known organizations and publicly recognized leaders, but also on many anonymous Americans engaged in the lawful pursuit of their goals for social change. Most often the goals of these people were meritorious, sometimes they were questionable, bizarre, or illegal. Rarely, however, was the information necessary for the proper maintenance of the Army's capacity to carry out its lawful mission. In the instances where the Army had a right to information as, for instance, with regard to attempts to induce dissent, the ability of military intelligence to carry out its responsibilities was heavily compromised by the overbroad nature of domestic collection. I will try to show later why this overbroad activity came about and what can be done about it.

Investigation of Army Intelligence in Domestic Affairs

When I left the Army in October 1968 I was very concerned about the nature and scope of military intelligence activities when those activities included surveillance operations, covert penetrations of organizations, and massive data keeping, sometimes with the use of computers. Examples of computer usage for domestic intelligence include the CIAB computer indexed microfilm data bank, the computerized data bank at Fort Holabird and similar if not as extensive data banks at Fortress Monroe, Virginia and the U. S. Strike Command at McDill Air Force Base. When I first became aware of the Army's interest in civilian affairs while assigned to Ft. Holabird in May 1966, I tended to dismiss any misgivings because of my impending departure for Korea and my lack of knowledge of the growing assault on privacy and a clear understanding of the damaging effects on First Amendment rights posed by the Army's surveillance activities.

After seeing the domestic intelligence effort expand, with no apparent end in sight, I decided to take positive action to curb what I now consider to be one of the greatest threats to civil liberties in my lifetime. Before I left the Army I had applied for an intelligence position as a civilian. I had planned to make my disclosures anonymously if I were employed by the Army. However, my plans changed when I became engaged and married shortly after leaving the Army and my wife convinced me that delaying a return to school was not in our interest. After informing the Army's Administrative Survey Detachment that I was no longer interested in employment I began to ponder the manner in which I could most effectively bring out the story of the military's monitoring of civilian activities.

Working with Christopher Pyle for over a year has brought me into contact with many former special agents and some active duty members of the Army's Intelligence Command. My study is far from over, but I would like to acquaint you with the experiences of a few of my sources to indicate the scope and involvement of military intelligence.

One agent, whom I will call Agent A, spent many hours following the Poor People's Campaign as its mule train passed through Georgia. He had the task of racing ahead of the mule train to alert the sheriff in each town to be reached. During the time he was with the mule train, he was expected to pick up as much information as possible. Equipped with an Army 35 mm. camera, he took as many pictures as he could, including photographs of the mules.

Agent B observed the preparations for the Poor People's Campaign in Seattle. With his camera he monitored the activities of the Seattle contingent to Washington. He was told to eavesdrop and obtain as much information as possible. His photographs were wanted so that military intelligence could identify the leaders of this small, totally non-violent group whose members were waiting for a bus. Unfortunately for Agent B, he used most of his film on the most militant-looking participant only to find out later that the man was a penetrant undercover agent who was accompanying the marchers. ("That's Mr. Brown. We don't need his picture!")

Agent C in New York City was far behind on his backlog of routine investigations. However, he had to do the work of two men because so many agents of the New York Field Office were checking train departures, bus charter companies and airlines to determine who was participating in the Poor People's Campaign. The same fate had befallen Agent C during the October 1967 Pentagon demonstration and, to a lesser degree, on numerous other occasions. He felt the general quality of background investigations in New York was minimal.

Agent D from the New York Field Office was sent with another agent to cover the October 1967 Pentagon protest. Although he was supposed to phone in any reports he heard suggesting plans for violence, he was also told to find out as much as possible about the leadership and membership of New York anti-war groups by posing as a demonstrator and joining an anti-war group.

Agent E, stationed in Washington, D. C., was known to be against the war so his superiors weren't too surprised when he marched as a demonstrator in an anti-war moratorium the day after he attended a similar rally to gather information on who was behind the protest and to report on what participants said.

Agent F was pulled off his routine assignment to attend the Republican National Convention in Miami in 1968. He was told to walk about the floor without specific instructions as to what to do. He was, not a part of the protective services and he was not armed. He simply walked around the floor

Agent G monitored reports on activities by informants working for military intelligence who reported on soldiers patronizing anti-war off-post coffee houses on the West Coast. These informants concerned themselves with reporting views on the war expressed by the soldier-patrons as well as by attempting to find out as much about the people who ran these activities as could be ascertained.

Agent H covertly attended a meeting of the sanitation workers' union in Atlanta, Georgia, in the late summer of 1968. He reported back on the progress of negotiations. Another informant stated that members of the 111th Military Intelligence Group videotaped this meeting, but I have been unable to confirm this so far.

Agent I spent a weekend watching drunk college students live it up in White, South Dakota. Shortly before this episode, a drunken brawl called Sip to Zap had resulted in a great deal of material damage to that little South Dakota town. The region commander for that area for the 113th Military Intelligence Group, Lt. Col. Matson, was somewhat less than happy that his agent was conducting liaison with the North Dakota National Guard at Bismarck while the kids had their spree and he determined that Army Intelligence would not miss out the second time.

Agent I's estimate of the possibility of Federal troop involvement was that no such possibility existed. He broke out laughing when I questioned him on that point and explained that his boss believed the Army should cover everything that happened in the region.

Agent J traveled to Milwaukee, Wisconsin, to conduct surveillance of mothers on welfare who wanted higher payments. Along with several other agents, he spent several days monitoring the protest and sending back spot reports.

Agent K, assigned to Washington, D. C., had a chauffer's assignment during the life of Resurrection City. His job was to drive a nervous black major who had penetrated Resurrection City to and from that area. Agent K reported that the major had orders to find out as much about the camp and the Southern Christian Leadership Conference as possible.

Agents of the U. S. Army Intelligence Command performed not only the duties cited above, but engaged in many more activities of a similar nature. Most, to their credit, recognized the absurdity or illegitimacy of their domestic intelligence assignment. I am currently contacting other sources with similar experiences. I have had to omit some sources' stores at this time because they are still in the service or working in a sensitive area.

Analysis

"What's wrong with the Army just because they're watching civilians?" "If people have nothing to hide, why should they care if the Army is interested in them?" I have been asked those questions by some people as I travelled through our country. Fortunately, the overwhelming majority of people with whom I have had contact understand the peril to civil liberties caused by military surveillance of civilian activities. I have answered as best I could those who do not understand this grave threat to our freedom.

Experts from the legal and academic world, such as Professor Arthur Miller and Mr. Pyle, have presented their views, perhaps more cogently than I have and certainly with more authority. As a past participant in domestic intelligence and an ongoing student of military surveillance, I would like to present my feelings and suggest a course of action.

Wherever we turn today we are exhorted to remember America's traditions. Conservatives remind us of loyalty and past accomplishments, many of which we can truly view with pride, and the radical left points out that our existence as a nation is founded on revolutionary action. Perhaps none of our traditions is so vital to the security of our form of government than the separation of civil-military responsibilities and the maintenance of civilian hegemony over the military. This tradition has been imperilled by the growth of the domestic intelligence operations of the U. S. Army, at times supported by similar activities of the Navy and the Air Force.

To further understand the problem we must recognize several key and immutable facets of military sociology and psychology. The professional soldier is trained for war, steeped in a tradition which emphasizes force as the final arbiter and instills a moral code which, however well suited to the exigencies of warfare and military service, has little relevance to the process of understanding and solving the complex urban and social problems of today. Isolated by assignment from the mainstream of American life and living an insular life in which conformity is prized and dissent is looked down upon or even forbidden, the professional soldier brings uniquely military paradigms to bear when confronted with civil problems. This is what has happened at the highest levels of military intelligence. The desperate search for information and the initiating of overbroad requirements are examples both of the deadly disease called bureaucratic accretion and the application of military and even combat standards to the American scene. The gulf between civil and military thinking is too great to be bridged and the framers of our Constitution realized this perhaps better than we do today. The reliance on force, the readiness to believe in conspiratorial theories, the lack of identification with social problems and the immense force of our military are sufficient pragmatic reasons for reinforcing the Constitutional mandate and long tradition or military non-involvement in civilian affairs.

A second major point to consider is the deleterious effect the involvement in CONUS intelligence has had on the ability of military intelligence to carry out its legitimate mission. Firstly, and I cannot stress this enough, the use of military intelligence agents in domestic situations causes a morale problem because it brings out very subjective attitudes and causes no small degree of polarization among the agents, particularly if black agents are involved. This polarization occurred in CIAB. The fact that the Army has no explicit statutory authority for such surveillance and data keeping only causes increased alienation and bitterness among the agents. Today the Army has tremendously reduced its activities in the area of domestic intelligence and the Intelligence Command is emphasizing compartmentalization and the exclusion of first termers from sensitive operations because of the fear of further unpleasant disclosures. This hardly addresses the real problem.

I have spoken of the attitude of the agents. What is the attitude of those surveilled? My experience has convinced me that while a few activists may dismiss the Army's activities as to be expected, the majority of people are genuinely inhibited in the exercise of Constitutionally protected rights.

I would like to mention a recent encounter which thoroughly chilled me. I participated in a TV talk show in Detroit hosted by a black community organizer. The format of the show allowed for questions from the audience which was composed entirely of blacks. Some were obvious supporters of militant groups. Others wore conservative dress and a few were college students. I was prepared for the usual questions which consist of "Who did what to whom?" The first person to get up asked me about the existence of a plan for the genocidal extinction of blacks through the use of military forces. I was about to dismiss my questioner's fears, perhaps casually, when I realized that his question had electrified the entire audience. After trying to convince him that I believed we had no Hitlers in our military and government, the rest of the audience began expressing their fears. These people believed that the Army must have a terribly malevolent intent in collecting this information and there was no dissuading them that something less dramatic, bureaucratic accretion and inappropriate paradigms, was responsible for the Army surveillance's and data keeping.

We can reverse the steady draining of the right to privacy and restore a measure of confidence in our military without endangering or weakening our internal security. The military must be permanently removed from the domestic intelligence picture. While I am hopeful that the courts will take a firm stand on this issue, I feel that legislation is necessary to hold the military in check. The recent statement by Secretary Laird, in which he insisted on a higher level of accountability, and the Army directive of Dec. 15, 1970, set the tone and indicated parameters for safeguarding Constitutional rights but past experience and study have convinced me that we cannot depend on the good intentions of individual bureaucrats nor can we rely on in-house directives to insure compliance when the present furor subsides.

Legislation is needed that will define the Army's legitimate concerns with regard to its security and its posture to effectively carry out its civil disturbance mission. I suggest the following guidelines:

- Domestic intelligence should be defined as the acquisition of knowledge by any means, covert or overt, about the political, social, economic, educational, and personal affairs of non-military Americans and the groups to which they belong.
- The military should have the right, and indeed it has the responsibility, to maintain accurate information on the access routes to American cities and the physical geography of such cities. As Senator Ervin has stated, the military's business is to know about bivouac areas, airports, parks, bridges, tunnels, and similar structures and facilities.
- The military should have the right to receive information from other agencies when the information directly concerns members or

employees of the Army or where a direct threat against the Army is evident.

• The military should be prohibited from gathering and maintaining information on the political and social, educational and economic affairs of civilians and the organizations to which they belong and the military should be prohibited from obtaining such information from any sources.

• Because so many military intelligence activities in the past were initiated by junior officers and civilians misinterpreting, reinterpreting or exceeding the scope of directives, legislation should provide for strict accountability from those few who may violate its provisions.

• Training is a vital part of indoctrinating a new agent and I believe that legislation should direct that an expanded course in civil liberties and the Army's position in American life be presented at all service intelligence schools and that such courses be monitored by civilian attorneys from the Army and/or the Department of Justice. Such a course can hardly be classified and the presence of civilian attorneys will at once emphasize the seriousness and resolve of the government to maintain the traditional civil-military relationship.

• Present files must be purged, through legislative requirements, with the right of inspection granted to cleared members of Congress. I have encountered too many incidents of deliberate evasion, continuing right to the present day, to believe that by administrative decree all subordinate commands will comply. As of last November the Army still could not locate all the copies of the Compendium which it desired destroyed.

The need for Congressional supervision cannot be too strongly stressed if we art to safeguard our Constitutional rights. Even when motivated by the best of intentions, the military will always view an issue more narrowly than the general populace of civilians and perceive threats where none exist. The military must protect itself from genuine threats to its security but too often it interprets every sign of dissent as a bugle call summoning enemies to destroy its structure and efficiency.

We now know what is wrong. We cannot stop until we have erected safeguards and effected remedies which will insure privacy for the individual and respect for his First Amendment rights, a renewed commitment to the concept of separation of civil-military relationships with the civil authorities firmly in control, and a paramount concern for the zealous preservation of First Amendment rights.

9

THE CONUS COVERUP

By Edward D. Sohier

In August 1970 I was separated from the Army, honorably, with the Army Commendation Medal and the rank of Specialist, 5, E-5. I had spent nearly three years on active duty, 15 months of which on duty with the Counterintelligence Analysis Division (CIAD), Directorate of Counterintelligence, Office of the Assistant Chief of Staff for Intelligence (OACSI). I had entered the Army in October 1967, taken basic training at Fort Bragg, North Carolina, and was trained as a military stenographer at Fort Benjamin Harrison, Indiana. In May 1968, I joined the 902d Military Intelligence Group, which then had administrative control of CIAD. In January 1970, when the 902d MI Group became part of the U. S. Army Intelligence Command, CIAD remained under the control of OACSI.

My first encounter with the so-called CONUS intelligence program was in my first job at CIAD. That was assisting in the preparation of the two-volume publication, *Personalities, Organizations, and Cities of Interest,* called by CIAD "the Compendium." This book, which was to be updated five times in the period I was with CIAD, was a compilation of information on individuals and organizations in this country which were regarded as potentially involved in domestic disturbances, in particular, in connection with anti-war and civil rights activities. Included in the lists were organizations such as Women's Strike for Peace, Southern Christian Leadership Conference, National Association for the Advancement of Colored People, American Civil Liberties Union, Quaker Action Committee, National Mobilization Committee (to End the War in Vietnam), American Friends Service Committee, and many other such peace and civil right groups, as well as more radical groups such as Students for a Democratic Society, Black Panther Party, and Weathermen. Individuals listed included the late Dr. Martin Luther King, Dr. Benjamin Spock, Dr. Ralph Abernathy, H. Rap Brown, and Eldridge Cleaver.

The Compendium was very widely distributed by OACSI. It was sent to elements of the armed forces in the continental U. S. (CONUS). and worldwide. It was sent to other branches of the government including the Justice Department (Federal Bureau of Investigation), Treasury Department (Secret Service), and State Department. It was augmented five times with changes (additions and deletions of pages of information), and, when the order was given to destroy all copies of the Compendium in the summer of 1970, a sixth change was in the works." The Compendium "was classified SECRET."

The CIAD also provided the armed forces and branches of the government with other publications regarding this area of interest. One was what was called an estimate, which provided an analysis of past events in the nation and an estimate of the potential for domestic disorders for the upcoming period. I believe this publication was prepared annually. Its purpose was to inform the Army commands of the potential need for Army support required to keep order in the nation in case of disorders.

The OACSI, and in particular, CIAD, was tasked with the responsibility of providing the Army with information regarding potentially disrupting situations in the United States. Since the Army has the responsibility of responding to a national call for aid in restoring order, it needs an agency to keep it informed of the potential for that call for aid, and thus, the potential for civil disturbances. In doing so OACSI kept a sharp eye and ear on potential "trouble-makers" both individuals and organizations, and their activities.

Much of the information was gathered by CIAD from the press. Most of the rest of the information was supplied by direct liaison with the Federal Bureau of Investigation, and, to a lesser extent, some other government investigative-type agencies. By far the largest supplier of information reports was the FBI, from whom CIAD almost daily received foot-high stacks of information reports. Naturally, the FBI was a recipient of CIDA reports, too, but CIAD received much more than it supplied. Another channel of information to the CIAD analysts was through the U.S. Army Intelligence Command's teletype, which would supply as many as 100 "spot reports" daily. These reports were forwarded to the Command at Fort Holabird, Maryland, for teletype distribution to other "interested" Army intelligence and investigative agencies. In almost all cases, the reports concerned meetings and minor incidents all over the country. Many of them were like the one which comes to mind, regarding simply a meeting of 200 people in a church in Philadelphia. The report would state that 200 people attended a meeting today in such-and-such church, and that there were no incidents. Almost all reports were read and discarded by CIAD analysts, and were generally regarded as worthless.

The CIAD analysts working in the domestic field maintained voluminous files. They were files of clippings from the press, FBI reports, and other information from other agencies, within and without the Army. A computerized index had been prepared for the files, though there was no computer at CIAB's office in Alexandria, Virginia. The computer experts at CIAD used card-punching and other facilities of OACSI in the Pentagon to prepare the index. Dossiers were frequently received by CIAD analysis from the U.S. Army Investigative Records Repository at Fort Holabird.

During the time I was at CIAD the domestic intelligence program grew immensely. When I joined the group there were perhaps ten members of the domestic section. When I left there were about twice that number. In that period the computerized index was developed. During that period the number of publications in this field produced by CIAD grew, and the number of reports received by CIAD analysts probably tripled.

In January 1970, OACSI was shocked by the publication of an article in *Washington Monthly* magazine by former Army Captain Christopher H. Pyle. The OACSI put together what it called a "Task Group" in one of its offices at the Pentagon to work on problems that stemmed from sudden disclosure of Army activities in this field. The Task Group originally numbered about eight persons, several of whom were from CIAD. I was one, the only enlisted member, and I joined them originally as a typist and administrative man. The Task Group, over the next few months, was responsible for formulating new Army policy to appease critics of the domestic intelligence program, and for replying to letters from Senators, Congressmen, and citizens. Although letters went out over the signatures of Major General McChristian, Assistant Chief of Staff for Intelligence, and others, nearly all were produced by this small group, put together for just this purpose.

The first reaction by CIAD to the Pyle article was, in typical fashion, to sit down and write a paragraph-by paragraph refutation of every charge that Mr. Pyle made. This went on for about two weeks, but there was no end result, for meanwhile the Task Group had been formed in the Pentagon to assume this fuction. The Task Group answered Congressional inquiries and press inquiries on this area of interest, and proceeded from the start to deny any and all charges, factual or otherwise. Eventually, with more and more Senators and Congressmen interested and informed, the group found it necessary to begin admitting some of the charges, but the Task Group, assumedly under orders from above, never admitted any more than it absolutely had to. It even went so far as to provide the Army's own General Counsel with misinformation at one point, so bent on denial was this group.

Time and time again replies that were prepared by the group to respond to Congressional and citizens' criticism admitted and denied charges at will, disregarding considerations concerning the truth of their statements.

This was, I believe, a natural reaction of members of what is referred to by its members as the "intelligence community." There is a definite feeling of privilege among members of this "community"—privilege in respect to access to information and immunity to probing questions not only from citizens but also from the Congress and other departments of the government. There is within the Army a general distrust of Congress anyway, for Congress, a body of civilians, holds the power of funds over the military; professional military men feel their job would be easier without civilian interference in military matters; this feeling is much magnified in the military intelligence community, where it is coupled with the feeling of privilege and immunity.

By the time of my separation from active duty, several directives had been issued to try to solve the problems that arose out of the "Pyle Case." First, the Compendium was ordered destroyed, and destruction certificates were directed to be forwarded to the Task Group. I was responsible for checking the list of Compendium recipients against the growing stack of destruction certificates, but it was generally understood that, because of a faulty system of accounting for that particular secret document, we were probably never to account for all the Compendia. In addition to this problem, many recipients of the Compendium had difficulty locating and accounting for the documents in their own offices. It is likely that OACSI will never guarantee that all copies distributed have been destroyed. Also, because the directive only ordered the destruction of those two volumes, not the information contained therein, I found that at least one recipient Xeroxed its copy of the book in order to be able to destroy its one official copy noted in OACSI records, while retaining a copy for further use. I have little doubt that this was done more than once. In fact, it was known at the time that the originating office for the Compendium, CIAD, had, in fact, microfilmed its own copy of the book for the same reason as above.

Other directives which were issued during the summer restricted the kinds of reports that could be sent over the Fort Holabird teletype, the kinds of activities agents in the field could be dispatched to cover, restrictions on the use of covert and "undercover" agents, and the kinds of files and filing techniques that could and could not be used for storing domestic intelligence information.

The restrictions on the use of convert agents were interesting, for, each time the Army was questioned on this subject, it immediately stated that it had express orders forbidding that type of activity. However, when the press finally was able to specify some incidents of this type of activity (for instance, 116th MI Group agents in Washington, D.C., posing as newsmen with a van marked "Midwest News," covering anti-war demonstrations), official Army replies stated simply that covert agent activities had been banned, except with the express permission of the Secretary of the Army.

Probably the most agile defensive moves were made by the Army concerning its computers. Replies to initial press and Congressional inquiries concerning Army computers were that there were none, period. This, of course, was done with full knowledge that there were computers, but without knowledge of, or, it appears, curiosity about, the kinds of work they were doing in the Army. Again, after heated exchanges with members of Congress and the press, the Army spokesmen (again, Task Group) were forced to go out and do some investigating on their own. The results were as surprising to Army brass in the Pentagon as to civilians and shortly thereafter orders were issued that computerized files may no longer be maintained or initiated on domestic intelligence activities, without the express permission of the Chief of Staff. Again, however, there were few restrictions on the type of information that may be kept; restrictions here only regarded what may or may not be kept in the *computerized* file.

Despite assurances by Army spokesmen that improper activities have been halted and will not begin again, my personal feeling is that a careful and constant watch will have to be maintained on the Army and other branches of the government which continue to harass and intimidate citizens with irresponsibly and clumsily constructed files. One of the most amazing discoveries I made during this period was concerning the nature of many of the files, and the criteria used to select those individuals and organizations "of interest" to Army intelligence. There were, in fact, *no* guidelines issued by the Army concerning persons and organizations of interest. Each office and command of the Army which had files in this area was responsible for determining for itself who and what would be included. There were, prior to the "Pyle Case," no Pentagon-issued directives giving criteria to be used in limiting files. Consequently, the program grew unchecked. With the increase in the number of civil disturbances and demonstrations in the nation, the Army likewise felt it necessary to expand its files and information-gathering activities. With no overall supervision, the agents and analysts could, in effect, expand the program as much as, and in whatever direction, they wished.

Even after some guidelines were finally laid down, it was questionable how long they would be adhered to. A career officer, a member of the Task Group when I left, and long an intelligence officer, told me that he did not think the restrictions in effect at that time would last long. He said that it is only natural for the domestic intelligence community to want to continue expanding the scope of its activities in order to ensure that it is carrying out its duties effectively.

In view of the blatant lying and unceasing string of mistatements made by Army spokesmen to Congressmen, members of the press, and citizens during 1970, I find it difficult to believe that we can take the official Army assurances at face value. The intelligence establishment and program are too powerful and too special to be left to their own devices. This can be seen in the way they have conducted themselves, essentially without supervision, over the past several years. In my estimation, some kind of civilian intelligence review board is needed, to watch over all the intelligence agencies of the U.S. government, including those within *and* without the military. This could prevent the kind of incursions into the civilian sector by the military we have witnessed, and would serve to make more efficient the intelligence operations that are necessary by eliminating duplication of efforts. Indeed, this is an important area of consideration, for it is doubtful that the Army's domestic intelligence program held any information not already held by other organizations, such as the FBI, and state and local law enforcement agencies.

10

KEEPING TRACK OF ELECTED OFFICIALS

By John M. O'Brien

I served in the United States Army for almost five years. My last four years on active duty were spent as an Army Intelligence Agent, the first three in Western Germany, where I was trained as and performed the duties of an Army Intelligence Case Officer. During these three years I worked in the defensive counter-espionage field and most of my work was directed against non-Americans, whose activities were thought to be inimical to the national defense interests of the United States. My last year on active duty with the United States Army was spent assigned to Region I, 113th Military Intelligence Group, in Evanston, Illinois. At Region I, I performed the duties of an Army Intelligence Case Officer. My duties at Region I were similar in nature to my duties while assigned to Western Europe, except that at Region I my activities were directed almost exclusively against United States citizens. I was honorably discharged from the United States Army on June 8, 1970, with the rank of Staff Sergeant.

From June 1969 until approximately December 1969, I was assigned to the Special Operations Section of Region I. During that period, I worked primarily in undercover operations. These undercover operations included the recruitment, training and controlling of undercover agents utilized by the United States Army. On several occasions I personally performed as an undercover agent as part of my assigned military duties. Special Operations activities at Region I consisted of the screening, investigation, recruitment, training, targeting, and controlling of individuals performing in an undercover capacity for the United States Army. Such activities were primarily directed against civilian organizations and individuals. Special Operations undercover activities were controlled from Fort Holabird. Prior to the initiation of an undercover operation, an operations plan for the implementation of the operation was written at either the Region or Group level and forwarded to Fort Holabird for approval. Once approval was authorized by Fort Holabird, all aspects of the operation were reported to Fort Holabird.

I also assisted the CONUS/Liaison Section at Region I. The CONUS/Liaison Section complied personalia information concerning and monitored organizations and individuals engaged in activities to oppose the United States military involvement in Vietnam and in other activities and associations thought to be inimical to the national defense interests of the United States. Individuals included within the sphere of interest of CONUS included Adlai Stevenson III, Abner Mikva, the individual plaintiffs in the trial in Chicago, and many others including, newspapermen, university professors, public officials and businessmen. At one period in late 1969 CONUS maintained dossiers concerning approximately 800 civilian organizations and individuals. These dossiers were commonly called the subversives files. The policy throughout Region I was to obtain any information available concerning organizations and individuals whose names were in a CONUS dossier. The dossiers contained, among other things, official military intelligence reports concerning the activities of the target organization or individual, copies of reports from other federal and non-federal investigative agencies, and copies of photographs taken by either military intelligence agents posing as members of the news media or as free-lance photographers or by members of the other investigative agencies. The CONUS dossiers at Region I filled approximately nine filing cabinets with four or five drawers per cabinet. All the dossiers were stamped confidiential.

The CONUS/Liaison activities in which I participated included the monitoring of civilian organizations which was carried out by military intelligence personnel who utilized radio cars, portable walkie-talkie equipment, photographic equipment, participation in demonstrations, and the like. Penetration was carried out by participation (without disclosure) in public demonstrations and activities.

In approximately January, 1970, my duties were changed. I was then assigned to the Special Investigations Branch of Region I. However, I continued at the request of the Region I Special Operations officer to participate in certain Special Operations activities and in assistance to CONUS/Liaison until approximately late May or early June 1970.

My new duties with the Special Investigations Branch included personnel background investigations of individuals under consideration for security clearance, participation in sabotage and espionage investigations, and the conduct of liaison with local investigative agencies within the area of the Evanston field office of Region I.

After my discharge from the United States Army I visited Region I approximately twice monthly until the first week of December, 1970. During these visits I learned from conversations with personnel assigned both to Special Operations and CONUS that the collection of information concerning the activities of civilians was still taking place, and that Special Operations continued to conduct undercover operations directed against civilian organizations.

My concern as to the legitimacy and necessity of my activities while assigned to Region I began in September 1969, when I witnessed the initiation of a file concerning Adlai Stevenson III. I concluded that such activities posed a threat to every American's right to freedom of expression and to the system of government under which we have lived in the United States since the inception of the United States Constitution.

11

MONITORING THE MILITANTS IN NEW YORK

By Joseph J. Levin, Jr.

From July of 1967 until February, 1969, I served as an agent and then as Special Agent in Charge (SAC) of the New York Field Office (NYFO) of the 108th Military Intelligence Group (108th MIG). My stint as SAC lasted from July, 1968 through January, 1969, when my tour of duty expired.

I have followed with great interest the unveiling of Army Intelligence activities with which I became so intimately familiar during my tour of duty in New York. I had always felt that the Army was dabbling in areas which were within the specific jurisdiction of the FBI and local police agencies.

During my tour of duty, many activist groups began to spring up in the New York area. The SDS (Students For a Democratic Society organization) was coming into full flower, Columbia University erupted, black militants were everywhere. The time span included the assassination of Senator Robert Kennedy and Dr. Martin Luther King, Jr., along with the ensuing violent disturbances.

As an agent part of my duties entailed investigations at City College of New York (CCNY), New York University (NYU—Bronx Campus) and Fordham University (FU—Bronx Campus). I was instructed to keep a close eye on all student activities on these campuses, in particular activities involving the local SDS chapters and their leaders. I was to collect all pamphlets, handouts, brochures, etc., which in any way involved student demonstrations re Vietnam or other issues. Liaison was established between various members of administrations (including ROTC units at each campus), and we found it relatively easy to know who was speaking where, when and about what. Agents were generally dispatched to listen to various speakers and to mingle with the crowd at demonstrations on these campuses. These activities took place not only on the campuses mentioned above, but also at Columbia, NYU (Washington Square) and the other schools and colleges serving the New York area.

Region I of the 108th MIG (which included the New York Field Office, the Brooklyn Field Office, White Plains Field Office and Garden City Field Office) set up an extensive Emergency Operations Center to deal with any civil disturbances which might arise. It was activated for a period of approximately one week following the King assassination. We were in constant contact with regular Army troops operating out of Fort Bragg. We had agents stationed in the Operations Center of the New York City Police Department in order to keep us advised as to conditions in the ghetto areas of the city. Agents were sent to midtown Manhatten to report back on disturbances allegedly occuring there. Perhaps all this was a legitimate function of the military. I had and still have serious doubts.

Our unit was required to send agents to Washington to mingle with and gather information on civilians participating in the Pentagon Demonstration. A number of them rode down on the special chartered buses leaving New York.

During the "Poor Peoples March" on Washington, I was personally dispatched to the 142nd Street Armory where demonstrators were staying overnight before beginning the trek to Washington on chartered buses. My job was to estimate the number of demonstrators, spot any "infamous" leaders, and follow the buses until they had left the city, informing our Operations Officers of the route of exit.

Agents from our office were sent with regularity to attend almost every anti-war rally which could potentially draw a crowd. We were even required to check out and submit reports on welfare recipients who demonstrated at City Hall.

A Negro agent stationed in our Special Investigative Branch was sent to special Black Studies courses at New York University, Washington Square, during either summer or fall 1968. His tuition was paid by the Army and his job was to report back on the activities and members of the class.

The Continental U.S. Intelligence (CONUS) Section of Region I was a real bundle of information on all kinds of civilian organizations and individuals. It was undoubtedly second only in its scope to the information complied at Intelligence Headquarters, Fort Holabird.

12

COVERT OPERATIONS IN WASHINGTON, D. C.

BY QUENTIN L. BURGESS

I am a former military intelligence agent, honorably discharged in April 1969, with the rank of First Lieutenant, the recipient of a Bronze Star and a Vietnam veteran. I am a 1965 graduate of Central State College, one year's experience working with the federally-sponsored Job Corps at Camp Kilmer, New Jersey, prior to my induction. I am currently the special assistant to the president of a management consultant and research firm, here in Washington, D.C.

As a result of a NBC news program, "First Tuesday," broadcast on December 2, 1970, which carried a feature on the Army's monitoring activities, I wrote a letter to NBC TV network. In essence the letter listed a number of my activities while in military intelligence, but more importantly, the fact that NBC through oversight or time limitations omitted a very important part. That was that "the Delimitations Agreement of 1947," which all American intelligence agencies were a party to, outlined the areas of responsibility in the collection of intelligence information. That agreement stated, briefly, that (1) the CIA would have the foreign area of responsibility, (2) the FBI would have domestic responsibility, and (3) the three military intelligence agencies would be limited to various internal and physical security responsibilities, along with their clear mandate for the conduct of personnel security investigations of military and civilian employees engaged in various classified job activities.

As a result of my letter to NBC, I appeared on the NBC Nightly News interview on December 18, 1970, when I detailed some of the activities that I had been aware of or had taken part in. Subsequent to that interview, Mr. Lawrence Baskir, counsel of the Senate Subcommittee on Constitutional Rights, and I discussed at length my activities in Army Intelligence.

My experiences with the Army's monitoring activities were limited to a nine-month period from September 1968 to my discharge in April 1969, with the 116th Military Intelligence Group, Washington, D.C.

On my arrival in the 116th, I was initially assigned to the Personnel Security Investigation (PSI) Division, which accounted for approximately 90 percent of my activities in the 116th during my nine-month tenure. The other 10 percent consisted of surveillance of individuals and monitoring of events.

The first of my covert activities was to attend an anti-war meeting which was to be held in or around the St. Thomas Episcopal Church on 18th Street, N.W. There were no additional instructions or orders given. The night of the so-called meeting the church and rectory doors were locked. There was no meeting.

During October and November, 1968, there was a series of minor civil disturbances as a result of several shooting incidents involving the Metropolitan Police Department, and subsequent rumors throughout the inner city area. One rumor, which heightened the involvement of adolescents and teenagers claimed James Brown had been killed by a white person. As a result of these incidents, I was assigned, with my partner, to walk or ride throughout those areas, reporting on anything suspicious or incidents, gatherings which might possibly develop into a civil disturbance. To the best of my knowledge we never reported anything of significant value.

I did, however, on one occasion, suffer from what I thought was a fatal overdose of tear gas, which was administered by the D.C. Police Department.

On another occasion, we responded to a sniper report arriving on the scene prior to some of the police units. It turned out to be a criminal incident—a policeman had wounded a burglary suspect. While on mobile patrol in an unmarked radio-equipped car, we would occasionally hear other reports from similar units, such as the number of men standing on a corner or in a crowd gathered at a McDonald's Hamburger shop. None of which would have been reported by trained observers, sensitive to the environs of any large metropolitan area, particularly Washington, D.C. with its large black population.

We participated in monitoring events at Howard and George Washington Universities, when guest speakers who had been labeled "radical" or "militant" appeared on their respective campuses. There have been other similar allegations about Army's involvement at college campuses, but my partner and I were probably the only two agents involved with the activities of an elementary school in N. E. Washington. We were sent there to cover a Halloween party for neighborhood children, obstensibly because Rufus "Catfish" Mayfield had procured the party ingredients from various food stores in the area.

Another incident had me following one of America's 1968 Olympic heroes, John Carlos, who was accompanied by Dr. Harry Edwards, Stokely Carmichael and others whose only "crime" had been to protest the inequality that Black Americans face in every facet of our lives in a form of government which "guarantees liberty and justice for all." Mr. Carlos and his entourage were followed from National Airport and throughout the city including Howard University campus.

Agents from our unit were detailed to attend a conference of dissenting priests from throughout the Washington Archdiocese who were protesting the position that Archbishop O'Boyle had taken in reference to the birth control pill.

Throughout my nine months in the 116th I know of no activities involved in the surveillance or monitoring of political figures. But because of the Army's involvement in anti-war and black affairs, I would think that any political figure active in those areas would have had his or her presence noted at rallies, meetings, conferences, etc., and their speeches noted. It is safe to say that in the recent D.C. primary for non-voting delegate to the House, that three of the seven candidates had at one time cards made up on them by Army Intelligence. It would also be safe to assume that in the general election in March that the Democratic nominee and at least two of the registered independents had file cards on them registered with the Army.

As noted previously, my role in the Army covert activities here in Washington was rather limited. I was used usually to supplement those individuals who were assigned to the Special Operations Division of the 116th and would have measurably more information on the activities of Army Intelligence here in the Capitol of the free world, Washington, D.C.

As a Black American I support efforts to protect the constitutional rights of us all, and hope someday that the dream will be reality.

13

SNOOPING ON STUDENTS

By Malcolm Moos

My criticisms of government practice in the information and intelligence areas does not assume that a few individuals with malevolent motives have suddenly found themselves in positions to act out their political views at the expense of others. Rather, I believe that information is being indiscriminately collected without adequate safeguards as to its purpose; and information is being shared across agencies for purposes that have little or nothing to do with the original reasons for collecting it.

As a general operating rule, I believe information ought to be collected only for specified and known purposes and then restricted as to its use to those or clearly related purposes. Where citizens have provided information to their government, they should be assured that the data will not be used for purposes other than those specified with fair notice and due process of appeal when changed uses are contemplated.

Our experience at the University of Minnesota, documented in Mr. Eidenberg's report,[1] demonstrate clearly that the practices I describe are not limited to national government. The tendency to allow slippage when the individuals involved believe that they are working within broad administrative or policy mandate is great. In addition, I do not want my remarks to be taken to mean I am assigning responsibility for what happened on our campus to the Army alone. As President of the University of Minnesota, I must and do take full responsibility for past practices and for making necessary changes in our own operations.

Nonetheless, it is the case that military intelligence agents, normally assigned to conduct security clearance interviews on individuals seeking employment or commissions that required such clearances, began in 1967 to engage in systematic surveillance of the University of Minnesota campus. Liaison was established with the University Police Department and the Office of Admissions and Records. In the latter case, agents obtained total access to confidential student records without demonstrating that the student had granted permission for the investigation. The relationship with the University Police Department was less detailed but equally profound. It involved conversations about the political life on the campus, occasional identification of individuals in photos taken by military intelligence agents, and in at least one instance, the transfer of University police photographs to agents of the military intelligence.

The report that Mr. Eidenberg has prepared at my request documents the character of our local problem in controlling and regulating the development and use of university information.

What the report is unable to specify is the extent of photo-surveillance on the campus by military intelligence agents; the precise percentage of military intelligence inquiries to our Admissions and Records Office that were simply fishing expeditions to gather background information on people suspected of holding views contrary to government policy or the uses to which such information was later put when funneled through the data processing equipment at Fort Holabird. Clearly the contacts between military intelligence agents and units of the university were carefully orchestrated by the military intelligence to generate maximum access to information about the political activities on our campus. The purpose of such data was never specified beyond the general explanation that military intelligence had been assigned to keep the Department of the Army informed as to events that might escalate beyond the control of local law enforcement and therefore might ultimately require the use of federal troops.

To explain fully the character of the military intelligence liaison with our Police Department requires an understanding of a professional ethic in law enforcement. Law enforcement agencies typically share information with each other. That the mission of one agency might be substantially different from another does not diminish the overriding tendency by enforcement personnel to exchange information between agencies with similar if not identical missions.

The agents of military intelligence made regular visits to the University Police Department to develop personal relationships with officers in our department. The purpose was clear: to obtain access to information that was outside the scope of both university policy and, in my judgment, the needs of the Army.

What conceivable purpose is served by maintaining a file of photographs of individuals and events on our campus if the Army's mission were solely to respond to the unlikely need for federal troops? Simply stated, what we have here are members of a large organization carrying out what they assumed were their responsibilities. But what resulted was the collection of information that was irrelevant to their mission and could only be used to further enlarge national data banks with information on individuals who were pursuing peaceful and lawful, although perhaps unpopular, causes.

Let me be clear. I am inclined to explain these events as the logical and predictable consequences of uncontrolled and indiscriminate information collection; not as the result of complex conspiracies involving federal, state and local agencies. But the consequences are just as damaging to the fabric of a free society. Information can be mishandled or misused or it can be deliberately collected and employed for purposes that debase the principles of free speech and inquiry. The results are the same, but an understanding of the causes of such practices are critical if we are to develop sensible public policy to deal with the problem.

At least two reinforcing solutions need to be pursued. Locally we must develop clear and precise policy and administrative guidance for agencies and people who manage information that can be put to purposes that are either damaging to individuals or unrelated to the responsibilities of the collecting agency. Second, the federal government must develop an appreciation for the local consequences of national policy and practice. That the Army was called upon to assist in controlling a civil disturbance in Detroit in 1967 is hardly justification for the establishment of a policy which assigns to the Army a role which ought only be performed by local law enforcement.

If federalism as a concept continues to have meaning, it must include a re-affirmation of the principle which opposes a national police force. I suspect that if we get a national police force in this country, it will come not because of a positive act by the Congress, but because of administrative and information sharing practices that make federal agencies the repository for information and data which can be used at the will of government officials far removed from the events that generated the information in the first place. The consequence of such practices is a growing dependency by local agencies upon national government for information which only it can afford to collect and maintain.

The federal police power must not follow either the federal dollar or federal information systems.

What has happened at Minnesota, if allowed to continue unchecked, diminishes responsible local control and accountability over our own institutions. There can be no other result when national government seeks by deliberate action and policy to use local agencies to accomplish their purposes outside local lines of control.

To whom is a local police chief accountable when agents of the federal government establish their own investigatory and surveillance functions in the name of Executive Orders of the President or Acts of Congress assigning campus jurisdiction to the FBI wherever federal dollars are involve?

The response to such confusion at the local level is equally disturbing. Revelations of military surveillance on our campus have produced demands for a total closure of the University and its records to outside agencies—even when the individual involved desires that his records be made available. The paradox is clear: abuses in a free society lead to panic-responses which seek to close off institutions as a defense against higher authority expanding its influence and activity outside the constraints of citizen preference and control.

How we shape public policy so that rights of privacy, association and expression continue to have meaning at a time when there appears to be an irresistible appetite for information about our citizens remains the challenge for the Congress.

Let me conclude by stating what is perhaps obvious but is at the heart of the hearings conducted by the Senate Subcommittee on Constitutional Rights. If one student, faculty member, or any member of the university community at Minnesota is dissuaded from expressing his political views because of haunting fear of being recorded hangs over him like a deadly mist, then freedom for all Americans is threatened by an expanding encirclement; and academic freedom as an operating principle of American higher education has suffered a setback. These consequences cannot be dismissed as unlikely or unrelated to the purposes and intent of the Army in particular, or the government in general. That the military has and presumably continues to engage in domestic political surveillance of the sort we uncovered at Minnesota is *per se* a serious infringement on the right to free speech. The Bill of Rights protects every citizen equally. Those ten amendments have meaning only when they are enforced during times of stress and tension. Freedom to speak and advocate is hollow indeed if it is only tolerated during periods of relative calm and consensus in the nation. Freedom of speech has substance when hard questions are being raised, when fundamental concerns are being expressed, and when reactions to dissent are fierce and intense.

If an institution of higher learning is subjected to constant and close surveillance by government, then what substance is there to our assertions that the academy is a place where free thought goes on; where unpopular and untried ideas can be expressed and advocated?

In that context, I would like to emphasize my sense of concern about the pervasiveness of political surveillance and information gathering by government. Even if the military were to end its domestic political surveillance, the network of official information systems remains.

Mr. Eidenberg points out in his report that there are charges being made by foreign students that United States government officials are cooperating with representatives from foreign governments in keeping tabs on students from those nations on our campuses. What are the policies and practices of the State Department in this regard? How widely has the data developed by military intelligence been shared?

In short, what are the ways and means that effective controls can be placed on information systems so that information is collected for legitimate purposes and used for the purposes for which it was originally collected?

14

WHAT HAPPENED AT THE UNIVERSITY OF MINNESOTA

By Eugene Eidenberg

This report has been prepared after careful research and analysis of information given to me by individuals who have been in a position to know about the relationship between federal intelligence agencies and the University of Minnesota.

While I have talked with many people in conducting the inquiry, no one reading this report should assume that all persons with knowledge of the issues involved has been reached. Necessary limits of time and relevance of information have required that I make some judgments about the limits of the investigation and about what would constitute necessary and sufficient information to answer fully the questions before the university.

This report was prepared after more than twenty interviews with people who had information that would be helpful to the inquiry. Relevant documents, photographs, memoranda, and newspaper articles have been collected and analyzed, and I have conducted a thorough search of the University Police Department's files in the course of the investigation.

All personnel and units of the university involved have beeen fully cooperative in assisting me in gathering as full a picture as possible of university practices in the area of information recording and dissemination. In addition, former agents of Military Intelligence have been extremely helpful in putting in broader perspective some of the charges that have been made but only partially reported in the media. Finally, the Department of Defense was of considerable assistance in the person of Assistant Secretary Robert Froehlke who provided me with a full statement of his perspective with respect to national policy governing the activities of the Department of the Army in domestic intelligence. In short, I complete this study with the strong feeling that I do know the full context of university-government relations in this area; that there is truth in the charges that have been made, but a truth which must be viewed in the full context of events; and that there have been administrative practices in several units of the university that require change in order to assure students and staff that there will not be either the improper collection or use of confidential information in the future.

Finally and significantly, I am fully confident that the changes that are necessary can be specified in clear administrative policy and that the personnel of the units involved are anxious to have such a clarification of policy to govern their responsibilities in this area. It is in no way an apology of or justification for the improper use of information to report at the outset that it is my judgment that no one on the staff of the university has maliciously or knowingly sought to violate either university policy or standards of common sense. Nonetheless, it is equally clear to me that both existing policy and standards of good judgment have not always been the determinants of behavior in this delicate area.

On December 1, 1970, the NBC television program "First Tuesday" reported that there existed an extensive network of domestic military intelligence in the United States which collected and maintained information on the political beliefs and activities of organizations and citizens. Specifically, the program reported that such intelligence activity existed in the Twin Cities area and included surveillance on the campus of the University of Minnesota and that certain information had been provided agents from the 113th Military Intelligence Group, Region V headquartered at Fort Snelling by the University Police Department.

On January 1, 1791, CBS Evening News carried a report from Mr. Richard Kasson, former Military Intelligence Agent assigned to the Special Investigations Branch of the 113th, Region V, that confirmed the earlier NBC program and further alleged that agents from the 113th had ready and complete access to the files of the university's Admissions and Records Department, and that foreign students had been subjected to lie detector tests administered by officials of the 113th unit. Two photographs alleged to have come from the files of the University of Minnesota Police Department were displayed on the program as examples of the information sharing practices between the police department and military intelligence.

Charges Involving the Department of Admissions and Records

It appears that investigating officers of federal agencies have had regular access to student records and files in the Office of Admissions.

Before January of 1968 the Office of Admissions and Records functioned under an information disclosure policy that had been developed internally within that office. While that policy indicated that confidential information was to be restricted in its availability, the written policy did not define what constituted information, and explicitly excluded federal and other investigating agents from any limitations imposed on the dissemination of confidential information. That policy statement included the following language: "FBI agents and Department of Protection and Investigation agents when identified are privileged to full access to all information without questions. Military security agents are also entitled to full information upon identification. U.S. Probation Officers—o.k."

Apparently this policy had been in effect for some period of time, although there is no written record of the data of approval of the policy.

On January 12, 1968, the Board of Regents adopted a "Policy on Student Records."[2] That policy creates the presumption of nondisclosure of student academic records except for certain specified "public information" (i.e., date of enrollment in the University, address, and degrees earned) and except to the student himself, his parents or guardian; or to individuals and organizations the student has given authority to see such records. The only other exception to these rules is that data in student records can be used within the university for appropriate "research, educational, and university administrative service functions."

Following the adoption of this policy, the Regents statement was circulated to appropriate administrative officials responsible for the management of student records. On March 18, two months later, a memo was distributed to all Record Bureaus by W. Donald Beatty, University Recorder, calling attention to the Regents policy. The Beatty memo noted that "this action (the Regents policy) does not materially change the general policy which we have followed."

Furthermore, and significantly, the March 18 memo re-stated that FBI, military security, and other Department of Protection agents were "entitled" to full information upon identification. This memo is reported to have been authorized by the late Dean R. E. Summers, then Dean of Admissions and Records.

Apart from the question of whether the March 18th memo is an accurate interpretation of the Regents January 1968 policy, it appears that this was the only administrative interpretation of the Regents statement that clerical and professional personnel in Admissions and Records received until January 7, 1970.

During the two year period January 68-January 70, Military intelligence and other security or government agents merely had to identify themselves to the appropriate clerk to receive any data included in the students file. Indeed, any such agents were given the file to work with at a desk in the Admissions and Records offices. On January 7, 1970, file access to government investigators was discontinued except in twenty-nine instances that remain unexplained.

These skeletal facts do not tell the full story, however. Several important points must be reported to fully understand this situation:

• On the personal testimony of the military intelligence agents themselves, 90-98% of their inquiries to Admissions and Records were for the purpose of conducting so-called "Personal Security Clearance" checks which had been authorized by the student at the time he applied for a job with the government or sought a commission in the army which required a security clearance. The agents had come to know the clerical staff in Admissions and Records and therefore were not required to show identification or evidence of the student's permission to see information in his files. It was the latter practice which permitted the federal agents to gather information on individuals who had not authorized such access to their files.

• The administrative and personnel structure of the Office of Admissions and Records was undergoing major change during the period immediately following the adoption of the Regents policy. The Office of Vice President for Student Affairs was just being created in the period February to July 1968, and the new Vice President assumed responsibility for the Office of Admissions and Records during this period. During the subsequent year (between July 1968-July 1969) personnel shifts were made which resulted in T. E. Kellogg being appointed Associate Dean of Admissions and Records (with operational responsibility for the Office of Admissions and Records) and Dean R. E. Summers being appointed Special Assistant to the Vice President for Student Affairs and Dean of Admissions and Records. The new administration raised the question of whether information disclosure practices were consistent with the January 1968 Regent's policy.

Discussions between July 1969 and Dec. 1969 between the Office of Admissions and Records and the Vice President for Student Affairs resulted in the following decisions in January 1970: no transcript data would be released without the written release of the students; and no information would be given to investigating officers (such as military intelligence) without the written release of the student.

From this point on any request for information from Admissions and Records by a federal investigating officer was handled by T. E. Kellogg or his first assistant John Fisher, who confirmed the fact of the student release. There are 29 minor exceptions to this in which Military Intelligence agents received student record files although with the proper release. The new administrative policy requires that a staff member in Admissions and Records answer agents' questions and not physicially turn the file over to the agent for his study. These appear to be exceptions based on genuine misunderstanding of policy and steps have been taken to prevent any recurrence.

(It should be noted parenthetically that the full transfer of responsibility for Admissions and Records to T. E. Kellogg did not take place until July 1970 when he was named Director of Admissions and Records and Dean Summers retired. In short, for 18 months after the Regents policy was adopted, the management structure and practices in this area was undergoing change. Many clerical and staff personnel apparently did not appreciate the significance of the new Regents' policy in their spheres of responsibilty because of previous practice—reinforced by the March 1968 memo—which was not altered until administrative authority had been effectively transferred to the new administration of Admissions and Records between July 1969 and January 1970.)

University Police—Military Intelligence

Former agents in Military Intelligence have alleged that they were on an information sharing basis with officers of the University Police Department. Specifically, it is alleged that photographs taken by the University Police Department during political rallies and demonstrations have been shown to and in some instances given to the Military Intelligence agents.

There is no doubt that agents of Military Intelligence did with some regularity (average of once per week) between 1968-1970 visit the University Police Department for the purpose of soliciting information about rallies, demonstrations, and other events. The source of Military Intelligence's interest in this information is a 1967 Executive Order of the President of the United States which explicitly assigned to the Army the responsibility for gathering information that would be necessary if the Army were called upon to operate in an American city to quell a civil disturbance. The White House and Department of

Defense felt this need quite directly after the summer of 1967 when federal troops were used in Detroit with almost no advance information available regarding that situation.

Apparently the judgment about what information was appropriate to collect was left to the commanding officers of the regional intelligence units, but according to testimony of former agents the effort was to collect as much information as possible about the activities of groups, organizations, and individuals who *might* be involved in events that *might* be beyond the competence of local law enforcement to handle.

In pursuing its mission, Military Intelligence routinely developed liaison with officers in local law enforcement agencies.

The University Police Department was no exception. The Police Department's view of its relationship with Military Intelligence varies with the people one talks with, but the common thread in all reports from Police Department and Military Intelligence interactions are:

- 90-98% of the contacts were precipitated by and limited to legitimate security clearance record checks with the permission of the student (although during periods of tension on the campus, such as Spring 1970, the agents devoted all of their time to watching events and situations that might escalate beyond the control of local law enforcement).
- Most conversations about political action on the campus between the University Police Department and Military Intelligence were of a highly general nature about events rather than people;
- A major share of the information received by Military Intelligence from the University Police Department was publicly available from other sources (copies of handbills, flyers, and the Minnesota *Daily*);
- Military Intelligence was never permitted to study or otherwise routinely go through Police Department records and files; and
- The Police Department—Military Intelligence link was built on the traditional law enforcement assumption of cooperation between "enforcement" agencies with similar if not identical missions.

Notwithstanding the above, several findings of my inquiry raise disturbing questions about University Police Department practices and suggest the need for specific additional administrative policy to regulate them.

- On at least one occasion Military Intelligence did secure copies of University Police Department photographs at the request of the Military Intelligence agent, but in direct violation of existing university policy regarding the use of photographic records of political rallies and events. It should be noted that Military Intelligence has its own photo-surveillance capability and routinely photographs demonstrations on the campus. There appears to be no way that university policy can prevent this practice.

• The University Police Department has regularly gathered information from student records in the Office of Admissions and Records under an interpretation of section 2, page 1 and section F, page 2 of the 1968 Regents' policy providing for the use of student record data for University "administrative service functions". The University Police Department has gathered information on approximately 4-5 students per week for the indefinite past and has done so without reporting to any officer of the university the purposes for which such information was being collected.

• The University Police Department does have stored photographs of events in apparent violation of university policy regarding the disposition of such photographs.

• The University Police Department does maintain an event file which lists individuals who have participated in particular demonstrations and rallies.

• While the university policy on photo-surveillance of rallies and demonstrations requires the police to seek when possible to notify the organizers of the rally of the intended photo-surveillance, the police have not, in general, explicitly provided such notifications. However, it should also be pointed out that the University Police Department has never sought to conduct photo-surveillance in a covert manner. Officers with cameras, although in plain clothes, were in the main known to the organizers of the events photographed during the past several years, and there was no effort by the police to masquerade their identity. Such photographic records have been used in court as evidence in several prosecutions.

• There is no written internal administrative policy within the University Police Department to interpret or enforce either the Regents' policy on Student Records or the Photographic Policy administratively adopted in November 1966.

These practices by the University Police Department indicate the need for clarified policy and lines of responsibility. Under present administrative practice, the chief does not provide policy guidance for his personnel in this area. The entire range of issues surrounding inter-agency cooperation, records and file maintenance, Regents' and Central Administrative policy pertaining to information disclosure have never been the subjects for staff discussion within the Police Department.

The fact that the University Police Department gathers intelligence is not difficult to understand or defend in the light of events during the past several years:

- The occupation of Morill Hall in January 1968.
- The demolition of a University Police Department squad car by explosives which but for unusual luck would have killed or injured members of the University Police Department.
- The SDS "trashing" raid on the Department of Criminal Justice Studies.
- The Spring 1970 strike and its attendant disruptions.
- The earlier uncovering of a dynamite cache in the West Bank area.
- Attempt at deliberate burning of the ROTC armory this fall.
- The national and local rash of bombings during the past summer and fall.
- The steady, if low level, rate of anonymous threats, public demands, and confrontations.

During this period three major areas of activity developed: (1) substantive curricula and governance reform to meet legitimate grievances when articulated; (2) frequent and time-consuming contingency planning to avoid over- and/or under-reaction to specific events; and (3) the development of minimally necesary information to make the contingency planning process something more than random guess work.

It seems clear that the University Police Department's mission to protect people and property on and around the campus requires that they become involved in this process. The question then is not whether the police should be developing basic information, but whether this necessary activity is being conducted under proper civilian controls and lines of accountability. I think it fair to say that while conversation between central administration and the administration of the Police Department has been frequent and intensive in the last two years, this conversation has been largely directed toward specific contingency planning, and has not developed clear policy guidelines beyond those provided in the earlier statement on photographic surveillance, nor clear procedures defining the form and nature of the reporting and accountability to be asked from the Department. Thus guidance from central administration in this area has been casual, and the Department itself has not developed explicit policy guidance for its officers, nor effective communication to university administration of decision-issues arising from the Regents' policy on information, and the Administrative policy on photo-surveillance.

Foreign Student Surveillance

Charges have been made that foreign students have from time to time been subjected to political surveillance and been "coerced" into taking lie detector tests.

According to testimony of former Military Intelligence agents, several foreign students who had applied for commissions in the armed services or had sought employment for which a security clearance was required were requested to submit to lie detector tests to corroborate statements about their background which couldn't otherwise be checked in the field. The questionnaire did, apparently, include items about the individual's political beliefs and about his sexual practices. The latter were included when independently generated information suggested a possible problem that might affect the security clearance. Both questions were defended on grounds that they (a) provide parameters against which to read the results of the test; and (b) the substantive answers might make a difference as to whether the security clearance would be given.

I have not been able to secure the testimony of any individual foreign student to either confirm or deny that such students have been coerced into taking the tests.

The University Police Department did not administer lie detector tests to foreign students for Military Intelligence. The department has on two accasions conducted lie detector tests at the written request of the foreign students involved to clear them of certain criminal charges that were pending. The prosecuting agency in both cases indicated its willingness to accept positive results and to ignore negative results.

The Office of Foreign Student Advisor does provide federal agencies with character reference interviews upon proper identification and with the student's consent. In the course of such character reference interviews, the staff does provide positive information. If information is derogatory, it is not revealed, and a check is made with the student as to how he wishes the staff to respond.

Towards the end of my investigation a memorandum was received describing extensive political surveillance of Taiwanese students and Chinese students from Taiwan at American universities by agents from the Chinese Embassy and regional Chinese consulates. The charges in this memorandum do not go to practices and policies of the University of Minnesota . . . I have found no evidence that university officials have provided information to representatives of foreign governments regarding the activities of students who are foreign nationals.[8] The issues raised in this memo go to national policy governing the behavior of foreign diplomats assigned to missions in the United States

Other University Practices

Given the nature of the charges being made I have made explicit inquiry into the practices of other university units which maintain records and data files.

- The Student Health Service has never provided information to any investigating agency without the explicit permission of the student, and then data was provided by an M.D. who used his professional judgment in determining what information would be given.
- The Student Counseling Bureau has not provided investigating agents data on students who have used its services.
- The ROTC has not provided data on students to investigating agents except where germane to a background investigation prior to a cadet's commissioning. Military Intelligence has (and continues to) maintain liaison with ROTC during periods when anti- ROTC demonstrations presented potential threats to the ROTC armory or other government property associated with the ROTC program.
- The Student Life Studies Bureau, which conducts various studies on student attitudes and behavior, has not provided data from its research to investigating agents.
- The State Adjutant General's Office has prepared for the Governor's office a weekly summary of major events in Minnesota that might require the use of the National Guard. The University Police Department has been routinely contacted (along with other law enforcement agencies) during the time this summary was being prepared for the Governor's office. The information solicited and provided was solely related to events and appears to pose no problem within University policy. The state Adjutant General's Office neither sought nor was given access to any files or records of the University.

Summary and Recommendations

It is clear that Military Intelligence and other government investigating agents have had access to student records and information in the Office of Admissions and Records and have received verbal reports and some photos from the University Police Department on a basis that violates university policy.

Gaps in administrative policy in the Office of Admissions and Records have been corrected by T. E. Kellogg's memo of January 11, 1971 to the staff of his office. Further discussions should be held between Kellogg and the Vice President for Student Affairs to examine any remaining administrative gaps that need to be filled.

I am satisfied that the staff of Admissions and Records deeply regrets any past practices (basically pre- Jan. 1970) that violated university policy or in any way compromised the confidence of the university community in the integrity of the records system. They mean to restore that confidence by explicit administrative action and controls already in force.

The University Police Department's practices are more difficult to summarize. The police mission to protect people and property requires that they observe rallies and demonstrations and take preventive or enforcement action when required. While the University of Minnesota has not been subjected to much violent protest during the past several years, there certainly has been enough to justify prudent police presence and observation of situations that contain the potential for violence and violation of law. Such police presence is necessary both to prevent violation of law, and to protect people who are not participating in a thoroughly peaceful and lawful manner.

The issue goes to what kind of information is required for the police to meet their responsibilities; and where the decision and control points are in deciding what data and action are required for effective police protection of the university.

With respect to the former issue, I believe the University Police Department has developed information that is not necessary for them to meet their responsibilities, and the Department ought to be instructed to destroy any files or listing of individuals who have participated in lawful, non-violent events. In addition, photographs in police files of rallies and demonstrations ought to be destroyed or turned over to the university archives pursuant to existing university policy. (In general, I would recommend that photographing of events on the campus by the police be limited to events where reasonable presumption of law violation or university policy violation exists, and where the photographs are useful for evidentiary purposes.)

The matter of effective decisional and policy control will in part be dealt with in the reorganization of the administration of the university Police Department. The creation of the position of Director of Police Services and Development with explicit authority and responsibility for helping to make and administer policy in this area will provide necessary central direction for the Police Department in this field. In addition, the establishment of the Assistant Vice Prendency for Administration that I now hold will assure continuing central administrative review of practices and policies of the Department. Without either of these positions the Vice President for Administration has simply been unable to devote sufficient time to provide the necessary central review in this area.

I would further recommend that the University Police Department not have access to university records and files except on the basis of explicit administrative decision on a case-by-case basis justifying the access. The University Police Department has full police powers and therefore, ought to be subject to the same civilian review and control that we expect of any policy agency. The excesses that have occurred in practices by the University Police Department are directly attributable to professional and agency protocols within the law enforcement profession and not to individual efforts within the Department to suppress political dissent or to intimidate members of the University community in the exercise of their rights.

In short, the police mission at this point in history is sufficiently delicate that the police ought *not* to be required to bear the burden of decisions about what information they require to meet their responsibilities. Policy decisions in law enforcement work ought to be made by individuals who are directly responsible to the President of the University and the Board of Regents. It is unfair to the police agency itself to have it any other way.

There do not appear to be any other areas of university policy and practice which have been violated in the collection or dissemination of records and information. It is my belief that the university does not need a new Regents' policy, but that there are administrative gaps which can be and already are being filled.

Conclusion

The political and national turmoil of the past decade has produced a new phenomenon on the American scene, political and civil violence, which has required the use of local police and federal troops in new and demanding circumstances. The felt need for information at the national level has resulted in policies and practices which can only be effectively reviewed and evaluated at national policy levels. However, there are obviously issues which have been raised which go to the significant matter of the use of information in a free society and its effect on citizens' rights to privacy and political expression. Every local institution such as the University of Minnesota bears the responsibility to insure that its practices and policies do not contribute to a pattern of events that in their collective impact have a chilling effect on free speech in the society at large. Had the office of Admissions and Records or the University Police Department not responded to even the small percentage of requests for information that were outside the scope of University policy, then that portion of the national pattern described on the "First Tuesday" program would have been eliminated.

Because I have been mindful of these very large issues, I have sought to report more than specific matters of fact in chronological order. A full understanding of what has happened here at Minnesota requires an effort at placing specific events into context. This I have tried to do.

All of the former Military Intelligence agents who have been assigned to the University of Minnesota, and with whom I have talked, have indicated their own concern that news accounts have distorted the real nature of what has happened on our campus. The risks are real enough, but there appear to be no practices that cannot be easily and permanently changed (if they have not already been altered) through administrative action and on-going attention. Our policy goal has been that information provided to the university or generated within the university must always be used for fully legitimate purposes, under proper lines of responsibility and accountability.

We in the administration bear a share of the responsibility for failure to meet this goal in the past. But I am certain that all units of the university that have responsibilities in this area are anxious to fill whatever administrative policy gaps exist. I feel that no one on this campus need fear any deliberate effort to circumscribe anyone's rights or privileges.

---

1. Items which might be found in a student file are:

- Completed application forms
- Transcripts from high school or other colleges
- Memos placing holds on registration or on transcript release
- Memos clearing holds
- Residence applications and supporting documents
- Letters from counselors, or parents or the student himself concerning academic records or achievement
- Petitions for exceptions to rules
- Evaluations of work at other colleges
- Achieve ment and aptitude test scores
- University transcripts
- Letters of inquiry
- Copies of university correspondence with student
- Counseling report summaries
- Name changes
- Joint registration applications
- Student request that his file (including public information) be sealed to persons outside the university

The file does not contain medical records, employment records, character references (except as a letter from a school about a new applicant might be so defined), counseling records, information about membership in university organizations or activities or any type of university disciplinary records.

Also it should be noted that the Office of Admissions and Records contains other types of files, such as paid fee statements, authorizations for billing for fees, college action on academic standing and registration blanks. None of these items are placed in the student file.

2. A survey reveals that the Regents Policy was distributed throughout the university on an uneven basis. The Institute of Agriculture reports no evidence that the policy was ever transmitted to them and the college of Liberal Arts reports the policy was received only upon request.

3. When students from USSR are on the campus, we are obliged to respond to inquiries from the FBI because of the travel restrictions imposed on such students in this country. There are at present no students from the USSR at the University of Minnesota.

15

THE INVISIBLE POLICE

BY JOSEPH R. LUNDY

Direct police infiltration of political groups is no longer merely a hypothetical possibility in America. The increasing use of police spies and undercover agents may have put us on the way to America's experience with "political police."

Developments during the conspiracy trial of the Chicago 8 relied heavily on evidence gathered by police undercover agents. Louis Salzberg, a newspaper photographer who, the *New York Times* stated, "had become a regular fixture at radical gatherings in New York City," revealed that he had been a paid informer for the FBI since 1967. A few days later, William Frapolly, a member of the Chicago Police Department since 1966, described how he had enrolled at Northeast Illinois State College, where he joined the SDS, the Student Mobilization Committee and the Chicago Peace Council. Earlier in the trial, Officer Robert L. Pierson repeated testimony he had given in 1969 to the House Un-American Activities Committee to the effect that he had infiltrated the Youth International Party in order to monitor its plans to disrupt the Democratic National Convention. The recent disclosure of documents stolen from the FBI office in Media, Pennsylvania, seem to confirm this omnious trend.

Spies and undercover agents are nothing new in law enforcement. For years, the Bureau of Narcotics has used undercover agents to solicit sales from the pushers. The FBI's best-known undercover operatives was Herbert Philbrick, whose *I Led Three Lives* was a best seller during the early 1950s; but the Bureau has employed the technique in other cases. A *New York Times* report in early 1966 indicated that the FBI had infiltrated the Ku Klux Klan hierarchy "to the Cabinet level." In August 1967, FBI undercover operative Herbert Itkin was revealed as the key figure in exposure of James Marcus' underworld contacts in New York City. In March 1968, seven Minutemen were arrested for conspiring to hold up four Spokane banks, the evidence being provided by an FBI secret agent.

If the undercover agent has been an occasional convenience in cases of conspiracy, he has been a regular fixture of the FBI's war on organized crime. Herbert Itkin had worked within the New York Mafia for several years before he was "surfaced" in order to provide testimony against Marcus. A Boston businessman, Charles W. Grinnel, related in *The Saturday Evening Post* how he volunteered to spy on Mafia representatives who approached him in conection with the "juice," or usurious loan racket.

If Americans have tolerated police use of spies and agents, especially in cases of organized crime or consensual offenses which present difficult problems of proof, they have never been happy about it. In 1798 Rep. Edward Livingston expressed to the House of Representatives of the Fifth Congress his revulsion against a practice which immigrants from the continent had learned to fear. "The system of espionage being thus established, the country will swarm with informers, spies, delators, and all the odious reptile tribe that breed in the sunshine of despotic power. The hours of most unsuspected confidence, the intimacies of friendship or the recesses of domestic retirement, will afford no security."

This unfortunate European tradition reached what was probably its fullest flower under the despotisms of Adolf Hitler and Joseph Stalin. Allen Dulles, former director of Central Intelligence, was convinced that "it can't happen here." In *The Craft of Intelligence*, he wrote: "Our Government in its very nature—and our open society in all its instincts under the Constitution and the Bill of Rights—automatically outlaws intelligence organizations of the kind that have developed in police states." Recent examples of police reliance on secret agents raise doubts that the Constitution's protections are quite as "automatic" as Mr. Dulles thought.

The variety of clandestine investigative techniques employed by the police has always been considerable, but never as great as it is today, when science and technology have increased tenfold the possibilities of snooping. Wire tapping, the most feared, or at least the most widely recognized, has recently been brought under the supervision of the Fourth Amendment's ban on unreasonable searches and seizures. Theoretically, after the rulings in *Berger v. New York* (1967) and *Katz v. United States* (1967), wire tapping is subject to all the requirements of a judicial warrant that have always applied to more traditional forms of search and seizure. What about secret agents?

Police secret agents may be distinguished roughly by what function they perform, at whose initiative they work, and what kind of accompanying gadgetry they carry. A fourth distinguishing factor, and a crucial one, seems to have been little considered by the courts—the kind of alleged criminal activity being investigated.

Informers are the best-known type of police secret operative. Working on their own, they need not be, and often are not, full-time informants. Informers usually live on the fringes of crime, and can readily provide useful information in return for small police favors, protection or guarantees against harassment. The Supreme Court has given some constitutional sanction to their use by carving out an "informer's privilege" as an exception to the rule that police must divulge the sources of information on which "probable cause" for arrest is based. On the other hand, the Court has said that if divulgence of an informer's identity is necessary to guarantee a defendant's fair trial, as opposed merely to providing probable cause for his arrest, that identity must be revealed.

Informers are among the most innocuous of the secret agents, for they work on their own, usually do nothing beyond mere information gathering, and carry no concealed transmitters or recorders. In the same category can be placed plea bargainers, known in England as "approvers," who supply information to the police by turning state's evidence once they are in custody.

Decoys and stool pigeons are used by the police, usually at an officer's initiative, to lure would-be criminals into action. To the extent that the decoy does not provoke the crime, or implant a criminal intent in the suspect's mind, his activities have been uncensured. When the agent, whether an outsider working at police instigation or a member of some official law-enforcement organization, strays over the line and stimulates some other person to commit a crime, the courts have protected the object of such provocation under the theory of "entrapment." Difficult as the distinction may be an already present intent and one implanted from outside, the defense of entrapment does provide some protection against the wiles of the *agent provocateur*. Its deterrent effect on police resort to secret agents, however, has been minimal.

The types of police secret agents that seem to have been most recently in vogue, and with whom we should be most concerned, are the spy and the undercover agent. A spy is a non-policeman who is hired, targeted, trained, managed and paid by the police to gather information about some target group. The undercover agent performs the same function, but is himself a police officer who has assumed a "cover" identity. Such spy or under cover agent may have several functions, which can be discussed in a review of the Supreme Court's evolving attitude toward such persons.

The Supreme Court first dealt with the secret agent problem in the case of *Gouled v. United States* in 1921. A government secret agent had gained access to the defendant's office by misrepresenting his identity and later, while the defendant was out of the room, had searched his desk and papers. The Court, equating entry by force and by deceit, held that a search where access was obtained by deception was barred by the Fourth Amendment ban against unreasonable searches and seizures.

More recent cases have often involved the use of electronic devises. In 1952, the Court held that a miniaturized transmitter carried by a government spy, which enabled a nacotics agent stationed nearby to monitor the defendant's criminal proposition, did not violate the Fourth Amendment. A more difficult case was presented in 1963 when a government agent carried a miniature recorder to preserve for evidence the defendant's bribe offer. Here again, the Court approved, although it can be argued that the decision does not really apply to secret agent situations because the defendant knew that the person to whom he was offering the bribe was a law-enforcement official. Finally, in 1966, the Court approved the FBI's seeking approval from a federal judge before sending an agent to record a bribe offer in the case of James Hoffa. As in the 1963 decision, however, the FBI agent was not "secret," in the sense that he did nothing to conceal his identity.

It was not until 1966 that the Supreme Court reviewed two cases involving secret agents, unaccompanied by electronic devices, who merely infiltrated, listened, and reported. In *Hoffa v. United States* and *Lewis v. United States,* the Court decided that using unwired undercover agents for information gathering was not "*per se* unconstitutional." On the other hand, Justice Stewart, writing for a majority of four Justices in *Hoffa,* cautioned that "this is not to say that a secret government agent is to the slightest degree more free from all relevant constitutional restrictions than is any other government agent." What is included in "all relevant constitutional restrictions" the Court did not feel compelled to say.

The *Lewis* case involved a situation which has become commonplace in modern law enforcement—use of an undercover agent to buy narcotics from a suspect. Aside from the government agent's telephone offer to buy narcotics and consummation of the sale in the defendant's home, the officer's conduct was innocuous. Lewis, the defendant; did not even raise the question of entrapment. The combination of a serious crime, the agent's neutral behavior, the absence of socially useful activity which might be discouraged by the undercover technique, and the difficulty of procuring evidence of "selling crimes," all make it likely that the *Lewis* precedent will stand for years to come—at least until some alternative approach is found to the problems of narcotics addiction.

The *Hoffa* decision rests on far shakier ground. In the first place, only seven Justices participated in the decision—and only four concurred in approving the government's use of a former friend of Hoffa, who had recently been released from jail and infiltrated Hoffa's coterie, as an undercover agent. Chief Justice Warren dissented vigorously from the four majority Justices, arguing that the Court's supervisory power over federal courts allowed it to control such use of secret agents by the federal agencies, even if the practice was not unconstitutional.

Most significant, the *Hoffa* case involved a crime—jury tampering—which, like narcotics peddling, would be extremely difficult to prove without undercover investigative activity. Moreover, it is difficult to conceive of any socially useful activity which Hoffa could claim might be discouraged by the use of secret agents in jury tampering cases. In this respect, jury tampering is like narcotics peddling, prostitution, gambling or other consensual or sumptuary crimes.

What is most disappointing about the opinion of the four-Justice majority in *Hoffa* is its failure to deal forthrightly with the competing social interests involved in police use of undercover agents in a free society. Perhaps it was too early to anticipate the widespread use of police spies and undercover agents in the peace movement, the anti-war/anti-draft movement, and even the civil rights movement. (This kind of use, Norman Mailer noted in *Armies of the Night,* is "now accepted as a chronic joke" by participants in New Left politics.) But certainly the Court's overconceptualistic approach was unsatisfactory.

The *Hoffa* majority based its decision primarily on the "assumption of risk" or "misplaced confidence" argument. "Assumption of risk" is a phrase borrowed from the law of torts. But the first requirement of "assumption of risk" in torts is that the assumer should have had an accurate knowledge of the nature of the risk he was taking, and taken it anyway. In a secret agent case, by definition, the target individual does *not* know the nature of the risk. If Justice Stewart meant to say that the defendant waives the right to protection of his privacy when he "'agrees" to deal with a secret agent, there is a similar conflict with previous Court decisions requiring that waivers of constitutional rights be knowing, intelligent and specific.

What Justice Stewart and his three colleagues in the *Hoffa* majority believed, whether they said so or not, was that regardless of the apparent unfairness of using secret agents to gather evidence of crime, these agents are necessary *in some circumstances*, that their use *in certain cases* is itself of benefit to society. The fact that secret agents are *sometimes* necessary and do serve *some* useful purposes does not, however, mean that they should always be allowed. That is undoubtedly what Justice Stewart meant by saying that "all relevant constitutional restrictions" apply to police spies and undercover agents. But by failing to specify those situations in which secret agents *would* violate the protections of the Fourth Amendment, the Court has left the field open for infiltration of political and quasi-political groups by Red Squads, Congressional investigators and secret agents of all kinds.

Another danger of secret agents which the Court ignored in *Hoffa* was recently emphasized when Partin, the informer whose evidence convicted Hoffa, partially recanted his earlier testimony. The corrosive effect of such changes of heart by government agents can seriously damage the integrity of the judicial system. They are bound to occur—although they may not always come to light—as long as informer testimony is accepted without proper judicial scrutiny.

It is not easy to measure how great a threat police secret agents present to the traditional American values of free speech and free political debate. Lack of information on the extent of police use of undercover agents, reluctance of law-enforcement officials to discuss their clandestine operations, and the absence of publicity about and recorded public reaction to police spies have combined to frustrate the balancing of conflicting social interests. But the balancing process is necessary, for when the Court decides that one must "assume the risk" of speaking, not, as one supposes, to a friend, relative or business associate, but to a secret government agent, it takes a position whose implications endanger the essence of a free society.

Application of the Fourth Amendment to secret agents who move into political groups would not ban their use elsewhere. It would not, if the Court chose so to limit its decision, affect their infiltration of such nonpolitical activities as dope peddling, gambling or prostitution. Nor would it even absolutely preclude their use against groups which call themselves political, but which are actually aimed at violence, destruction of property, or other illegal activity. The Fourth Amendment's ban is only against "unreasonable" searches and seizures. But the determination of when a search is reasonable is one which the Constitution wisely leaves not to the police, but to a neutral judicial officer. Thus the issue is not that secret agents should never be used against groups which claim to be political; it is *who shall decide* when such use is appropriate. That decision should rest with a court, not with a policeman.

The Supreme Court is not alone in having avoided the difficult problems of secret agents in a free society. State legislatures and Congress, as well as police agencies at all levels of government, have done little to provide guidelines. In fact, it could be argued on the basis of past experience with judicial warrant procedures that even when the warrant requirement is in effect it offers minimal protection. Moreover, any judicial guidelines for the use of police spies will inevitably require elaboration in state rules of criminal procedure or police administrative regulations. Thus Supreme Court action would be only a first step to protect sensitive First Amendment activities against police espionage.

The examples noted earlier of secret police operations in political contexts are only a few of many which could be cited. In recent years the training of Americans in military and civilian intelligence has made sophisticated agents, formerly confined almost exclusively to the FBI, available to police departments at state and local levels. The existence of "special investigation" units in state and local law-enforcement agencies was documented by the Organized Crime Task Force of the President's Commission on Law Enforcement and Administration of Justice. It noted that in 1966 there were "effective intelligence programs" in only a handful of jurisdictions. How many *ineffective* programs exist, the Task Force report did not say. Activities of the Chicago, New York, San Francisco and Los Angeles city police departments are discussed briefly in the report.

The extent of police "intelligence" operations cannot be precisely documented. A survey of such activity, made for the President's Crime Commission by Prof. G. Robert Blakey and entitled *Local Law Enforcement Response to Organized Crime,* has been suppressed by the Justice Department, despite specific requests that it be made public. A report in the February *Chicago Journalism Review* indicated that in Chicago, at least, the police intelligence unit is active enough to keep under surveillance a member of the City Council—a member who also happens to be black.

Former FBI agent William Turner has noted how hard it is to assure unbiased use of police undercover agents, especially in a time of growing political activism among police officers. "Every department of any size has what is variously called a Subversive Squad, an Intelligence Unit, or a Red Squad. With their jurisdiction tenuously hinged on archaic state anti-radical syndicalist or anti-anarchy laws, or no law at all, they constantly pry into the public and private activities of Communists and Socialists, liberals and intellectuals, beatnik and peaceniks, et al., while ignoring the subversive menace from the right."

Senators Hart of Michigan and Long of Missouri said in dissenting from the Senate Judiciary Committee's report on the Omnibus Crime Control and Safe Streets Act that "traditional military intelligence has furnished [to local law-enforcement agencies] both the vocabulary and the tools by which it wages constant war upon [organized crime]. Almost every metropolitan police department and almost every major State has a bureau engaged exclusively in the collection of criminal—and political—intelligence. It was particularly interesting to find that these bureaus had no direct responsibility to investigate any specific crimes." The Omnibus Crime Control and Safe Streets Act specifically authorized federal money and FBI technical assistance to local police departments to develop "special" investigative capabilities.

The New York Times reported recently that the Justice Department has begun its program of assisting local law-enforcement agencies by demonstrating "tiny electronic listening devices [and] undercover agents. . . ." Ironically, the officials to whom these new techniques were being demonstrated were from the South, an area which may not need instruction in undercover techniques. In 1964 the Subversives Unit of the Alabama Department of Public Safety was reported to be secretly compiling dossiers on civil rights workers, including some officials of the Justice Department's Civil Rights Division.

More information on the extent of police use of secret agents against various types of alleged illegal activity is the first requirement. It is no coincidence that the Supreme Court's decision to bring wire tapping within the protection of the Fourth Amendment followed shortly after revelation of the extent of government wire tapping and the public's increasing fear of it. The necessary information could come through legislative inquiries, through administrative reviews brought about by political pressure on mayors and governors, and through tough-minded journalistic investigating. Once the extent of the practice is known, some hard decisions will have to be made—by courts, by legislatures and by the mayors and governors who ultimately control the police.

As Norman Mailer said, the infiltration of political groups by police secret agents had become, in 1968, a chronic joke. In a country whose traditions include what Justice Brandeis called "the opportunity to discuss freely supposed grievances and proposed remedies," and which continues to pride itself on unfettered political exchange, it is not a very funny joke. (Reprinted by permission of *The Nation*).

16

ETHICS FOR DATA BANKS

By Senator Charles McC. Mathias

As the investigations of the Senate Subcommittee on Constitutional Rights have dramatized, our basic freedoms—the right of privacy, freedom of speech, freedom of association—are at the mercy of an amoral technology. Thanks to "good old American know-how," we now know how to find out so much about each other that we are in imminent danger of trampling what Justice Brandeis called "the right most valued by civilized men, the right to be let alone."

In 1967 a survey of all federal agencies by the Senate Judiciary Subcommittee on Administrative Practices and Procedures disclosed that, as of about July 1, 1967, federal files included more than 3.1 billion personrecords—records about individual citizens. These 3.1 billion records included over 27.2 billion names, over 2.3 billion current and past address, 264.5 million police histories, 279.6 million psychiatric histories, 916.4 million records on alcoholism and drug addiction and over 1.2 billion income records. Of these billions of bits of information, about 48 per cent were then, in 1967, retrievable by companies. I would guess that both the total and the percentage on comhave risen substantially during the last four years.

If knowledge is power, this encyclopedic knowledge gives government raw materials of tyranny. Surveys have already revealed many instances — some foolish, some frightening — in which information about American citizens has been improperly sought, stored or shared by agencies of government.

To date the primary checks against abuse have been bureaucratic self-restraint and the energies of the press. We need far more reliable and consistent controls. It is time for us to insure that the need to know, strictly defined, will rein in our ability to find out.

I would like to focus particular attention on problems of controlling data and data banks in one particular area: the field of law enforcement and the administration of justice. Clearly in this area, more than in many others, there is a legitimate need for public agencies to have considerable information about individuals. At the same time, there is an especially urgent need to protect individuals against arbitrary or excessive exercises of the awesome police powers of the state.

In some instances equity may require police or courts to know more, rather than less, about an individual. For instance, when John Q. Public is being sentenced following conviction, it is not enough for the sentencing judge to know that Mr. Public has a record of five previous arrests. The judge should also know whether those arrests were for speeding or for assault, and what disposition was made of each charge.

On the other hand, Mr. Public should have some assurance that a youthful indiscretion will not follow him all the days of his life. For example, if a youth receives a suspended sentence at age 18 for possession of marijuana, or for involvement in a campus demonstration, that fact could pop up for years to jeopardize his applications for jobs, for credit cards, and for home loans.

As one grim example, the Bureau of Narcotics and Dangerous Drugs (BNDD) maintains computerized files on narcotics users. As of October 30, 1970, those files covered over 64,000 individuals—including three boys under three years old! Will that item be buried in statistical reports, surfacing only as a curiosity? Or will three boys be pursued for life by the tragic fact that they were exposed to narcotics before they could talk?

We are now witnessing a tremendous surge in the development and use of computerized data banks by law enforcement agencies throughout the nation. Although no single, nationwide federal-state-local system for collecting and transmitting personal histories has yet been established, all signs show that law enforcement agencies are hurtling in this direction, fueled largely by federal funds and unrestrained by any consistent controls.

Within the Department of Justice there are several large, active computerized data banks: the FBI's National Crime Information Center on wanted persons; the BNDD file on narcotics users; the FBI's Known Professional Check Passers File; the Organized Crime Intelligence System; the Civil Disturbance System; a file on offenders, based on federal penitentiary records; and the records of the Immigration and Naturalization Service.

While each of these data banks is currently separately maintained, the contents of each—with the exception of some intelligence data—

is made available when needed not just within the Justice Department, but also to other federal agencies with even marginal law enforcement mandates, to state and local agencies, and in some cases to private establishments such as national banks. The federal stamp of course gives all such data the force and validity of gospel. Federal law, in fact, encourages the collection and exchange of criminal records under the aegis of law enforcement.

At the same time that these federal files are growing, nearly every state and many cities are establishing their own data banks often with funds provided under the Safe Streets Act of 1968.

On July 17, 1970, I asked the Law Enforcement Assistance Administration for a full list of all automated data banks on individuals which had received LEAA funds, including the purpose of each project and the amount of each grant. In September I was advised that "a complete list should be available in about one month." Unfortunately, after considering my request for a total of seven and a half months, LEAA spokesmen have now decided that a full report cannot be assembled and no partial list will be made available at this time.

The LEAA annual report for fiscal 1970 does provide some pieces of the picture. For example, a comprehensive LEAA field survey of criminal justice information systems concluded that

". . . more than 30 states and the District of Columbia are engaged in developing law enforcement and criminal justice information systems. These systems range in scope of design from a limited police information system with online access to a few state files, such as driver records and vehicle registration, and an NCIC interface to those including all components of the criminal justice system and a variety of online and offline applications. There is also a wide disparity in the state of systems development . . .

"In all states the initial emphasis has been on police applications. This development focused on developing an NCIC interface, a message switching capability and online access to such key files as warrants and wanted persons, stolen vehicles, stolen property, stolen guns, driver records, vehicle registration, criminal histories and statistics."

The survey notes that information systems are also being developed in many states to serve the courts and correctional systems, including parole and juvenile agencies, and concludes: "The future promises an even greater rate of growth: most of the 1970 state plans contain requests for funds for computerized information systems. In addition, numerous discretionary fund proposals were received for information system development."

It is obvious that such state and local systems vary enormously in scope, sophistication, and the types of information and intelligence embraced. Yet, while disbursing uncounted millions to promote such systems, LEAA has not promulgated any regulations or standards. As Associate Administrator Richard W. Velde advised me last September, "Each system is governed by the appropriate state law."

State and local law enforcement agencies do not necessarily have any fewer scruples than federal bureaus about keeping personal histories confidential, or about jealously guarding criminal intelligence and raw investigatory files. But computers are bringing the ammunition for persecution, harassment and idle gossip within the reach of every prosecutor and parti-time deputy sheriff in the land. Just as one example, the Kansas City, Missouri, ALERT System includes the following "categories of information" in its computerized Warrant/ Want Real Time Files:

Outstanding Traffic and Parking Warrants
Outstanding City General Warrants
Outstanding Felony Warrants
Outstanding KCMOPD Pickup Orders
Local and National Intelligence Subjects
Persons on Parole Status
Active Adult and Juvenile Arrest Records with Abstract Date
KCMOPD Civilian/Law Enforcement Personnel
Area Dignitaries
Stolen Vehicles/License Plates
FBI Finger Print Classification and FBI Number
Moniker File (at a later date)
Persons with a history of mental disturbance
Persons known to have confronted or opposed law-enforcement personnel in the performance of their duty
College students known to have participated in disturbances, primarily on college campus areas
Persons known to assault Policemen
Persons known to be involved in shoplifting cases.

A description notes that "local area dignitaries" will be included in this system "with their appropriate titles" only if they so desire. Others in the above categories apparently have no choice.

I do not know that the Kansas City system has been abused. I do believe that it is myopic for Congress to fund hundreds and thousands of such catalogues, and wait until abuses surface before exercising oversight or imposing order.

It is encouraging that the most extensive new data system, Project SEARCH, has been extremely sensitive to problems of individual privacy. Project SEARCH is the ten-state System for Electronic Analysis and Retrieval of Criminal Histories which in December completed an 18-month demonstration period at a combined federal-state cost of $2.5 million. During that period, the SEARCH Project Group developed not only the technical capacity to collect and exchange standardized criminal histories, but also an impressive Code of Ethics and related policies "to assure that the most sophisticated measures are employed and the most perceptive judgments are made in the development and operation of the System to optimize the protection of individual privacy."

The philosophy summarized in this Code of Ethics is amplified in Technical Report No. 2, prepared by the Project SEARCH Committee on Security and Privacy. Among other steps, this report prescribes procedures for

• limiting data to that "with the characteristics of public records," recorded "only upon the report of a crime," and excluding such irrelevant data and unreliable material as unverified intelligence tips;

• continuously re-evaluating included data for its accuracy and completeness, and purging such items as "the record of first offenders where criminal proceedings have resulted in a determination in favor of such persons;"

• developing a "high level of computer, legal, physical, information, communications, and personnel security methods" to protect the system and give full protection to all information included; and

• developing "procedures for an individual to learn the contents of the arrest record kept about him and for the correction of inaccuracies or prejudicial omissions in a person's arrest record." (Quotes from Code of Ethics)

Overall, Technical Report No. 2 is a perceptive, challenging and generally successful attempt to come to grips with the problems inherent in an efficient, nationwide criminal justice data bank. Obviously, this approach has its critics. For instance, after reviewing an early draft of Technical Report No. 2, an FBI spokesman called it "very objectionable."

On December 9, 1970, LEAA approved a new grant of $1,552,060 to Project SEARCH for calendar year 1971 "to further develop and make operational an offender-record based criminal justice information system." On December 10, 1970, in an internal directive which was not publicly released, the Attorney General transferred the prime responsibility for future development of a nationwide system for exchanging criminal histories from LEAA to the FBI. I have been advised that this brief directive made no reference to privacy issues or the fate of the standards so carefully shaped by the SEARCH Project Group. Nor was the FBI's new mandate mentioned at all when the LEAA grant to Project SEARCH was routinely announced on December 16.

Congress should establish some reasonable rules to govern such operations. Some argue that the needs of law enforcement are so great that new technology should not be fettered by precious concerns for the niceties of privacy. Others assert that any regulatory efforts in this field are an unwarranted reflection on the integrity of our hallowed system of criminal justice. Still others maintain that the regulatory chore should be left to the states, as it was in the days when a criminal record could be transmitted across the country only by mail. In response we must consider Juvenal's question: *Sed quis custodiet ipsos custodes?* But who guards the guardians?

In my judgment it is not only proper but essential for Congress to enact, at minimum, controls over three types of criminal justice data systems: all those developed and maintained by agencies of the federal government; all those operated by state or local agencies but supported wholly or partly by federal funds; and all those interfacing with federal systems.

As I have suggested, these criteria embrace a vast and mushrooming field. By enacting definite standards for federal data banks, Congress can inject order into operations now subject to great misunderstanding and suspicion, and promote public confidence in those data collection systems which are necessary. By imposing basic requirements on other systems involving federal funds or linkages, Congress can guide the states and take a long step toward insuring that any state or local data bank abuses or excesses will remain localized.

While I personally believe that we should begin from recommendations such as those of the SEARCH Project Group, I am frank to admit that right now Congress simply does not know enough to prepare sound, durable legislation overnight. Accordingly, last year I sponsored and Congress approved the following amendment to the Omnibus Crime Control and Safe Streets Act Amendments of 1970: "Not later than May 1, 1971, the Administration (LEAA) shall submit to the President and to the Congress recommendations for legislation . . . with respect to promoting the integrity and accuracy of criminal justice data collection, processing and dissemination systems funded in whole or in part by the Federal Government, and protecting the constitutional rights of all persons covered or affected by such systems." (P.L. 91-644, Sec. 7).

Lest there be any doubt, let me emphasize that this directive means exactly what it says. The report to Congress is to be a comprehensive one, recommending legislation to cover *all* criminal justice data systems of *all* federal agencies — including those in the arena of national security—plus all non-federal systems which enjoy any federal financial support. It is not to be, for example, simply a status report on Project SEARCH or a pious assertion that there is no problem. Rather, the report should reflect a somber self-examination by the executive branch and a serious effort to work with the Congress in this difficult field.

In conclusion, I do not believe that we are doomed to perpetual war between computers and the Constitution. Rather, I am confident that—through hard work and constant watchfulness—we can civilize our technology so as to promote both justice and liberty.

17

INVASION OF THE HOME

By Ralph Nader

Invasion of privacy used to carry an almost luxurious connotation, a concept reserved for special public figures whose private lives were invaded by scandalmongers or seekers of vicarious thrills. It is no longer an elitist term. Hundreds of bits of information filed in dossiers on millions of individual Americans today constitute a massive assault on privacy whose ramifications are just beginning to be realized.

Most adults have at some time sought credit (or a credit card) and bought insurance. If you have done these things, there are probably at least two dossiers with your name on them.

When you seek to borrow money, your creditor receives a file from the credit bureau to establish your "credit rating." This dossier contains all the personal facts the credit bureau can assemble—your job, salary, length of time on the present job, marital status, a list of present and past debts and their payment history, any criminal record, any lawsuits of any kind, and any real estate you may own. The dossier may include your employer's opinion of your job performance or even your IQ rating from a high school test. By the time the creditor has finished talking to the credit bureau, he is likely to know more about your personal life than your mother-in-law does.

When you try to buy life insurance a file of even more intimate information about you is compiled by the "inspection agency." The insurance company finds out not only about your health but also about your drinking habits (how often, how much, with others or alone, and even what beverage), your net worth, salary, debts, domestic troubles, reputation, associates, manner of living, and standing in the community. The investigator is also asked to inquire of your neighbors and associates whether there is "any criticism of character or morals," and he must state whether he recommends that the insurance be declined.

Credit bureaus and inspection agencies are the major sources of information about individuals. But government, schools, employers, and banks are also collectors, and sometimes suppliers, of information. Employers frequently make information on their employees available to a credit bureau or inspection agency. They may also exchange information among themselves. *The Wall Street Journal* has reported that department stores in many cities have formed "mutual protection associations" that trade the names of former workers who were fired for suspected theft. This information-trading means that an individual may be denied a job on the basis of a former employer's untested—and unrefuted—suspicions.

Anyone processing an individual's bank records—now extensively recorded on computers—can reconstruct his associations, movements, habits, and life-style. The recently enacted Foreign Bank Secrecy Act can be used to require every FDIC-insured bank to make a reproduction of each check you draw on it and keep those reproductions for up to six years. The purpose is to ensure records of large quantities of money going out of the country so as to prevent tax evasions through the use of secret Swiss bank accounts. But the act contains no protection for the depositor by limiting in any way the banks' use of these records. Conceivably, a bank could sell them to a credit bureau or investigation agency.

It is the rare American who does not live in the shadow of his dossier. The "dossier industry" is a huge and growing business. There are 105 million files kept by the Association of Credit Bureaus of America (ACBA). Retail Credit Company of Atlanta, Georgia, the giant of the industry, has forty-five million files and makes thirty-five million reports each year. Credit Data Corporation, the second largest firm, has twenty-seven million files and adds seven million new dossiers each year.

These economic interests have almost total control over the information they collect and sell. They are not accountable to anyone except those who seek to purchase information. Further, for reasons of profit, these companies place a premium on the derogatory information they assemble. Except in three states, citizens do not have the right even to see these dossiers in order to correct inaccuracies. They will have that right for the first time when a federal law, the Fair Credit Reporting Act, goes into effect April 25, 1971. But they still will not have the right to control access to the information, on which there are in effect no legal restrictions, or the right to control the kinds of information that can go into their dossiers.

Until there are adequate protective measures—an "information bill of rights" that protects him against invasion of privacy through information dissemination—the citizen's major recourse is to understand how these agencies operate and what are his limited rights under present and pending law.

The first problem of the dossier is accuracy. There is no doubt that inaccurate information comes into the files of credit bureaus and insurance inspection agencies. In fact, credit bureaus disclaim accuracy in their forms, because most of the material is obtained from others (merchants, employers) and not verified by them. The information "has been obtained from sources deemed reliable, the accuracy of which [the credit bureau] does not guarantee."

Illustrations of errors are legion. New York State Assemblyman Chester P. Straub was refused a credit card because his dossier revealed an outstanding judgment. The judgment actually was against another person with a similar name, but the bureau had erroneously put it against Straub's name. Testimony before a U. S. Senate committee has accused credit bureaus of using a "shotgun" approach to recording judgments against consumers—entering any judgment on all the records bearing the same name as the defendant's, or a similar name, without checking to see which individual was actually involved.

In addition to errors of identification, there are errors due to incomplete information. A woman ordered a rug, but the seller delivered one of the wrong color. He refused to take it back and sued for payment. Although his case was thrown out of court, her credit record showed only that she had been sued for non-payment, and she was unable to get credit elsewhere thereafter. Arrests and the filing of lawsuits are systematically collected by credit bureaus and rushed into dossiers, but the dismissal of charges or a suit is not reported in the newspaper and so the credit bureau never learns of, or records, the affirmative data.

Also, there is the problem of obsolescence of information, as shown by the man whose bureau dossier in the Sixties listed a lawsuit from the Thirties. It was a $5 scare suit for a magazine subscription he had never ordered, and "nothing had come of it"—except in regard to his credit rating.

The introduction of computers can create its own set of problems. Although mechanical errors in the handling of information by people may be reduced, the probability of machine error is increased. In addition, credit data are taken directly from a creditor's computer to a credit bureau's computer without discretion. Your payments may have been excused for two months, due to illness, but the computer does not know this, and it will only report that you missed two payments. Storage problems alone will prevent the explanation from being made. Your rating with that creditor may not be affected, but with all others it will be.

These credit bureau inaccuracies generally relate to "hard data," which are subject to verification or contradiction. The insurance inspection agency, on the other hand, reports "soft data," or gossip, and they are not subject to verification at all. This creates new sources of inaccuracies. Where the information is inherently uncheckable, the biased employee or the biased informant can easily introduce inaccuracies. Even where bias is not present, inneuendo or misunderstanding can create error, while a vindictive inspector can abuse his power for personal reasons.

Why don't inspectors check the accusations made by informants with the accused? One reason is they don't have time. If they must make ten or fifteen reports a day, they can spend only forty minutes on an average report, including transportation and typing it up. This allows no time for checking accusations, or even facts.

A more vicious reason is the agency's penchant for derogatory information and the fact that it records on both a weekly and a monthly basis the percentage of cases in which an inspector recommends declines. He must file a certain percentage of derogatory reports (at one time 8 per cent for life and 10 per cent for auto reports) if he is to be known as a "good digger." If he has not met his "quota," the temptation to use any rumor, without confirmation, may be overwhelming. These quotas may be regarded by the agency as a necessary control device to prevent inspectors from filing fake reports without investigation, but they show a reckless disregard for the safety of the investigated public.

Gossip-mongering with a quota on unfavorable comments can lead the harried inspector to rely on innuendo. A vivid illustration of the problems in insurance reporting is the case of two successful young businesswomen who applied for a life insurance policy required for a particular business transaction. On completion of a routine report, Retail Credit Company advised the insurance company not to issue the policy. It reported "severe criticism of the morals of both women, particularly regarding habits, and Lesbian activities." The investigator's information came from neighbors. None of these neighbors actually stated they had seen any illicit activity, but innuendo accomplished the same result. "Informants [unidentified] will not come out and state that applicant is Lesbian, but hint and hedge around and do everything but state it." The insurance company followed Retail Credit's advice and denied the policy.

Until passage of the Fair Credit Reporting Act, the law offered no protection against an inaccurate report, except in three states. There was no way one could even see a report to correct it. However, this new act offers some solutions to problems of accuracy.

1) It requires users of reports to notify consumers of the name and address of the consumer reporting agency whenever the user (e.g., creditor, insurer, or employer) takes adverse action on the basis of the agency's report.

2) It gives the consumer the right to know "the nature and substance of all information" on him in the agency's files, except medical information and the sources of "investigative information" (i.e., gossip). The limitation on sources of gossip is a serious weakness. Such sources can be discovered in litigation, however, and a suit is made easy to bring. Thus, *the agency can no longer guarantee the confidentiality of its sources.*

3) If a dispute arises between the consumer and the agency about the accuracy of an item, the agency must reinvestigate and *reverify* or delete the information. This will usually mean going back to the same neighbors and obtaining the same gossip. If the dispute is not settled by reinvestigation, the item must be noted as disputed. This leaves the user free to believe the agency.

These provisions are the strongest in the bill. They are weak from the consumer's point of view in two areas: The consumer should be allowed to learn the sources of gossip before litigation so that he can effectively rebut inaccurate gossip; further, he should be provided a quick, simple procedure for obtaining a declaratory judgment on the truth of any item.

4) The act also provides for enforcement through private actions if the agency is negligent. Negligence is easy to allege, but may be difficult to prove. Only time will tell what standards the courts will set.

Even though the agency's secrecy is now partially broken, relief may still not be available because most agencies are granted immunity for agency libel. Under the law of most states, the agencies are given a "conditional privilege" to publish false statements; so the libel action will not succeed. The privilege is granted on the grounds that they are fulfilling a private duty by providing businessmen with information they need in the conduct of their affairs. Georgia and Idaho (and England) do not grant the agencies such a privilege on the grounds the privilege itself does not benefit the general public, but only a profit-oriented enterprise, and that individual rights take precedence over the self-interest of the enterprise.

In the states granting the privilege, it is conditioned on the agency's 1) disclosing the information only to those with the requisite commercial interest, and 2) acting in good faith and without malice. However, proof of malice requires more than just the falsity of the report. In the past this has conferred an effective immunity on false reports. Malice, however, may be shown by the quota systems of the agencies or by their secrecy. Arguably, these company policies show a "wanton and reckless disregard of the rights of another, as is an ill will equivalent." Such theories, however, have not yet been tested in court.

There is no regulation on sale of the extensive personal information collected by credit bureau, insurance agencies, and employers. The dossiers are considered their "property," and they may do what they wish with it. The only influence to limit availability is an economic one, arising from the condition on the privilege for publishing libel—the report can be given only to subscribers of the service or others claiming a legitimate interest in its subject matter. However, claims of interest are easy to make and are not often scrutinized.

Furthermore, the citizen never knows when these dossiers are opened to someone. His consent is not sought before release of the information. He is not warned when someone new obtains the information, or told who they are—unless, under the new law, they take adverse action. There are no pressures on the information agencies to account to the subject of the dossier, nor have these agencies shown any willingness to assume such responsibility.

Credit bureaus may follow the Associated Credit Bureau guidelines and release information only to those who certify that they will use it in a "legitimate business transaction." This, of course, includes not only credit granters but also employers, landlords, insurers, and dozens of others. But even these weak guidelines are unenforceable by the association, and a CBS study found that half the bureaus they contacted furnished information to CBS without checking the legitimacy of their business purpose. Announced policies of inspection agencies also require a showing of a business purpose. But this includes anyone who has $5 and announces himself as a "prospective employer."

In April, the Fair Credit Reporting Act will impose a restriction on the release of information, but it is no better than those presently available. An agency will be able to sell information to anyone having "a legitimate business need" for the information. There are no economic or legal restrictions preventing any credit bureau or inspection agency from giving out their dossiers indiscriminately to anyone who can pay.

The consequences of making highly personal information easily available have only begun to be recognized. Credit reporting agencies may serve as private detectives for corporations that want to intimidate a critic. Recently the press reported that American Home Products, a drug manufacturer with more than $1-billion in sales, hired Retail Credit Company to investigate the personal affairs of Jay B. Constantine, an aide to the Senate Finance Committee who had helped draft legislation opposed by the drug industry. The investigation was stopped only "after their stupidity was uncovered," according to Senator Russell Long, Finance Committee chairman, who also said that the company had tendered "a complete letter of apology."

The introduction of computers furnishes other possibilities for use and misuse of personal information. Arthur R. Miller, in his new book, *The Assault on Privacy,* reports that MIT students in Project MAC (Machine Aided Cognition) were able to tap into computers handling classified Strategic Air Command data. If they can do this, any timesharing user can tap into a computer data bank. There is no way at present that computer people can guarantee their control over access. They cannot even guarantee that they can prevent rewriting of the information in the computer by outsiders.

What can be done to control the availability of these dossiers? Primarily, anyone obtaining information on you should be required to obtain your express consent to the release before receiving the information. This would recognize your interest in preserving the privacy of your own personality. It would allow you to decide whether any particular transaction was worth the invasion of your privacy by the other party.

Even if the information in the dossier is completely accurate and available only to creditors, insurers, and employers, there may be personal or private details—perhaps irrelevant to the demands of the credit-insurance industries—that people want kept to themselves. Some kinds of information may be so personal that their storage and sale are offensive. For example, it is possible to assemble a list of the books a person reads by observing his bookshelves, talking to his neighbors, or obtaining the records of the public library. An employer or insurer could manufacture a "business purpose" for obtaining such information—to determine the subject's knowledge or intelligence, generally, or in a specific field. There is little doubt that such an effort would be offensive to most people, violating their privilege of private thoughts and opinions. It would be offensive even if accurate.

Currently, the information gathered in most dossiers includes a subject's past educational, marital, employment, and bill-paying records. His "club life," drinking habits, and associates are recorded. Also included are an employer's opinion of his work habits and his neighbors' opinion of his reputation, character, and morals, which probably includes gossip about old neighborhood feuds.

Insurance company underwriters indicate that many do not use some questions (e.g., "What social clubs does he belong to?"). Some questions are overdrafted (e.g., the query "Who are his associates?" is useful to them only as "Does he have any criminal associates?"—a quite different version). The reason for asking what *kind* of alcoholic beverage an applicant drank was incomprehensible to at least two underwriters.

When asked whether they ever sought to have unnecessary questions struck from the form, the response was "Why should we? It's just as easy to skip over them when reading." There was no indication that they had any scruples about, or even any understanding of, the problem as an invasion of privacy.

Credit bureaus and investigation agencies do not generally gather such information as test scores or personality traits. Nor are lists of books assembled—yet. But there is nothing to prevent these investigators from adding this information to the standard items in their dossiers. The FBI has tried a similar form of investigation. Common law doctrines seem not to cover these problems, and, until recently, legislatures and relevant administrative bodies have shown no interest. Most information agencies have no announced policies that would preclude them from including any type of question. Thus, the only reason such information is not gathered is an economic one: No one is sufficiently interested to request and pay for it.

New technology is also tipping the balance against the individual's right of privacy as far as kinds of information are concerned. With problems of storage and transmittal solved, the technological tendency is to collect more data on individuals, inevitably more sensitive data.

The way information is gathered also has ominous implications for the individual's privacy. Credit bureaus gather their information from employers, newspapers, and credit-granters who are members of the bureau. They also collect data from the "welcome wagon" woman who visits homes and notes what buying "needs" you have so that you can be dunned by the right merchant. American Airlines' computer can give anyone information about what trips you have taken in the last two or three months. Further, it can give your seat number and be used to determine who sat next to you, perhaps inferentially describing your associates. In addition, it can tell your telephone contact number and, from this, determine where you or your associates stayed in each city of departure. Credit Card accounts can do much the same thing, telling what you have bought recently (to establish standard of living and life-style) and where you shop.

Each of these methods of inquiry constitutes a serious invasion of privacy, but the most serious invasion is the neighborhood investigation by the inspection agency. Here information is gathered by questioning your neighbors, building superintendent, grocer, or postmaster about what you do while you are in your own home. There is the threat not only of gossip-mongering and slander, but of the creation of a kind of surveillance on your home. For most people, the only available private place is "home." Here, even though observed by neighbors perhaps, the individual can feel free to discard his social role and be more expressive of his own personality. It is here that the "neighborhood check" of the inspection agency is most frightening.

How does an inspector go about obtaining information from your neighbors? Frederick King of Hooper-Holmes candidly described the procedures used when a married man is suspected of an extramarital affair. "You go to a neighbor and establish rapport. Then you ask, 'What's your opinion of him as a family man?' This will usually elicit some hint—through the expression on his face or the way he answers. Then you start digging. You press him as far as he will go, and if he becomes recalcitrant you go somewhere else. If you go to enough people, you get it."

Do present laws give you any protection from these invasions of your privacy in regard to either the types of information stored and sold or the manner in which they are gathered? Probably not.

There is a tort cause of action for invasion of privacy, but instead of furnishing a broad protection device, the courts have established four subcategories of the right. Two of these subcategories related to the gathering and publication of personal material are "public disclosures of private facts" and "intrusion."

Public disclosure of private facts has not been actionable without a finding of "unreasonable publication," and publication to a "small group" would include the subscribers of a credit bureau or investigation agency, in much the same way that publication of defamation to such groups has been held privileged. The exemption is based on the same reasoning that sustains the conditional privilege to defamation and has the same dangers to the subject, who may not be able to correct falsehoods or defend himself against the consequences of having intimate details of his life revealed to the business community in his town.

Intrusion has been found most often in cases involving physical intrusion. Peering through windows, wiretapping, and eavesdropping seem to strike a more responsive chord in court than does interviewing your neighbors or acquaintances. This tort is usually held to require an "extreme" or "shocking" violation of your privacy, and physical trespasses are most easily perceived as shocking.

In a New York Court of Appeals decision involving the author and General Motors, the court went beyond physical intrusions to include surveillance for an unreasonable time. However, even this decision makes actionable only those intrusions that are for the purpose of gathering confidential information. The question whether this doctrine covers investigations seeking to discover marital relationships, sexual habits, or housekeeping abilities has not been presented to the courts since the New York decision. However, three of the court's judges specifically stated that the four recognized subcategories of the right to privacy are neither frozen nor exhaustive.

If judicial protection against the collection and sale of overly personal information is limited, legislative protection is still nonexistent, even after passage of the Fair Credit Reporting Act. That statute may provide accuracy protection, but the Senate conferees refused to accept any provisions that would limit the types of data about you that can be gathered and sold.

The invasion of privacy should more accurately be called the invasion of self. The right to protect himself against an informational assault is basic to the inviolability of the individual. On the one hand, we recognize that an arrest record may haunt an individual, and there is precedent for a wrong arrest that is thrown out of court to be expunged from the record. But we have not yet recognized that the bits of information contained in dossiers kept on 105 million Americans may be just as decisive and just as damaging to their lives.

The individual's right to privacy of self is crucial to the functioning of our society. Suppose you walked into a courtroom and picked up a pamphlet relating everything the judge had ever done in his personal life. What would that information do to your interaction with that court? To some extent it is absolutely necessary to preserve barriers of privacy and protection about people's lives in order to permit ordinary interaction between people, an interaction that is to a significant degree based on trust.

Our Founding Fathers developed Constitutional safeguards in the Bill of Rights against the arbitrary authority of government. The rights against unreasonable search and seizure and against self-incrimination were examples of basic rights of privacy deemed critical for a free people. Generations passed and the country developed private organizations possessed of a potential for arbitrary authority not foreseen by the early Constitutional draftsmen. Most pervasive and embracing of these organizations is the modern corporation. Aggressive by its motivational nature, the corporation, in a credit-insurance economy spurred by computer gathering and retrieval efficiency, has created new dimensions to information as the currency of power over individuals. The secret gathering and use of such true or false information by any bank, finance company, insurance firm, other business concern, or employer place the individual in a world of unknowns. He is inhibited, has less power to speak out, is less free, and develops his own elaborate self-censorship.

What this costs in individual freedom and social justice cannot be measured. It can only be felt by the daily contacts with human beings in invisible chains reluctant to challenge or question what they believe to be wrong since, from some secret corporate dossier, irrelevant but damaging information may be brought to bear on them. The law and technology have provided the "dossier industry" with powerful tools to obtain and use information against people in an unjust way—whether knowingly or negligently. The defenseless citizen now requires specific rights to defend against and deter such invasions of privacy.

What You Can Do

What can you do to protect yourself from your dossiers? The Fair Credit Reporting Act allows you to protect yourself, but only if you take action. Let me use, as an example, the ordinary purchase of a life insurance policy. After you have decided to purchase some life insurance, you should first consider how much of an invasion of privacy you are willing to suffer in order to get it.

If a character investigation will be made, you are entitled under the act to be told automatically only that it will be made, and you are told that fact three days after the investigation has been ordered. Once you have been informed, it is up to you to take any further initiative. You must request in writing additional information. Once you have made that request, the insurer must reveal "the nature and scope" of the investigation. According to Representative Leonor K. Sullivan of Missouri, the House manager of the bill, this means they must tell you "all the items of questions which the investigation will cover. The best method of meeting this criterion is for the agency to give the consumer [you] a blank copy of any standardized form used." Unfortunately, all of this happens at least three days after you have signed the contract.

However, you can still insist on receiving this information before you sign the contract. Nothing in the law prevents you from obtaining this information earlier. The agent and the insurer are both anxious to sell you insurance. If you don't like too much snooping, demand that the scope of the investigation be revealed before you buy. If you think it is overzealous, complain to both the agent and the insurer and be specific about what you think is too intrusive. If the company will not listen to your complaints, find another one—or consider using group insurance. It is an interesting fact that group insurance does not usually require an investigation, and its use has been growing.

Once the privacy problems have been settled between you and the insurer, you must also worry about the accuracy of the report. If you are turned down or high-rated by the insurer, due in part to an investigation and report, the insurer must tell you that it was due to a report and give you the name and address of the agency making the report.

This entitles you to go to the agency and demand that it disclose "the nature and substance of all the information (except medical information) in its files." According to the House manager of the bill, this means disclosure of "all information in the file relevant to a prudent businessman's judgment" in reviewing an insurance application. If you have demanded a blank copy of the agency's standard form, you will know whether you have been told all that you are entitled to know.

If you disagree with any information in your file, tell the agency. The agency is then required to reinvestigate and reverify or delete the information. If they do not claim reverification, make certain that they delete the information, and then personally notify all prior recipients that it has been deleted. If they do claim reverification, ask how they reverified, from whom, and exactly what was said. Don't be satisfied with general answers because you cannot refute specific accusations with generalities. Although the act does not give you access on request to the names of those who lied about you, it does give you access to those names if you file suit under the act. Thus, the names cannot be protected forever. Many reputable agencies should see this and be willing to attempt to settle disputes with you without litigation. Even if the agency claims reverification, you can still have the item listed as disputed if it is in error, and file a brief statement outlining your side of the story.

A second common example is the credit card company that charges you improperly and will not answer your letter of complaint, but continues to bill you and threatens to ruin your credit rating if you don't pay. You can follow the procedure discussed earlier and wait until some other creditor turns you down, then go and get the file corrected. It may be better, however, to go and check your file at the local credit bureau periodically, so that you can correct errors before they are reported and you are turned down.

The Fair Credit Reporting Act is an essential step toward solving some of the problems of accuracy in individual dossiers. For the first time, people may find out what credit bureaus and inspection agencies are saying about them, and they now have some means of correcting inaccuracies. But there are still no restraints on availability of this information or on the kinds of information gathered. Unless citizens are provided with an "information bill of rights" enabling them to see, correct, and know the uses of these dossiers, and to impose liability on wrongdoers, they can be reduced to a new form of computer-indentured slavery. The law must begin to teach the corporation about the inviolability of the individual as it has striven to teach the state. (Reprinted by permission of the American Civil Liberties Union.)

SELECTED BIBLIOGRAPHY

(Compiled by Christopher Pyle)

Congressional Documents

Hearings of the Senate Subcommittee on Constitutional Rights, Committee on the Judiciary: *Wiretapping, Eavesdropping, and the Bill of Rights* (1959); *The Rights of Government Employees, Psychiatric Exams, and Psychological Tests.* (1965); *Protecting Privacy and the Rights of Federal Employees* (1967).

Hearings of the Senate Subcommittee on Administrative Practice and Procedure, Committee on the Judiciary: *Invasions of Privacy* (1965); *Hearings on S. 928*—Right of Privacy Act of 1967 (1967); *Government Dossier* (1967); *Computer Privacy* (1968).

Hearings of other Senate Subcommittees: Subcommittee on Anti-Trust and Monopoly, Committee on the Judiciary—*Credit Bureaus* (1968); Subcommittee on Financial Institutions, Committee on Banking and Currency—*Fair Credit Reporting* (1969).

Hearings of the House (Gallagher) Subcommittee on Government Operations: *Privacy and the National Data Bank Concept* (1968); *The Computer and Invasion of Privacy* (1966); *Data Processing Management in the Federal Government* (1967).

Hearings of the House (Moss) Subcommittee on Government Operations: *The Use of Polygraphs as "Lie Detectors"* (1964 and 1965).

Hearings of the Special Subcommittee on the Invasion of Privacy of the Committee on Government Operations: *Invasion of Privacy* (1965); *Retail Credit Companies* (1968).

Hearings of other House Committees: Ad Hoc Subcommittee of the Committee on Education and Labor — *National Research Data Processing and Information Retrieval Center* (1963); Committee on the Post Office and Civil Service: *1970 Census Questions* (1966); Special Subcommittee of the Committee on the Armed Services: *The Capability of the National Guard to Cope With Civil Disturbances* (1967).

Leading Books

Miller, Arthur R. *The Assault on Privacy: Computers, Data Banks, and Dossiers,* 1971.
Packard, Vance. *The Naked Society,* 1964.
Westin, Alan F. *Privacy and Freedom,* 1967.
Wheeler, S. (ed). *On Record: Files and Dossiers in American Life,* 1969.

The Functions of Privacy

Ardrey, Robert. *The Territorial Imperative,* 1966.
Bates. "Privacy—A Useful Concept?" 42 *Social Forces* 429 (1964).
Bloustein. "Privacy as an Aspect of Human Dignity: An Answer to Dean Prosser," 39 *New York University Law Review* 962 (1964).
Carpenter, C. R. "Territoriality: A Review of Concepts and Problems, *Behavior and Evolution,* 1958.
Halmos, Paul. *Solitude and Privacy,* 1952.
Jourand, Sidney M. "Some Psychological Aspects of Privacy," 31 *Law and Contemporary Problems* 307 (1966).
Konvitz, Milton R. "Privacy and the Law: A Philosophical Prelude," 31 *Law and Contemporary Problems* 272 (1966).
Neumann, Franz L. "The Concept of Political Freedom," 53 *Columbia Law Review* 901 (1953).
Prosser, William. "Privacy," 48 *Columbia Law Review* 383 (1960).
Shils, Edward. "Privacy: Its Constitution and Vicissitudes," 31 *Law and Contemporary Problems* 281 (1966).
Warren, Samuel, and Louis D. Brandeis. "The Right to Privacy," 4 *Harvard Law Review* 193 (1890).

Threats to Privacy

"Big Corporations Can Have Their Own CIA," *New Republic,* February 18, 1967.
Brenton, Myron. *The Privacy Invaders,* 1964.
Douglas, William O. "The Black Silence of Fear," *New York Times Magazine,* May 13, 1952.
Franklin, Ben A. "Surveillance of Citizens Stirs Debate," *New York Times,* December 27, 1970.
Hamilton, Peter. "Espionage and Subversion in an Industrial Society," *The Nation,* December 11, 1967.
Heckscher, August. "The Invasion of Privacy: The Reshaping of Privacy," 28 *American Scholar* 13 (1959).

Kalven, J., Jr. "Problems of Privacy in the Year 2000," *Daedalus,* (Summer 1967).

Lasswell, H. D. "The Threat to Privacy," in R. M. MacIver (ed.), *The Conflict of Loyalties,* 1952.

Rovere, Richard. "The Invasion of Privacy: Technology and the Claims of Community," 27 *American Scholar* 416 (1958).

DATA SURVEILLANCE

Baran. "On Distributed Communications: Security, Secrecy, and Tamper-Free Considerations," *Rand Corporation Memorandum,* RM-3765-PR. 1964.

Franklin, Ben A. "Federal Computers Amass Files on Suspect Citizens," *New York Times,* June 28, 1970.

Hirsch, Phil. "Data Banks: The Punchcard Snooper," *The Nation,* October 16, 1967.

Hoffman. "Computers and Privacy: A Survey," 1 *Computing Surveys* 85 (1969).

Information Sharing: The Hidden Challenge in Criminal Justice. Brochure of the New York State Identification and Intelligence System, 1966-67.

Kaysen, Carl. "Data Banks and Dossiers," *The Public Interest,* Spring 1967.

"National Data Center and Personal Privacy," *Atlantic,* November 1967.

Note, "Privacy and Efficient Government: Proposals for a National Data Center," 82 *Harvard Law Review* 400 (1968).

Office of Science and Technology of the Executive Office of the President, *Privacy and Behavioral Research,* 1967.

Packard, Vance. "Don't Tell It to the Computer," *New York Times Magazine,* January 8, 1967.

Prisendorf, Anthony. "National Data Center: The Computer vs. the Bill of Rights," *The Nation,* October 31, 1966.

Project, "The Computerization of Government Files: What Impact on the Individual?" 15 *University of California at Los Angeles Law Review* 1371 (1968).

Rosenberg, Jerry. *The Death of Privacy,* 1969.

Sawyer and Schechter. "Computers, Privacy, and the National Data Center: The Responsibility of Social Scientists," 23 *American Psychologist* 810 (1968).

Ware. "Security and Privacy in Computer Systems," 30 *AFIPS Conference Proceedings* 279 (1967).

Westin, Alan F. "The Snooping Machine," *Playboy,* May 1968.

Wheeler, S., (ed.). *On Record: Files and Dossiers in American Life,* 1969.

ELECTRONIC SURVEILLANCE

Bishop, Joseph W. "Privacy vs. Protection—The Bugged Society," *New York Times Magazine,* June 8, 1969.

Brown, Robert M. *The Electronic Invasion,* 1967.

Clark, Ramsey. *Crime in America,* 1970. (Chapter 17, "The Wiretap: Destroyer of Integrity").

Dash, Samuel. *The Eavesdroppers,* 1959.

Edwards. "Effect of the Electronic Age Upon Invasion of Privacy," in *American Bar Association Section of Individual Rights and Responsibilities,* 1967.

Kessler, Ronald. "FBI Wiretapping: How Widespread?" *Washington Post,* February 7, 1971.

Kessler, Ronald. "Private Wiretapping: How Extensive?" *Washington Post,* February 8, 1971.

Long, Edward V. *The Intruders: The Invasion of Privacy by Government and Industry,* 1967.

Murphy, Walter. *Wiretapping on Trial,* 1965.

Schwartz, Herman. "The Legitimation of Electronic Eavesdropping: The Politics of Law and Order." 76 *Michigan Law Review* 455 1969).

U.S. Senate. Subcommittee on Constitutional Rights, Committee on the Judiciary. *Hearings on Wiretapping, Eavesdropping, and the Bill of Rights.* 86th Cong., 1st Sess., 1959.

PHYSICAL SURVEILLENCE

Donnelly. "Judicial Control of Informants, Spies, Stool Pigeons, and Agents Provocateur," 60 *Yale Law Journal* 1091 (1951).

Dubin. "The Informer's Privilege Versus the Constitution: A Doctrinal Dilemma," 50 *Journal of Criminal Law* 554 (1960).

"How Police Infiltrate the Press," *Chicago Journalism Review,* January 1971.

Lundy, Joseph R. "The Invisible Police," *The Nation,* December 8, 1969.

Mikell. "Judicial Control of Secret Agents." 76 *Yale Law Journal* 994 (1967).

Mikell. "The Doctrine of Entrapment in the Federal Courts." 90 *University of Pennsylvania Law Review* 245 (1942).

Neirs, D. R. "Informers and Agents Provocateurs—The Judicial Response," 120 *New Law Journal* 577 (June 18, 25, 1970).

Note, "An Informer's Tale: Its Use in Judicial and Administrative Proceedings," 63 *Yale Law Journal* 206 (1953).

Note, "Concealment of an Informant's Identity—A Governmental Privilege," 1959 *Washington University Law Quarterly* 296.

Note, "Police Undercover Agents: New Treat to First Amendment Freedoms," 37 *Georgetown Law Review* 634 (1969).

Orfield. "Defense of Entrapment: A Plea for Constitutional Standards." 20 *University of Florida Law Review* 63 (1967).

"Police Agent Jailed in Hobart Inquiry," *New York Times,* July 25, 1970.

"Police Infiltration of Dissident Groups," 61 *Journal of Criminal Law, Criminology, and Police Science* 181 (1970).

"Where are the Clark Kents of Yesteryear?" *Ramparts,* November, 1970.

PSYCHOLOGICAL SURVEILLANCE

Gross, M. L. *The Brain Watchers.* 1962.

Miller, Arthur R. "Psychological Testing: Can We Minimize Its Perils?," *Think,* May-June 1969.

THE DOMESTIC INTELLIGENCE COMMUNITY (*General*)

Donner, Frank. "The Theory and Practice of American Political Intelligence," *New York Review of Books,* April 22, 1971.

Elliff, John T. *Crime, Dissent, and the Attorney General,* 1971.

"Federal Civil Disturbance Intelligence Network," *The National Journal,* June 6, 1970.

Kondracke, Morton. "The Boom in Snoopery," *The Progressive,* June 1970.

Lang, John S. "Big Brother (U.S.) Is Watching You," *Boston Herald Traveler,* April 19, 1970.

Lundy, Joseph R. "The Invisible Police," *The Nation,* December 8, 1969.

Ottenberg, Miriam. *The Federal Investigators,* 1962.

POLICE INTELLIGENCE UNITS

Bouza, Anthony. Thesis on New York's Bureau of Special Services,

1968. (On file in the John Jay College of Criminal Justice Library).
Dreifus, Claudia. "Boss is Watching," *The Nation, January 25,* 1971.
Goulden, Joseph C. "The Cops Hit the Jackpot," *The Nation,* November 23, 1970.
LaFave and Remington. "Controlling the Police: The Judge's Role in Making Law Enforcement Decisions." 63 *Michigan Law Review* 987 (1965).
Turner, William. *The Police Establishment,* 1968.

THE JUSTICE DEPARTMENT

Cummings, Homer and Carl McFarland. *Federal Justice.* 1937.
Eliff, John T. *Crime, Dissent, and the Attorney General,* 1971.
Goulden, Joseph C. "The Cops Hit the Jackpot," *The Nation,* November 23, 1970.
Halloran, Richard. "Dissidence Unit Has Dossier on 14,000," *New York Times,* April 2, 1971.
Kondracke, Morton. "Army Conditions Met on Civilian Intelligence Files?" *Chicago Sun-Times,* March 8, 1970.
National Popular Government League. *Report on the Illegal Practices of the United States Department of Justice,* 1920.
Naughton, James M. "United States To Tighten Surveillance of Radicals," *New York Times,* April 12, 1970.

THE FEDERAL BUREAU OF INVESTIGATION

Collins, F. L. *The FBI in Peace and War,* 1962.
Cook, Fred J. *The FBI Nobody Knows,* 1964.
Hoover, J. Edgar. "Civil Liberties and Law Enforcement," 49 *Northwestern University Law Review* 333 (1954).
Latham, Aaron. "FBI: Top Secrets at at Top Prices," *Washington Post,* July 25, 1970.
Lowenthal, Max. *The Federal Bureau of Investigation,* 1950.
Mason, Alpheus T. *Harlan Fiske Stone: Pillar of the Law,* 1956. (Discussion of appointment of J. Edgar Hoover at pp. 149-53).
Navasky, Victor W. "The Government and Martin Luther King," *Atlantic,* November 1970.
Overstreet, Harry, *The FBI In Our Open Society,* 1969.
Whitehead, Don. *The FBI Story,* 1956.
Wilson, H. H. "The FBI Today," *The Nation,* February 8, 1971.

THE SECRET SERVICE

"Card Carrying Reader," *New Republic,* July 15, 1970.

Ervin, Sam J., Jr. "Secret Service Guidelines," *Congressional Record,* December 15, 1969, p. S16721.

"Search for the Maryland Bomber Widens," *New York Times,* March 14, 1970.

ARMY COUNTERINTELLIGENCE

Holloran, Richard. "Army Spied on 18,000 Civilians in 2-Year Operation, *New York Times,* January 18, 1970.

Maffre, John. "Army Riot Unit Marks Time," *Washington Post,* August 11, 1968. (Directorate of Civil Disturbance Planning and Operations).

Mikva, Abner *et al.* "Military Surveillance Over Civilians," *Congressional Record,* December 18, 1970.

Pyle, Christopher H. "CONUS Intelligence: The Army Watches Civilian Politics," *Washington Monthly,* January, 1970.

Pyle, Christopher H. "CONUS Revisited: The Army Covers Up," *Washington Monthly,* July, 1970.

Stout, Jared "Big Brother Pentagon: Keping Tabs on Civilians," *The Nation, December* 28, 1970.

THE CIVIL SERVICE COMMISSION

Doyle, James. "CSC Keeps 'Security File,'" *Washington Evening Star,* April 22, 1970.

THE MILITARY ROLE IN LAW ENFORCEMENT

Clark, Ramsey. *Crime in America: Observations on Its Nature, Causes, Prevention and Control,* 1970. (Chapter 16, "Soldiers, Safety and Freedom")

Rankin, Robert S. *Freedom and Emergency Powers in the Cold War,* 1964.

Report of the National Advisory Commission on Civil Disorders, 1968.

Yarmolinsky, Adam. *The Military Establishment,* 1971. (Chapter 11, "The Traditional Federal Role in Civil Disorders," and Chapter 12, "Use of Troops in Recent Domestic Disorders.").

PRIVACY AND THE LAW

American Bar Association Standing Committee on Law & Technology. *Computers and the Law,* 1969.

Askin, Frank. "Police Dossiers and Emerging Principles of First Amendment Adjudication," 22 *Stanford Law Review* 196 (1970).

Beaney, William M. "The Right to Privacy and American Law," 31 *Law and Contemporary Problems* 253 (1966).

Bishop, J. W., Jr. "The Executive's Right of Privacy: An Unresolved Constitutional Question," 66 *Yale Law Journal* 477 (1957).

Blakey, G. Robert. "Aspects of the Evidence Gathering Process in Organized Crime Cases," in *The President's Commission on Law Enforcement and Administration of Justice, Task Force Report: Organized Crime,* 1967.

Bloustein. "Privacy as an Aspect of Human Dignity: An Answer to Dean Prosser," 39 *New York University Law Review* 962 (1964).

Bloustein. "Privacy, Tort Law, and the Constitution: Is Warren and Brandeis' Tort Petty and Unconstitutional As Well?" 46 *Texas Law Review* 611 (1968).

Buchenwald, Donald. "Eavesdropping, Informers and the Right of Privacy: A Judicial Tightrope,' 52 *Cornell Law Quarterly* 975 (1967).

Comment, "Electronic Surveillance by Law Enforcement Officers," 64 *Northwestern University Law Review* 63 (1969).

Comment, "Privacy, Defamation, and the First Amendment: The Implications of *Time, Inc. v. Hill,*" 67 *Columbia Law Review,* 926 1967).

"Consent Problem in Wiretapping and Eavesdropping: Surreptitious Monitoring with the Consent of a Participant in a Conversation," 68 *Columbia Law Review* 189 (1968).

Creech, William A. "The Privacy of Government Employees," 31 *Law and Contemporary Problems* 413 (1966).

Dixon. "The Griswold Penumbra: Constitutional Charter for an Expanded Law of Privacy?" 64 *Michigan Law Review* 197 (1965).

Fried. "Privacy," 77 *Yale Law Journal* 475 (1968).

Green, Harold P. "The New Technological Era: A View from the Law," *Bulletin of Atomic Scientists,* November 1967.

Handler, Joel and Margaret K. Rosenheim. "Privacy in Welfare: Public Assistance and Juvenile Justice," 31 *Law and Contemporary Problems* 377 (1966).

Helfeld, David M. "A Study of the Justice Department's Policies on Wiretapping," 9 *Lawyers Guild Review* 57 (1949).

Hofstader, Samuel H., and George Horowitz. *The Right of Privacy,* 1964.

Hoover, J. Edgar, "The Confidential Nature of FBI Reports," 8 *Syracuse Law Review* 2 (1956).

Jacob & Jacob. "Confidential Communications," *New Law Journal,* February 6, 1969, p. 133.

Kalven, Harry Jr. "Privacy in Tort Law—Were Warren and Brandeis Wrong?" 31 *Law and Contemporary Problems* 326 (1966).

Kamisar, Yale. "The Wiretapping-Eavesdropping Problem," 44 *Minnesota Law Review* 891 (1960).

Karst, Kenneth L. "The Files: Legal Controls Over the Accuracy and Accessibility of Stored Personal Data," 31 *Law and Contemporary Problems* 342 (1966).

Konvitz, Milton R. "Privacy and the Law: A Philosophical Prelude," 31 *Law and Contemporary Problems* 272 (1966).

Lewin, Nathan. "Privacy and the 'Third-Party Bug,' " *New Republic,* April 17, 1971.

Michael, D. N. "Speculation on the Relation of the Computer to Individual Freedom and the Right of Privacy," 33 *George Washington Law Review* 270-86 (1964).

Nizer, Louis. "The Right of Privacy: A Half Century's Development," 39 *Michigan Law Review* 526 (1951).

Note, "Credit Investigations and the Right to Privacy: Quest for a Remedy," 57 *Georgetown Law Journal* 509 (1969).

Note, "From Private Places to Personal Privacy," 43 *New York University Law Review* 968 (1968).

Pemberton. "On the Dangers, Legal Aspects, and Remedies," in "Symposium—Computers, Data Banks, and Individual Privacy," 63 *Minnesota Law Review* 211 (1968).

Pipe. "Privacy: Establishing Restrictions on Government Inquiry," 18 *American University Law Review* 516 (1969).

"Police Liability for Invasion of Privacy." 16 *Cleveland and Marshall Law Review* 428 (1967).

Project, "The Computerization of Government Files," 15 *University of California at Los Angeles Law Review* 1371 (1968).

Prosser, William. "Privacy," 48 *Columbia Law Review* 393 (1960).

Rogers, William P. "The Case for Wire Tapping,' 63 *Yale Law Journal* 792 (1954).

Silver. "Privacy and the First Amendment," 34 *Fordham Law Review* 553 (1966).

Spritzer, Ralph S. "Electronic Surveillance by Leave of the Magistrate," 118 *University of Pennsylvannia Law Review* 169 (1969).

Warren, Samuel, and Louis D. Brandeis. "The Right to Privacy," 4 *Harvard Law Review* 193 (1890).

Westin, Alan. "Civil Liberties and Computerized Data Systems," in *Computers, Communications and the Public Interest* (1971).

SURVEILLANCE AND THE FIRST AMENDMPT

ACLU v. Laird: Brief for the Appellants, U.S. Court of Appeals, 7th Circuit, No. 71-1159. Illinois Division, American Civil Liberties Union, 1971.

Askin, Frank. "Police Dossiers and Emerging Principles of Frist Amendment Adjudication." 22 *Stanford Law Review* 196 (1970).

Comment, "Chilling Political Expression By Use of Police Intelligence Files." 5 *Harvard Civil Rights, Civil Liberties Law Review* 71 (1970).

Myerson. "Right of Association Extended to Curtail Harrassment of Political Associations Through Criminal Investigations," 1969 *Utah Law Review* 383 (1969).

Note, "Anderson v. Sills: The Constitutionality of Police Intelligence Gathering," 65 *Northwestern University Law Review* 461 (1970).

Note, "Freedom of Speech: State Police Intelligence System Focusing on Public Protesters Declared Unconstitutional, Anderson v. Sills," 83 *Harvard Law Review* 935 (1970).

Tatum v. Laird: Brief for the Appellants, U.S. Court of Appeals, District of Columbia Circuit, No. 24,203. American Civil Liberties Union, New York, 1970.

INDIVIDUAL LIBERTIES IN TIMES OF CRISIS

Allen, Charles R., Jr. *Concentration Camps, U.S.A.* Citizens Committee for Constitutional Liberities, 1966.

Coben, Stanley. *A. Mitchell Palmer, Politician,* 1963.

Douglas, William O. "The Black Silence of Fear," *New York Times Magazine,* May 13, 1952.

Harris. "The Black Panthers: The Cornered Cats," *The Nation,* July 8, 1968.

Hoyt, Edwin P. *The Palmer Raids,* 1969.

Jensen, Joan M. *The Price of Vigilance,* 1968.

Lazarsfeld, Paul and Wagner Thielens. *The Academic Mind,* 1959. (Study of effect of "McCarthyism" on professors).

Levy, Leonard W. *Freedom of Speech and Press in Early American History.*

Murray, Robert K. *Red Scare: A Study in National Hysteria, 1919-20,* 1955.

Myerson. "Concentration Camps: Whose Fantasy?" 260 *Civil Liberties* 8-10 (1969).

Preston, William, Jr. *Aliens and Dissenters: Federal Suppression of Radicals, 1903-1933,* 1963.

van dan Haag, Ernest. "Controlling Subversive Groups," 300 *Annals of the American Academy of Political and Social Science* 62 (1955).

BIBLIOGRAPHIES

Emerson, Haber and Dorsen. *Political and Civil Rights in the United States,* 1967.

Harrison, Annette. *The Problem of Privacy in the Computer Age.* 1967.